11/19

2/25

MW00787700

ASIS

PHILOSOPHY UNMASKED

A Skeptic's Critique

PHILOSOPHY UNMASKED

A Skeptic's Critique

Laurie Calhoun

UNIVERSITY PRESS OF KANSAS

Part of Chapter One first appeared in "A 231-Word Refutation of Churchland's 'Vision'," *Reason Papers* 19 (Fall 1994): 98.

Parts of Chapter Two first appeared in "Institutions and Deviance: Art and Psychiatry," *Critical Review* 8(3) (Summer 1994): 393–409, and "The Intentional Fallacy," *Philosophy and Literature* 18 (Fall 1994): 337–38.

Parts of Chapter Three first appeared in "Some Simple Problems with Simplicity," *Reason Papers* 20 (Fall 1995): 109–12, "A Two-Minute Defense of van Fraassen's View on Scientists and Belief," *Explorations in Knowledge* 12(1) (1995): 17–18, and "Scientistic Confusion and Metaethical Relativism," *Ethica* 7(2) (1995): 53–72.

Parts of Chapter Four first appeared in "The Underdetermination of Theory by Data, 'Inference to the Best Explanation,' and the Impotence of Argumentation," *Philosophical Forum* 27(2) (Winter 1996): 146–60.

Published by the University Press of Kansas (Lawrence, Kansas 66049), which was organized by the Kansas Board of Regents and is operated and funded by Emporia State University, Fort Hays State University, Kansas State University, Pittsburg State University, the University of Kansas, and Wichita State University

Library of Congress Cataloging-in-Publication Data

Calhoun, Laurie.
    Philosophy unmasked : a skeptic's critique / Laurie Calhoun.
      p. cm.
    Includes bibliographical references and index.
    ISBN 0-7006-0833-8 (alk. paper)
    1. Philosophy. 2. Perspective (Philosophy). 3. Absolute, The—
Controversial literature. I. Title.
    BD348.C35 1997
    101—dc21   97-1484

British Library Cataloguing in Publication Data is available.

Printed in the United States of America

10 9 8 7 6 5 4 3 2 1

The paper used in this publication meets the minimum requirements of the American National Standard for Permanence of Paper for Printed Library Materials Z39.48–1984.

For Ted Jr.

Contents

Preface

This text is a radical work of metaphilosophy, which begins in a deceptively simple and straightforward way, as an investigation into the implications of the metaphysical question: "What would the world be like if perspectivism were true?" The work is self-referential and multiply layered and offers what I believe to be an innovative explanation of how analytic philosophy, with its excessive attention to argumentation, has gone awry. Because it is a reflection upon not only philosophy, but society as well, this work also provides some insights into the nature of cultural criticism.

Through the discussion of the theses of perspectivism and absolutism, which are defined so as to form an exclusive and exhaustive disjunction, it emerges that features of "the world" would simply be interpreted along different lines in the two cases. While institutions and methods of conflict resolution would be the same in either a perspectivist or an absolutist world, our understanding of what makes a person in a given domain an "expert" would differ. The institutions of the art world, psychiatry, and academic philosophy are considered in this connection.

These interpretive findings bear directly upon an understanding of the nature of philosophy. Because philosophy is essentially concerned with unanswered questions, as opposed to facts, "the world of philosophy" is a microcosm of what our interpretation of the world would be, if perspectivism were true. This means that the results about the nature of institutions in a perspectivist world are directly applicable to philosophy, yielding a metaphilosophical view according to which philosophical debates must, of necessity, be resolved by the nonrational means of seduction or conversion. This metaphilosophical view is fully compatible with, and indeed implies, a skepticism about lower-order philosophical theories, as is explained and repeatedly exemplified throughout this work.

The chapter entitled "Homilies and Diatribes" provides a concrete example of the thesis of this work, that "All of philosophy is seduction or conversion." According to the thesis itself, no argument could bring a reader to belief in the thesis. Rather, he would have to be either seduced or converted to the view. In other words, the inclusion of this admittedly radical portion of the text is essential to the overall integrity of the work. The sometimes blatant use of repetition is similarly justified in the light of the primary metaphilosophical thesis. Repetition is an integral part of the work, since if it is true that philosophy involves a great deal of conversion (the culmination of the process of indoctrination described early on and itself repeated throughout the text, self-referentially exemplifying what philosophers are claimed to do much of the time), and one of the most effective techniques of indoctrination is repetition, then the text itself, a work of philosophy, should include this feature.

This exemplification of the process of indoctrination is further accomplished through the choice of tone for the narrator's voice in "My Private Fantasy," of Chapter Six. The tone is that of a proselytizing bible-thumper, who repeatedly and doggedly assaults the reader with a variety of theses, for example: "Intuitions are not logical. Intuitions are atomic. . . . Intuitions are beliefs. Beliefs are hypotheses. Hypotheses are gods. Therefore, intuitions are gods." This section aims to indoctrinate the reader to the belief that philosophers are not authorities about anything, while at the same time making it patently clear that the narrator is himself in the process of bashing his prospective proselytes over the head with his own personal beliefs, his little "gods," in precisely the manner of those whom he criticizes. According to the theory being advanced, philosophers wake up (find themselves) with their idiosyncratic beliefs and devise theories and arguments that make themselves seem reasonable and/or pleasing to others. But, because this is but one of the views presumably being exposed, it, too, must finally be acknowledged to be no more than another possible "story." The postscript reiterates this idea. In fact, the work ends with the words, "the end."

Perhaps the most persistent thesis of this work is that doing philosophy involves imposing one's own values upon the phenomena with which one is confronted, and this is an essentially subjective enterprise. The view is certainly not new, and may have been expressed by Socrates, through his famous exhortations to "know thyself." "The message" of this text is that there is no message (not even that message), in the sense of "absolute truth," in philosophy. This idea is repeatedly exemplified or, to use Wittgenstein's idiom, "shown," to the reader in a variety of ways and on different levels. The view is undeniably paradoxical, and throughout history it may have been articulated (or gestured toward) in provocative ways by Socrates (who wrote nothing), Wittgenstein (who left behind books and books of fragments), and Nietzsche (who wrote thousands of aphorisms).

Many philosophers have become disillusioned with analytic philosophy, which has grown inordinately specialized in recent decades and has left the fundamental questions of the classical philosophers behind. I hope that this work will help contemporary philosophers come to an understanding of the shortcomings of the approach that has dominated Anglo-American philosophy throughout the twentieth century. Please note that the epilogue does not summarize the content of *Philosophy Unmasked*. Rather, it is an essay on the structure and content of *Philosophy Unmasked* in its relation to the work of Richard Rorty.

I would like to thank Gilbert Harman, Charles Crittenden, James Kellenberger, Berel Lang, Jane Cullen, and Stanley Corngold, all of whom read this work during the Spring of 1993 and encouraged me to pursue publication. I would also like to thank Barry Allen and an anonymous reader for the University Press of Kansas for providing the thoughtful criticisms that prompted my composition of the epilogue to this work. Two early comments by Jim Kellenberger, one regarding "fictional existence" and another regarding the necessity of "concern" to the writing of philosophy, have been incorporated directly into my text.

Some of the editors of the journals in which certain portions of this text previously appeared deserve special mention here, not only for agreeing to publish my articles and allowing me to reprint them, but also for evincing such enthusiasm for my work. Thanks to Jeffrey Friedman (*Critical Review*), Denis Dutton and Patrick Henry (*Philosophy and Literature*), Tibor Machan (*Reason Papers*), and the editors of *Ethica, Explorations in Knowledge,* and *The Philosophical Forum*.

Finally, above all, I would like to thank Peggy DesAutels, Dick Jeffrey, Scott Soames, Ermanno Bencivenga, and, again, Gilbert Harman, whose strong emotive reactions to my work persuaded me to believe that what I have to say is important indeed.

Introduction

"Perspectivism" can be characterized in at least two different ways: one is banal; another is, according to some, preposterous.

That any thing can be regarded from a variety of perspectives is incontestable and uninteresting. An extended object can obviously be viewed from an infinity of different vantage points, and so a type of perspectivism is true even with regard to spatial perspective alone. The same extended object can furthermore be viewed in different manners depending upon one's interests and values. A book can be regarded as a source of information, edification, or diversion, as a paper weight or book end, or as fuel for a fire.

Nelson Goodman espouses the extreme view that there are only perspectives. "The world" does not exist, and we speak and interact in "worlds" no one of which is best or authoritative. According to Goodman, there are many worlds, described by different world versions, but there is no underlying basic world of which these are different perspectives. However he might decide to describe "the skies," to which he refers in the following passage, would itself lead to talk in terms of some other theoretical constructs (mutatis mutandis, ad infinitum):

> Now as we thus make constellations by picking out and putting together certain stars rather than others, so we make stars by drawing certain boundaries rather than others. Nothing dictates whether the skies shall be marked off into constellations or other objects. We have to make what we find, be it the Great Dipper, Sirius, food, fuel, or a stereo system. [or the skies . . .][1]

> Still, if stars like constellations are made by versions, how can the stars have been there eons before all versions? Plainly, through being made by a version that puts the stars much earlier than itself in its own space-time.[2]

1

Since according to his view we in effect determine the historical date of the creation of the stars through our construction of a theory about the stars, Goodman's idea is thoroughly radical and not to be confused with the banal observation that we can look at our (given) objects from a variety of different perspectives. According to Goodman, there are no given objects. The objects of worlds depend for their existence upon us, and their properties are determined by the manner in which we conceptualize and perceive them. Worlds comprise objects, and the view according to which we literally make worlds is the strongest form of perspectivism. In saying that "a representational system determines the sorts of things its world consists of"[3] Goodman seems to be advocating a neo-Kantian view, according to which the constitution of things that we experience is ultimately dependent upon our peculiar conceptual and perceptual faculties. But, unlike Kant, Goodman does not posit the existence of a realm of noumema distinct from and underlying our conceptualized worlds. The question whether "the noumena" are distinct from "the phenomena" presupposes the existence of a point inaccessible to us and is, in his view, nonsensical. Moreover, Goodman denies even that any unique objective world might be determined by "the phenomena" generated by our peculiar conceptual and perceptual faculties. In contrast to Kant, he offers no "deduction" of the necessary categories through which we achieve "the phenomena." The manners in which we might conceptualize things are not constrained a priori by some sort of faculty of pure reason.[4] Any theory according to which we were able to conceptualize only in a fixed, predetermined number of ways would itself constitute only one abandonable view about how we conceptualize.

> The non-Kantian theme of multiplicity of worlds is closely akin to the Kantian theme of the vacuity of the notion of pure content. The one denies a unique world, the other the common stuff of which worlds are made. Together these theses defy our intuitive demand for something solid underneath, and threaten to leave us uncontrolled, spinning out our own inconsequent fantasies.[5]

We find ourselves located in worlds that we transform through the creation of new, more fully determined objects. If perspectivism is correct, then I am conducting this discussion in a world that I share with you. You have found yourself with this object, a text, which you will more fully determine through the creative interpretation of the words that you find before your eyes. This work will begin with an elaboration of what seem plausibly to be some of the implications of the provocative idea that "we literally make worlds" and then employ this hypothesis as a tool for investigating some facets of this world. The issues that I shall discuss are of general interest.

ONE

Perspectivism, Interpretation, and "The World"

According to perspectivism, objects are dependent for their existence upon human beings, whose conceptualization creates and determines worlds. Worlds are not "answerable" to some external, antecedent, and nonhuman thing, "the world." There is no uniform underlying reality beyond the appearance of the worlds which we create. Because we literally make all of the worlds which we inhabit and about which we discourse, if we did not exist, those worlds would not either. Every world depends for its existence upon human conceptualizers, and the world of any larger community can be built up from a single individual's through an expansion of the intersubjective community, through the addition of other community members. Although this might seem to be a slightly artificial manner in which to look at the construction of worlds, given that we find ourselves in intersubjectively inhabited worlds, it is important to recognize the importance of the subject's perspective and the role it plays in the choice of communities in which one participates. The intimate connection between conceptualization and comprehensibility plays a crucial role in our decisions about which communities to join and remain a part of. There is a sense in which we choose to participate in particular traditions and to be members of certain communities, which, if perspectivism is true, literally determine the worlds which we inhabit. Worlds vary due to the heterogeneous constitutions of their communities, which determine the objects of discourse in a world. The objects of science are determined by the set of all scientists, whose current best views set the scientific facts. Within science there are many smaller worlds, such as chemistry, geology, botany, zoology, etc., which are incommensurable with one another, involving as they do, disparate vocabularies and concepts, and, therefore, objects.

Depending upon how finely worlds are partitioned, ordinary language might assimilate radically disparate "things" under crude systems of differentiation. Intersubjectively shared language picks out a sort of "lowest common denominator" of features commonly taken to be essential to the type of object in question. Since perspectivism asserts that all distinctions are world-constrained, it denies that "essential" and "accidental" properties are stable through all worlds. The description under, or the perspective from which anything is regarded substantively contributes to the identity of the thing, so substantively, in fact, that it is constitutive. What we would normally conceive of as a single object existing in the world, that is, subsisting under a variety of perspectives which might be taken toward it, is in fact a group of distinct objects. For example, the molecular structure of vinegar, $HC_2H_3O_2$, is not essential to it, unless it is being considered under its description as a chemical substance. Vinegar qua constituent of salad dressing, is a distinct object from vinegar qua acetic acid, in some worlds, if perspectivism is true. Our language is quasi-absolutistic, whether or not absolutism is true, but our words refer to what have been intersubjectively agreed upon, by a community, to be essences. So in the example just described, the word 'vinegar' can be used to pick out two distinct objects, in some worlds, if perspectivism is true. This is not to deny that in other worlds a single object might be susceptible of multiple characterizations. In those worlds, a quasi-absolutistic distinction between accidental and essential properties is assumed.

If "we make worlds" through our conceptualizations and representations, then who are "we"? Perhaps we should begin with "me." My properties are those conferred upon me by some conceptualizer in some world. But, in general, the smallest community contained within any other larger community is a single individual. For example, while van Gogh was a member of his society, insofar as he interacted with other members of that community, he also inhabited worlds alone, containing their own sets of facts. Since facts are a matter of convention, if perspectivism is true, the intersubjectively determined facts within a world inhabited by a single individual will coincide with his current best view, which is the view which he currently holds. Of course, members of society simultaneously occupy a variety of distinct worlds, so they will determine "the facts" only in those worlds in which they are experts about the domain of objects of the world. But an individual determines the facts in every world which he inhabits alone. Although a person, as ordinarily conceived, can change his view diachronically, he cannot disagree with himself synchronically, so instantaneously partitioned time slices of "a person" occupy worlds inhabited by the individual alone and in which he is the absolute. In worlds inhabited by me alone, I determine all of the properties which I possess, since which properties a thing possesses is a matter of fact, but facts are a matter of convention, if perspectivism is true. A synchronically individuated individual cannot disagree with himself, so whatever he takes himself to be is what he is at that moment.

The philosophical question of what "the subject" must be was raised by Descartes, who located the essential feature of a thinking subject in his thinking (doubting). Descartes' further extrapolations from this datum have been rejected by numerous thinkers through history, but it seems undeniable that, in retrospective reflection upon what he takes himself to be during a moment of doubting, "the doubter" sees what he takes himself to be as having been a doubter. Nietzsche's enumeration of the theories presupposed by Descartes' conclusion reminds the would-be Cartesian that conclusions must be expressed in language and therefore necessarily presuppose theories, and that things can be spoken of only in language. These observations are devastating to foundationalistic absolutists, but would be most congenial to perspectivists:

> Der Philosoph muß sich sagen: wenn ich den Vorgang zerlege in dem Satz "ich denke" ausgedrückt ist, so bekomme ich eine Reihe von verwegnen Behauptungen, deren Begründung schwer, vielleicht unmöglich ist,—zum Beispiel, daß *ich* es bin, der denkt, daß überhaupt ein Etwas es sein muß, das denkt, daß Denken eine Tätigkeit und Wirkung seitens eines Wesens ist, welches als Ursache gedacht wird, daß es ein "Ich" gibt, endlich, daß es bereits feststeht, was mit Denken zu bezeichnen ist—daß ich *weiß*, was Denken ist.[1]

> [The philosopher must say to himself: When I analyze the process which is expressed in the sentence, "I think," I find a whole series of daring assertions, which would be difficult, perhaps impossible, to prove; for example, that it is *I* who think, that there must necessarily be something which thinks, that thinking is an activity and operation on the part of a being who is thought of as a cause, that there is an "ego," and, finally, that it has already been established what is to be designated by thinking—that I *know* what thinking is.]

A Cartesian solus ipse, an isolated metaphysical subject, would have to occupy "the noumena" underlying all worlds. But perspectivism denies that the idea of a distinction between some "noumenon" and "the phenomena" makes sense. The self-reflective subject has only those properties which he confers upon himself, since all of the properties of a thing derive from its conceptualizer(s), but worlds in which a subject reflects upon himself contain only one conceptualizer, "the subject" himself.

What are the properties of a conceptualizer qua conceptualizer, in this world? A thing considered under the description of "conceptualizing thing" necessarily has those and only those properties which it has under that description (at that time). No "thing," ordinarily conceived of as susceptible of multiple interpretations, has any essential properties. But every thing, perspectivally conceived, has all and only its own properties necessarily. Far from being philosophically suspect, this consequence is tantamount to the tautology: "A thing is what it is."

It is of course possible to conceptualize things as human beings, one of the characteristics of which is the ability to conceptualize variously, so that the conceptualization in which a given individual might engage could differ from time to time. This conceptualizer's conceptualizations taken together would (disjunctively) determine his own concept of conceptualization. Such a "diachronic conceptualizer" would constitute a microcosmic model of a community of disparate synchronic conceptualizers. But, in both the synchronic and diachronic cases, individuals are individuated via the individuator's conception of them. There are no hidden aspects to a thing as conceived, it is nothing over and above what it is taken to be.[2]

Looking at conceptualization of extended objects as we might ordinarily, at least three distinguishable levels are involved. First, there is a fundamental or ontological level, at which crudely discriminated objects of the world are determined. Second, there is a perceptual level, at which different individuals attend to different facets or properties of the things conceived to exist at the first level. Third, there is a valuational level, at which different individuals perceive their partial representations of the objects from the first level tinged with their own values and interests. Given an agreed upon set of basic concepts and ontology, it remains for individual perceivers to interpret their environments, including "the events" which transpire.[3] This interpretive process involves decisions (whether conscious or not) to focus upon certain aspects of "the environment" rather than others. The only objects of a world inhabited by a single individual are those things to which he attends.

One might think that the basic "furniture" of our intersubjectively constituted world is agreed upon by all functional members of the community. But since, in the perspectivist's view, objects as we ordinarily conceive of them have no essential properties, he does not seem to be entitled to the distinction in levels proposed above. The ontological, selective, and valuational tiers all merge into one in the individual's interactions with objects in his own private world. This might seem to suggest a sense in which a form of solipsism is true, if perspectivism is correct. Arguments against the coherence of the concept of "the world" will apply, mutatis mutandis, to the combined worlds of all possible individuals. Individual worlds are inhabited by instantaneously existing individuals. Indeed, even if the validity of the three distinct levels of conceptualization is assumed, the community fragments at the second and third levels, no matter how it is delimited at the first. Crudely partitioning, one might think that one occupies the same world as those whose values are the same as one's own. But even that would imply that worlds are unique to individuals, indeed to individual time slices of individuals as ordinarily conceived, since people's interests and values transform diachronically, and according to perspectivism there is no subsistent self, since no properties of a person, as ordinarily (diachronically) conceived, are essential to him.

But all of this assumes that an individual occupies a single world. In fact, "I" occupy this world with you, but others with others, and some all alone. "I" simultaneously occupy the world which is the focus of my immediate attention while occupying many others passively. How can this be? Intersubjective worlds are delimited by their objects, including the conceptualizers whose agreement ensures the objects' existence. Language permits communication between conceptualizers who agree about some things, objects, which the language permits them to talk about. The other worlds which "I" inhabit are preserved by their other inhabitants while my attention is diverted. By reading this essay, you preserve the existence of a world which you share with me, though "I" may now be asleep. You constitute me as a writer. So long as someone is aware of the existence of the objects which it comprises, a world continues to exist.

World versions can be more and more finely or quite crudely discriminating, via language. But every world requires a conceptualizer. The intersection of all of the worlds which "I" inhabit is my concept of me as the pure conceptualizer. "I," stripped of all properties but one, the property of being a conceptualizer, persist through all of "my" worlds. The intersection of all of the worlds which "an individual" inhabits is "the individual." This is how "the subject" is defined. The pure conceptualizer is the "lowest common denominator" to all of the intersubjective worlds which "he" inhabits. "He" is an object in many different worlds, in each of which "he" is conceived of differently. Dressed in properties exceeding that of being a pure conceptualizer, "he" continues to exist in worlds to which he is not currently attending.

Worlds comprise all and only their objects. The identity of a world is uniquely determined by its objects. It suffices to annihilate an object, and therefore simultaneously destroy one and create another world, that one divert one's attention from it. It suffices to annihilate another conceptualizer and create one's own world that one refuse to speak to someone, since the only way to render oneself comprehensible to another is through language, and intersubjectively inhabited worlds comprise all and only their objects, including conceptualizers, who agree that their objects of discourse exist. If one never speaks with others, then one cannot know which objects one shares with them. Rich concepts of others require dialogue. You can limit your concept of others by not asking what they think, by not finding out which objects they share with you. One might infer from their actions that they believe in some objects. But the concepts of those objects in those worlds would be exhausted by the properties which one ascribes to them conjoined with the properties they appear to be committed to by their actions. It is precipitous to assume that another shares your objects. Why should he? It is impossible to know whether or not another believes in the existence of the same objects you do without his saying so. Does his saying that he believes in something settle the question? You still must decide to believe that you are talking about the same thing. It may emerge that you're not.

Individuals conceptualize, not societies. The standards of "reality" must involve the disjunction of the individuals' conceptualizations, whenever normal conceptualization is determined by a community with more than one member, so there is necessarily some variance tolerated. Even two agents with relevantly similar cognitive and perceptual faculties can only view "the same" extended "object" from different perspectives, since they do not and could never occupy the same point in space. Whether or not a substantial degree of variation (deviance) is tolerated might seem to depend upon the degree to which different individuals actually share similar cognitive and perceptual faculties.

The conventions governing language use impose the most obvious constraints, due to the crudeness with which it can be used to differentiate things. Language cannot ensure intersubjective similarity of phenomenological experience. But doesn't the problem of whether or not in a given case two people's qualia are relevantly similar presuppose a distinction between appearance and reality which is nonsensical to perspectivists? Language partitions different world versions in a manner which renders intersubjective communication possible, and this is because our crudest conceptualizations are in large part inculcated through language itself. Intersubjective language is "public"; it permits individuals to talk about what they believe to be relevantly similar experiences of what they agree to call the same objects.

If existence of worlds depended upon "public" language, then only "places" where intersubjective communication occurred would be worlds; the other "places" would be the void. It would be impossible for an individual non-language user to be located; he wouldn't be "grounded." But what could it mean for a real thing to inhabit an unreal world? How could "he" be nowhere? If perspectivism is true, then the subject of experience decides which worlds are permitted, and wherever one is, is "the world" relativized to himself. An isolated individual's concept of conceptualization permits the conceptualization of a world without language, of a world in which what we call "memory" and "imagination" are indistinguishable, where that distinction is not real.

If language makes objects, then all conceptualization presupposes language.[4] But a society of one individual (as ordinarily conceived) is nonetheless possible as the limiting case. Since objects comprise all and only their properties, through time as an individual changes he could be said to be having a sort of dialogue with "himself," in entertaining, creating, the objects of the world which he inhabits. "Solipsistic" world versions rapidly succeed one another with the consciousness of the passage of time. But memory permits the integration of a "self," as we ordinarily conceive of it. The distinction between memories and ideas or images is real, but what is real has been established by convention. In order to have the concept of that distinction, and therefore to be able to apply it to one's own experiences, correctly calling some things "memories" while others "figments of imagination," one must remain a member of the intersubjective community in which the convention was established. Without communication with others, all connections with them in what we ordinarily term "the world" are severed and one escapes to another, solipsistic, world.[5]

But solipsism is not a problem, since it presupposes that the others could be something beyond what I conceive of them to be. In this view, you are precisely what I take you to be, since I construct you. Your properties are all and only those properties which "I" confer upon you in all of the worlds which "we" share. If I believe you to share multiple worlds with me, this means that subtracting the properties which "you" do not possess in all of those worlds, my construction of you as a pure conceptualizer preserves your existence.[6] I determine the nature of the objects which persist through all of my world versions. My believing in the existence of other conceptualizers suffices for them to exist. I am the absolute relative to the worlds which I construct alone.

Although our conceptualizations may have been initially determined in large part through societal inculcation, individuals can continually metamorphose and enrich (or limit) worlds through recombination and selection of the elements with which they begin. Whether or not it can be said (with linguistic propriety) that some conceptualizations are "wrong" will depend upon which conceptualizers are counted among the community. If all people were counted members of the community, then it would be impossible for there to be an actual conceptualization which was wrong, since the standard is just determined by the actually operative conceptualizations. On the other hand, if only a subset of the entire human community were assumed to dictate the "standard," then there might be a sort of "majority (ochlocratic) rule" which constrained conceptions. In any case, since the decision of how to delimit the community is a decision, which must necessarily be constrained by some standards currently embraced by the individual making the decision, no possible conceptualization is precluded a priori. But communities are constrained conservatively by the conceptualizer.

"Epistemic conservatism" is the view that one is justified in believing what one believes in the absence of recalcitrant, disconfirmatory evidence. Of course what constitutes "disconfirmatory evidence" is also determined by the agent. So if a "conservative" were so disposed, he could retain a belief in the face of any putative "evidence," by refusing to admit it as disconfirmatory. In general, no one else can force another to abandon a belief, no matter how much "evidence" is adduced, since he must first accept that what is being called "evidence" is in fact evidence. In order to defer to "the experts," who present the putative evidence, one must oneself have already accepted "the experts" as the experts. Perspectivism is conservative, since any individual's decision to adopt any possible conception of conceptualization, is automatically sanctioned by his doing so.[7]

Some would reject the suggestion that we might be able to choose radically to reconceptualize, that is, to adopt another quite disparate world view about basic constructs,[8] but whether or not fundamental conceptions are freely revisable and abandonable, it is clear that communities can be diversely individuated, and so, through the judicious selection of community members, any conception whatsoever, which is realized by some actual conceptualizer, can be sanctioned. Within a given intersubjectively shared world (one where people are individuated ordinarily) the choice of a standard or "normal" community remains, and one necessarily includes oneself in that community, since the very selection of a community presupposes the soundness of one's own mind. In a different context, Husserl makes a pertinent Cartesian point:

Nun wissen wir wohl, daß es so etwas wie Abnormalitäten gibt. . . .
Aber die Abnormalitäten muß sich als solche selbst erst konstituieren
und kann es nur auf dem Grunde einer an sich vorangehenden
Normalität. . . . In Bezug auf das Tier ist der Mensch, konstitutiv
gesprochen, der Normalfall, wie ich selbst konstitutiv die Urnorm bin
für alle Menschen.[9]

[Now, we know that there are such things as abnormalities . . . but
abnormality must itself be constituted, and this can only be done from
the basis of an antecedently constituted normality. With respect to
animals, man is, constitutively spoken, the normal case, just as I myself
am constitutive of the normal standard for all people.]

It is not the case that "anything goes," because the selection of others to be included in one's community of conceptualizers requires that they be recognizable as conceptualizers. The other members of the community must be comprehensible to the conceptualizer, in order for him to entertain them as possible conceptualizers. To be capable of being understood constitutes at once the necessary and sufficient condition for being admitted to the class.

One would not choose persons who were comatose or catatonic as members of the intersubjective conceptual community, unless one believed oneself possibly able to understand what it would be like to conceptualize (assuming that they do) as they do.[10] Similarly, when others regard someone as insane, believing him to be "abnormal," *he* must think that *they* are ignorant or stupid (or otherwise "abnormal"). If they "saw" what he "sees," then they would understand. But they cannot see what he sees, because they are not he. They do not share his beliefs, perceptions, and values.

It is prima facie plausible that the ability to conceptualize another as a conceptualizer requires that he also be (potentially) able to conceptualize conceptualizers as conceptualizers. The agents would then be relevantly similar in the respect that they have some concept of conceptualization. Does having this concept presuppose the actual ability to view oneself as a conceptualizer? Is self-knowledge a requirement for conceptualizers? No, that would be a superfluous property. Some conceptualizers are self-consciously aware of their acts of conceptualization. Most people in most of the worlds which I inhabit are not. But they are still comprehensible to me.

If comprehensibility of other conceptualizers were transitive, then communities of conceptualizers would comprise all and only those individuals who understood one another. Normal language users in "the world," as we ordinarily conceive of it, understand one another to a high degree in discourse about the basic ontological categories of what they take to be "the world." Discourse ranges from strictly "literal," at the core of what might be metaphorically termed "the sphere of comprehensibility," to highly "metaphorical." Language use near the core is pedestrian and understood by all competent speakers of the language in question. As one moves farther out, language use becomes more and more nuanced and ultimately reaches its limits at the periphery, where the use of metaphor becomes obscure and recondite, readily comprehensible only to individuals whose past experiences and knowledge peculiarly equip them to understand the speaker's idiosyncratic usage in the instance in question. To transcend the sphere of intersubjective comprehensibility is to render oneself unfathomable and to escape to another world.

Location within the sphere of comprehensibility is a metaphor for the degree to which an instance of language use is metaphorical or literal, relative to a given language community. (If the metaphor is highly comprehensible to you, then it lies well within the bounds of our intersubjective sphere of comprehensibility.) Proximity to the periphery, or distance from the origin is a measure of "newness." At the core lies literal meaning, that is, instances of language use the governing conventions which are completely solidified. No competent language user, no inhabitant of the world in question, could fail to understand the utterances. Surrounding the core are somewhat less frozen metaphors. A little further out are what might be described as "slushy" metaphors. Near the periphery, language use is fluid. Outside the sphere, the liquid has transformed to gas; language use escapes all comprehension by leaving the original vessel, convention, behind. "Newness" and "comprehensibility" are inversely proportional to one another.

This metaphor should be extended to include cases of nonlinguistic symbolization, since the distinction between linguistic and nonlinguistic symbolization is itself conventional. For example, in some contexts the color purple definitively symbolizes royalty and black definitively symbolizes death. Again, the degree of fluidity of the symbolization is the degree to which conventions governing its interpretation have become standard and is finally a function of the relevant community.

"The origin" is necessarily determined by the community of language users; there is no absolute coordinate system by which it could be fixed. The attachment of words to things is at bottom arbitrary, if perspectivism is false. But if perspectivism is true, then the relations between words and things are no longer arbitrary, since discourse alone determines the properties of the things, even when names are attached to things which have antecedently been talked into existence. These attachments only seem arbitrary on the assumption that there might be an absolute coordinate system. They *are* arbitrary relative to the relativized notion of the absolute.

The "sphere of comprehensibility" is similar in many ways to Quine's "web of belief." Location within Quine's "web of belief" is a metaphor for the degree to which a belief is actually abandonable. In Quine's model, the beliefs furthest from the edges are deeply entrenched, dealing with basic logical facts, for example, the law of noncontradiction, "not-(p and not-p)," and the law of the excluded middle, "p or not-p." Those nearer to the edges are only tentatively held. They might be, for example, beliefs about current string theories. If language makes objects, and language presupposes logic, then reality must be logical. This would explain why consistency is the ultimate and incontestable constraint on all theories. Logic cannot be questioned, since the questioning would itself presuppose the object of investigation. It is impossible to derive a contradiction from a tautology.

Public language makes intersubjectively shared objects. So the connections between words and things are no more and no less tenuous if perspectivism is correct than if absolutism is. In the former case, stability of those objects is a function only of language, and in the latter it is also a function only of language, since the intersubjectively shared objects of society are fixed relative to the world version of society. We were inculcated at an early age to believe that tables and chairs exist. Today we can argue about whether this table is walnut or oak. But when we have decided, we enter a new world, since a world comprises all and only its objects and an object comprises all and only its properties. We can use the same label, "this table," to refer to what we ordinarily regard as the same thing underlying both descriptions.

That all language must begin as metaphorical might seem a commonplace to any reader of at least two languages. The words 'hell' in English and German, 'hier' in German and French, and 'pie' in French, Spanish, and English mean completely different things. Clearly there is no necessary connection between words and things.[11] That we have come to regard some language use as "literal" and other as "metaphorical" indicates only the stability of the conventions governing one type of usage vis-à-vis the other. The literal and metaphorical language distinction is itself a metaphor for the degree to which the conventions surrounding the language use have become standard. We assume that "literal" language literally refers, possibly in some quasi-tractarian sense, but the relation of reference is at bottom arbitrary, if it was stipulated by someone at some time in history.

If perspectivism is true, then worlds are not delimited only by languages, as ordinarily conceived, because what constitutes a language is also a matter of convention. The symbol '♪' could symbolize anything. A black dot could symbolize the sun just as 'le soleil', 'die Sonne', and 'el sol' do. The alphabets of non-Western languages exemplify, to nonspeakers of those languages, the aesthetic nature of linguistic symbols: テ`, ツ, д, Ж. Nothing prevents one from associating things with one another, including what we ordinarily call written symbols and things, or completely different kinds of things. To say that already established linguistic conventions limit possible worlds would be to assume that the worlds precede the conceptualizations and not vice versa, as perspectivism asserts.

Rousseau observes that written language is much cruder than spoken language,[12] which might seem obvious to one with an appreciation for the distinct pronunciations of 'pie' in French, 'pie' in Spanish, and 'pie' in English. (Since homonyms are very few in number, Rousseau's idea is not undermined by their existence.) Although they are spelled identically, these words are phonetically entirely distinct, as is evidenced by their spelling in the phonetic alphabet employed by French linguists: [pi], [piʝe], [paiʝ]. Of course, to say that 'pie' in French, Spanish, and English is the same word is to assume that the individual letters: 'p', 'i', and 'e' are interlingually identical, which some would dispute. To the frustration of many a foreign language learner upon arrival in the country where the language he has diligently studied is spoken, the "same" letter in two disparate languages, even when viewed as an isolated unit, may bear no relation to its counterpart in his maternal language. For example, anglophones often erroneously believe that hard consonants are to be aspirated in every language (much to the chagrin of the French). Recognizing that 'p' in French and 'p' in English are pronounced differently, one might deny that Rousseau's point is illustrated by the French phonetic spelling of the three words.[13] However, that the point is apt emerges incontrovertibly through a consideration of monolingual examples. English, to the dismay of many an ESL student, provides a panoply of examples. 'Lead' and 'lead' are indisputably orthographically indistinguishable in English, though phonetically and semantically distinct.

Rousseau apparently thinks that language is falsificatory,[14] insofar as it imposes a choice of level and a discrete abstraction upon a continuous phenomenon. This could be a recognition of what I shall call the "problem of selection" below. The following argument concludes that all hypotheses are underdetermined by the data which they cover:

> Language is symbolic.
> Symbols are discrete.
> All hypotheses are in language.
> So all hypotheses are discrete.
> But events are replete.
>
> ---
>
> Therefore: All hypotheses are underdetermined by
> the "data," events, which they cover.

If I were to ask you what you are doing right now, knowing that your eyes are open, you might answer, "I am reading," or "I am looking at your essay," or "I am interpreting the characters on this sheet of paper," or any infinite number of other statements, all of which are, in one sense or another, true, though also, in many ways, omissive. Another version of the problem of the underdetermination of theory by data is the skeptical problem where the theory to be confirmed is "X," the verbal description of the putative state of affairs, from the datum that "It is as though X," the fact being reported. To give one example, I might take as confirmatory of the fact that "I am typing right now," my observation that "it is as though I am typing right now." In the light of the theory-ladenness of what is ordinarily thought of as data, the problems would seem to be intimately related, though nonetheless distinguishable, since most people (nonskeptics) do not see the step from "it is as though X" to "X" as, in any sense, an inductive ascent, in the way in which they might view the move from "this emerald is green" to "all emeralds are green" as involving inductive ascent. A third version of the problem is Goodman's "new riddle of induction." I shall discuss all of these problems at greater length below. For now, let us simply observe that, if the first version is genuinely a problem, then Rousseau is right, spoken language is falsificatory, and written language is a fortiori falsificatory. So formalization of written languages is of course a fortiori falsificatory, since it abstracts from an already abstracted abstraction, oral language itself being an abstraction from replete events.

When usage becomes commonplace and history is forgotten, then some people (mainly monolingual anglophones) decide to look to language for insight into reality. But, Rousseau would query: "Comment est-ce qu'une étude de l'usage anglais puisse nous donner plus que des renseignements sur la langue anglaise et, peut-être, le peuple anglais?" [How could a study of English usage reveal anything about anything other than English language and, perhaps, anglophonic people?] Indeed, it might seem surprising that so many contemporary philosophers should have turned to language for information about "the world." However, this is fully comprehensible, given that most anglophones are monolingual, and it might be difficult to happen upon the above Rousseauian points without a speaking familiarity with at least one foreign language.

This model of language provides a means by which to understand the classical idea illustrated by the slave boy of Plato's *Meno* and expressed by Wittgenstein (perhaps facetiously) in the preface to the *Tractatus*:

> Dieses Buch wird vielleicht nur der verstehen, der die Gedanken, die darin ausgedrückt sind—oder ähnliche Gedanken—schon selbst einmal gedacht hat.

> [This book will perhaps only be understood by one who has already thought the thoughts, or similar thoughts, here expressed.]

"No one ever teaches anyone anything," if in order to understand the meaning of a sentence one must already understand how its parts function and what the speaker intends by his utterance. But how could one understand that, unless one had already had the same idea? How could one understand something "new"? If all language is originally metaphorical, due to the arbitrariness of the connection between any word and any object, then the distinction between literal and metaphorical language is just the distinction between language the governing conventions of which have been pervasively inculcated in the relevant community and language use which has no such agreed upon conventions. In that case, "newness" is nothing more and nothing less than a measure of the degree to which symbol use is metaphorical, that is, the degree to which the conventions governing interpretation in the way in which the speaker intends have not been accepted (or perhaps even previously introduced) in the community. So the classical idea, that "no one teaches anyone anything," might be an observation about the nature of "newness" of symbol use and the subjective nature of interpretation. Only individual conceptualizers interpret symbols, so only individual conceptualizers interpret correctly or incorrectly with respect to the standards of appropriateness of a world version. In a putative case of learning, either an individual interprets "normally," that is, correctly understands the speaker's meanings, in which case he himself generated the "new" idea, or he interprets "abnormally," that is, misunderstands the subject matter supposedly being taught. No one else can force the individual to interpret in one way over another, but "learning" requires a determinate, univocal interpretation. This means that only the individual himself can teach himself, that is, choose to interpret in the particular way desired by the teacher. The underdetermination of theory by data precludes the possibility of anyone's teaching another anything, because in order to learn what another is trying to teach, the individual must himself opt for the teacher's particular interpretation of the symbols being used. But any group of data is compatible with an infinite number of equally adequate stories, interpretations. Could this be why Socrates thought that "the subject" of philosophy is "the self"?

Worlds are nothing beyond the objects which they comprise. Since worlds comprise and are exhausted by their objects, no conceptualizer can occupy the null world. The other members of the world in which Goodman is an author are all and only his readers. Every person who reads and understands what he says, whether or not they agree, is a member of that world. Disagreements between language users might seem prima facie to indicate that they inhabit different worlds. But only those who do not comprehend one another occupy no common world; they have no shared objects of disagreement. Two conceptualizers who are completely incomprehensible to one another, having no shared objects in common, do not inhabit the same world. They are completely opaque to one another, for they share no objects of possible disagreement.

Worlds are delimited by their communities of conceptualizers, who comprehend one another in discoursing about objects which all members agree exist. Disagreements presuppose agreements about the objects of disagreement. Disputants comprehend each other and take themselves to be talking about the same objects. A single object and a conceptualizer suffice to create a world. If, by transitivity, any two conceptualizers who can discourse meaningfully about an object occupy the same world, then all functional English language users occupy a single world. There are many other smaller worlds too, for example, that of the community of string theorists who take themselves to be talking about the same objects. What we would ordinarily think of as a single person occupies a variety of these sorts of worlds, since he is a member of a variety of communities.

We believe in the existence of objects, which provide the material for our further investigations. We find ourselves with objects about which we can ask questions. We find ourselves with beliefs, which we can call into question, when we are so disposed. The provenance of these beliefs is irrelevant.[15] Sometimes we want to ask whether or not an object actually exists. Then the object of our investigation is no longer "the object," but the question, "does 'it' exist?" Turning to the putative object wouldn't settle anything, since if "it" doesn't exist, then "it" doesn't have any properties, so there is nothing to which to turn. We would have to appeal to other considerations in order to answer the question. We could appeal to other objects the existence of which is not in question.

In each world the objects of discourse are agreed upon by all members of the community. They disagree about the "essential" properties, relativized to that world, of the objects of discussion. "Essential" properties are stipulated within a world. Disagreements are battles over what those properties should be. The culmination of these battles coincides with the destruction of an old and the creation of a new world. It suffices that the experts of a community agree that some properties be "essential" in order for them to be essential.[16] Individuals attempt to make the properties which they value essential to objects of a world. If perspectivism is true, then in order to convince people that the properties which you deem valuable should be accepted as "essential" you must either convert or seduce them. They have to be converted, through indoctrination, or seduced, through deception, because there are no facts to show them. The facts are being settled, that is, determined, in these disputes.

"Conversion" is the culmination of a process, "indoctrination," by which individuals come to a change in view which they did not, in any sense, willfully seek. The most obvious examples of indoctrination are training procedures which involve repeated and intensive exposure to ideas to be assimilated or attitudes to be adopted. These procedures effect a change in belief or attitude (typically both) about some individual(s) or thing(s). In religious cults the change takes the form of a "realization" that some specific individual is "the messiah" or a deity. But any case in which an agent neither foresees nor intends that his following someone else's prescriptions for action will lead to the change in attitude or belief which it does effect, is a case of indoctrination. One such type of change in view is to come to believe that something, formerly not believed to exist, in fact exists. Although "conversion" might to some connote a change from one to another positive view, it can also be used to describe the process by which one changes from an agnostic to a positive position. "Conversion," in the most general sense, is a change to a positive view about something. To believe something not to exist is a positive view, which is not the same as not to believe that something exists. So whether atheists can with propriety be described as having been "converted" depends solely upon the means by which they arrived at their view.

A few salient features of this phenomenon warrant mention here, since they provide a ready means of understanding the tendency of people to find perspectivism preposterous, on their first exposure to the thesis. First of all, the indoctrinator/proselyte relationship is one of faith, since the proselyte must somehow come to the belief that he can trust the indoctrinator, which simultaneously requires his being able to accept that his own powers of judgment have until now failed to locate the truth, since previously he has failed to "see the light." He must both believe in his own powers of judgment, enough to trust them in selecting the guide as a guide, and disbelieve them insofar as they have previously led him astray. When the guide is thought of as serendipitously encountered, then the two ideas are not so problematic, since the proselyte can believe that his powers of judgment are sound, but he never before encountered the transmitter of "the word," who, being messianic, is of course unique. If people were able to discover "the word" on their own, then there would be no sense to the notion of "messiah." If perspectivism is correct, then the proselyte–indoctrinator relationship is essentially that of a nonexpert to an expert, since the former must trust the latter, being himself unqualified to render judgments upon the facts lying outside of his own area of expertise.

Unsurprisingly, debriefing is nearly impossible to effect by an individual himself, because he occupies a world of the indoctrinator's creation. He has come to depend upon him as an authority and to trust him. To come to believe that he is wrong requires his being able to believe not only that the indoctrinator is wrong and that he in some sense "tricked"[17] the proselyte into believing, but also that the proselyte himself was tricked. No one likes to play the fool. But it is equally difficult for outsiders to debrief cult members, since they must somehow convince the individual both that the "guide" is not to be trusted and that they, the debriefers, are. But if the individual was wrong in the first instance, and was led into the cult through the wiles of the cult leader, then why should he trust his own powers of judgment now? If he believes the debriefers, that his own powers of judgment are not to be trusted, then he should not believe the debriefers, since his own powers of judgment are not to be trusted. Given this dilemma, the simplest, most painless solution is to retain one's ardent commitment to the cult. If perspectivism is correct, then these dynamics explain people's tendency to believe that facts which they believe to be facts are genuinely facts, in the ordinary sense of the word, and that the world is not dependent for its existence upon human beings.

Many powers of psychological coercion have been used and continue to operate upon the individual. The other cult members all reinforce his belief that his is the true religion and that this is "the way." When everyone believes the same thing, then it sounds insane when one individual disagrees. To reject the received view of an entire intersubjective community in favor of one's own requires a sort of arrogance on the part of the individual. How could a person be so presumptuous as to think that he is right and all of the others are wrong? In a cult, exposure to outsiders is often proscribed, and not without reason. Interaction with outsiders might cause a cult member to realize that the seeming unanimity of his intersubjective community is illusory, merely a product of the homogeneous constitution of that sheltered group, comprising individuals who have already been persuaded by the cult leader to believe. Of course the cult leader won't tell the proselytes that; he says that outsiders are besotted, sullied, beclouded, lost. This is an explanation of the form of "group behavior" in which people form communities that involve an "us vs. them" dichotomy.

Initiation to a cult often requires a large financial sacrifice. But contrary to what some might think, the main reason for this is not to bring in new funds to the cult, which are easy to acquire by putting the members to work selling flowers, distributing pamphlets, etc. The sacrifice has the psychological effect of increasing the total investment of time, energy, and money to the cause. It would be very difficult, take an enormous amount of courage, for a person to be able to acknowledge that he had squandered his life's savings and years of his life for someone who had lured him through a beautiful forest down a long narrow path, which terminates abruptly at a desert. In general, the more one has invested oneself in one's projects, the more difficult it is to abandon them. This explains people's tendencies to embrace "idées fixes."

Another interesting feature is the means by which individuals may become dependent upon their indoctrinator, through being placed in positions of weakness and discomfort antecedent to their being "saved." This "discomfort" can be purely emotional or cognitive but probably usually involves both, for example, being in a state of uncertainty or ignorance, which seems generally to have the effect of producing anxiety in people. When the proselyte surrenders his powers of judgment to his indoctrinator, by accepting what he says on faith, the proselyte simultaneously becomes dependent upon him for access to the truth, "the word," since only he will know whether or not the facts have changed, when new facts have been discovered. Dependency is further strengthened by the fact that liberating oneself from an indoctrinator's control would require one to admit that one had wasted one's time and energy prostrating oneself before a mere mortal.

"Seduction" is the process by which a person is persuaded to believe something which he did not formerly believe to be true (e.g., that something exists or that something has some property) through the construction of a façade which suggests in some effective but deceptive sense that something more lies behind the appearance than "meets the eye." For example, a suggestible person can be led to infer an object's existence through a type of wishful thinking. He wants it to be the case that the façade is the real appearance of something substantive and diachronically stable. Although "seduction" might to some connote the process by which Emma Bovary, Johannes' Cordelia, and many other women have been lured into disreputable actions (i.e., as judged by the prevailing standards of their societies), it can also be used to describe any process leading to a change in attitude or belief the effectiveness of which depends upon the use of a façade, which exploits the agent's suggestibility and vulnerability to wishful thinking.

The most obvious example of seduction in contemporary society is of course advertising. Advertisements often present people with no essential connection to the products which they advertise. Yet their glamour or respectability or athletic prowess or other qualities increase consumers' tendency to buy. The consumers think, perhaps, that the connections between the people and the products are substantive, consist of something more than the beautiful models' or the successful athletes' having received an enormous amount of money to appear with or to appear to use the products being advertised. This example, however, misleadingly suggests that all seducers are self-consciously aware of what they are doing. If one believes in the existence of something, one may nonetheless construct a façade with the aim of persuading another to believe, on the grounds that the end justifies the means, and that it might be otherwise quite difficult to bring the other person to the belief, which, being true, should be acknowledged by all. This could in fact be the case for some advertisers, since they might believe that a product is good but that the best way to get people to use it would be by building such a façade, which the advertiser himself can see through, but which is justified by the end.

Seduction and indoctrination are most effective upon individuals who are in some sense dissatisfied with their current view (including about themselves), who are looking for "an answer." Cult leaders and advertisers are often keen psychologists, capable of detecting human frailties and exploiting them to their own benefit. Ardent believers in a cause or religion are very difficult to convert to a different, incompatible, cause or religion. Highly skeptical individuals are very difficult to seduce, since they typically disbelieve the sorts of connections insinuated in advertising and other realms. They tend to poke holes in façades, which reveal the emptiness behind. Skeptical agents are also very difficult to convert to religions. And some people prefer seduction to conversion. They will engage in dialogues with others, but they will not do what others tell them to do unless they can devise independent rationales for so doing. They would rather seduce themselves with language than allow others to convert them through indoctrination.

Given the sorts of dynamics involved in indoctrination and seduction, it is understandable why, if perspectivism is correct, people would tend toward a conservatism in their belief systems. No one likes to be made the fool. It is much easier to believe that what one has always regarded the absolute truth, the facts about the objective, external world, is in fact the truth, than to come to think that one has been continually indoctrinated and seduced by authorities who manipulated one into believing a bunch of lies.

It is an as of yet unsettled fact whether perspectivism or absolutism is correct. Since perspectivism is a meta-thesis, which therefore has no implications for action, the difference between absolutism and perspectivism lies only in the interpretation of facets of "the world," for example, why "the experts" are the experts. If perspectivism is correct, then most people do not know what they are doing, since they take themselves to be finding out facts about "the world," not creating them. Most people are deceived about what they are doing. People who do not know what "they" are doing are "self"-deceived.

Perspectivism is tantamount to the collapse of what we ordinarily regard as the fact/value dichotomy, since people's values determine what the facts will be. But it is not merely that the facts are biased, as many absolutists will admit. Values completely determine the facts. Every question is a question about values. Since every putative fact represents a perspective, perspectivism has won out over other perspectives through some process of seduction or conversion of the dissenters, or else they have escaped to another world, appointing themselves "the experts." For example, in order for us to have reached this point of accepting the fact that these words are written on a piece of paper, it had to have been decided by two disputants whether to consider its thinness essential to it or not. We do not call wooden planks "paper," even when they have writing on them, and even though they too derive from trees.

If absolutism is true, then the largest human community is nonetheless delimited by the language users. They disagree about some of the facts about the objects which they agree to exist. "The facts" are still determined by the outcomes of disputes. But this is interpreted in absolutist terms as having "located" the facts. The process, of either creating or discovering "the facts," appears to be the same in either case: intersubjective agreement is taken as criterional for truth. Whether absolutism or perspectivism is correct, we always defer to the experts. There is a sense in which our finitude forces us to depend upon the experts in areas unfamiliar to us, since we could not possibly undertake exhaustive investigations of everything relevant to our lives. So if "ought implies can," then such deference may not be criticizable as a whole, though it may be in particular cases.

Communities and their associated institutions tend toward conservatism, since those who disagree radically with the prevailing values of a system most often select other communities and careers where their interests and values are shared by the experts. Revolutionary overthrows of the value systems of communities and their associated institutions are nearly impossible to effect by individuals, since the systems all have built-in mechanisms for removing dissidents. Failure to agree with the experts of an institution is nearly always regarded as evidence of incompetence.

Consequently, institutions transform through time according to the anthropological model of punctuated equilibrium. Small disruptions are squelched or ignored, but this has the effect of volcano-capping, which eventually becomes prohibitively difficult and finally impossible. Those in authority can remove weeds from their own garden plots, but eventually history marches on, and change is effected. For example, despite many localized protests against U.S. slavery, the institution remained intact for centuries, since those in power were, of course, highly conservative. Only something of the magnitude of the Civil War could effect that radical change, switch a community's perspective, force people to invert the necker cube. If some of the plantation owners had tended their garden plots a bit more carefully, they might have postponed the war for five, ten, even twenty years. But everyone knows that weeds come from weeds, so when they were gone, history would have marched on, and what would they have accomplished? Now, looking back, we can see the type of self-deception which slave owners engaged in, persuading themselves that they were doing Negroes a favor, by providing them with the "opportunity" to eat, sleep, and reproduce.

If perspectivism is true, then people "choose" to impose their values upon the relevant community when they embark upon careers which will lead to their becoming the experts in a domain. It is fully comprehensible why, even if perspectivism were correct, experts would be avowedly absolutists. To deny that the facts are "out there" in "the world" to be discovered is tantamount to admitting that one has appointed oneself "the expert" in order to determine the reigning values of a community. Since experts would be unlikely to want to face up to this sort of responsibility,[18] it is understandable why they would include in the curricula of their training programs the idea that the subject matter is essentially factual. In fact, those who have come to a perspectival understanding of "the world" conduct themselves indistinguishably from absolutists; the difference emerges only when they ascend to a higher-order level, when they *interpret* their enterprises. On one interpretation, experts are serving "the cause" of the perpetuation of their own values; on the other interpretation, experts are serving "the cause" of Truth, Knowledge, Beauty, etc.

Goodman's espousal of a positive first-order aesthetic theory does not conflict with his claim that we make worlds. His rejection of resemblance as criterional for representation is made in a world in which a quasi-absolutistic distinction between appearance and reality is presupposed. A world is absolute vis-à-vis itself. It is built from choices about properties made according to individual conceptualizers' values. A certain conception of competence is presupposed by resemblance theory. The experts have access to "reality." But if perspectivism is true, the experts have access to "reality" because they are the most "powerful," the better proselytizers or seducers, in the domain in question. They have succeeded in determining, stipulating, the essential properties of the objects of that world.

How does this differ from absolutism? "Facts are biased" means that some details are selected as important, while others are ignored. But "focusing upon different details" is what is going on in both cases, right? What does it mean to say that we create objects? We destroy and create objects by imparting properties to "them," since an object has all and only its properties necessarily and within a world. One alteration, augmentation or diminution, of "its" numerous properties, destroys the object and creates another, in another world. If the "largest," that is, most comprehensive, world were redefined as "the world," then there would seem to be no distinction between such a view and absolutism. But perspectivism denies that the notion of a most comprehensive world, if that is supposed to include all worlds, makes sense. Why is that?

Perhaps the idea is similar to Russell's paradox. Suppose that S is the set of all sets. Let X be the set of all sets that are not elements of themselves. If X is an element of X, then it follows that X is not an element of X. But if X is not an element of X, then X is an element of X. Is this what the perspectivist means? A world is a set of objects, including its conceptualizer. The absolutist world would be the set of all worlds. But Russell's paradox is only applicable if the analogue to the set X described above is a conceptual possibility. Call w the world of all worlds which are not elements of themselves. What would it mean for a world to be "an element of itself"? I do not understand what it would mean for a world to be "an element of itself," so how would I know when I encountered one which was? Worlds are necessarily comprehensible to their conceptualizers. But that "world" is incomprehensible to me.

Another way of understanding the claim that "the world" does not exist would be as a thesis about the nature of facts. It might be thought, as outlined above, that facts are selective, necessarily omissive, since they are linguistic reports of events, which are themselves infinitely replete, continuous rather than discrete. Symbolic language is discrete, so facts necessarily reflect the values of the reporter, including his desire to communicate with his listener, conjoined with his perception of the listener's interests. Reports are meant to transmit relevant and interesting information, but these criteria are necessarily relative to contexts, including the communities in question. So it would be impossible to give a complete account of "the world" because we are finite and cannot offer an infinite number of descriptions of it. Indeed, it is impossible to capture even one event *completely*, since that would require an exhaustive description of all possible sensory impingement upon a single individual in a given instant. These ideas, however, are compatible with an absolutism about the real existence of a world independent of human conceptualization, so this must not be what the perspectivist has in mind.

Perhaps the idea is, rather, something like the following. "The world" would have to comprise all worlds. A thing has all and only its properties necessarily. One's properties are determined by one's experiences, but one's experiences are creative acts of conceptualization. The self constitutes its world, and each new act imparts a new property to the self. So each act is a "self"-destruction and a "self"-construction. I choose which new properties "my" new self will have by choosing to attend to some objects rather than others. I find myself with certain objects of belief about which I ask questions. At the culmination of each investigation a new fact emerges, and what "I" once was no longer exists, since I now have the property of having resolved that question. Worlds comprise all and only their objects, including their conceptualizers. But the hiatus between the conceptualizer and "his" conceptualization of "himself," which can only be retrospective reflection upon something which "he" no longer is, precludes the possibility of his grasping a world comprising all of his worlds, since his reflection upon that world necessarily changes him, creating a world which "he" now inhabits. In order to capture "the world," he would have to capture all of his antecedent worlds, but even if he were able to do that, his doing so would itself generate a new world. His reflection upon what he takes to be his former self (hypothetically entertaining all of his worlds) itself creates a new world, comprising the subsequent self (what he is now) and the former self, which is an object now believed to exist in the world which the conceptualizer currently inhabits.

So "the world" refers to nothing which I can fathom. When I try to capture "the world" I change it by adding a new fact to it. I destroy one world and create another by creating a new fact, that " 'I' captured 'the world'." Every conscious experience eradicates the world in which "I" was located and creates a new world which "I" subsequently inhabit, until "I" experience again. "The world" does not exist because it cannot be captured in the moment. So long as the subject lives he is creating objects, by imparting properties to them, in the worlds in which he exists. Conscious life is change, in this view, and "the subject" is continually creating "himself."

Assuming that this is an apt characterization of this view, the self is microcosmic of the world since "the self" cannot exist anymore than "the world." The self is constrained to worlds but it creates worlds and new selves by reflecting upon them. "The self" is nothing beyond what "it" takes itself to have been in an act of retrospective reflection, since "it" is the only thing which considers "it" as an object. Every act of reflection both destroys and creates a self. "The self" as pure conceptualizer is essentially "self"-destructive, since its property is to conceive, and its expansion of its concept of what "it" takes itself to have been effects the destruction of that object and the creation of a new one.

If the pure conceptualizer is essentially self-destructive, then responsibility and credit are self-deceptive interpretations. Self-deception is the seduction of the self by the self. One form of self-deception is a belief in one's "self," a reification of "the self," a belief that one is something substantive, more than the culmination of each momentary experience. Each creation of a new object through imparting a new property to it at the termination of an investigation concomitantly creates a new self. In this view there is a problem with egoism, since "you" don't survive any accomplishment, so it is unclear why "you" should be proud. "You" are not the same entity.

"The self" is Humean, if perspectivism is correct. A person is a concatenation or bundle of ideas and impressions. Another relevant model is the Buddhist, according to which no single thread, what could be interpreted as an "essence," runs through the lifetime of a person as ordinarily individuated. The existentialist idea that "l'existence précède l'essence" is apt, if perspectivism is correct; however, Sartre's concept of mauvaise foi is (ironically) a deceptive interpretation of others (as is this one of Sartre, as well). So either Sartre was not a perspectivist or he thought that he could better perpetuate his own values through writing as though others can with linguistic propriety be morally judged diachronically. Sartre's requirement of consistency or nonhypocrisy is an absolute value relative to the world version of all members of society or the functional intersubjective community. Logical consistency is a requirement for all intersubjectively shared languages, and it may be that Sartre thought that one's commitment to language in a community implicitly commits one to a value of consistency.[19] But people are not languages.

If perspectivism is correct, then it is impossible for someone to be hypocritical, and ascriptions of hypocrisy are judgments rendered upon concretized and erroneous conceptions of the other. This might seem to explain why no one ever seems able to "face up" to his own hypocrisy. If you asked the most "hypocritical" person you know whether he condones hypocrisy, he would insist that he does not. Hypocrisy, in the perspectivist view, is a simple conceptual impossibility, an interpretation of the comportment of others in a sort of self-congratulatory way.

Interpretation is conferring properties upon objects believed to exist, but about which there are open questions. The choice of properties simultaneously answers the questions and destroys and recreates a self and a "text." But the self is also a "text," since it acquires a new property with every experience. In fact, "Everything is a text," if perspectivism is correct, because things only exist in worlds constituted by conceptualizers who determine the properties of the object of discourse. The end of discourse about objects creates new facts and thereby new worlds. People select properties, which are completely determined by their own values, to impart to objects. So your immediately preceding time slice determined the identity of the object with which you now share a world. Your immediately preceding time slice changed into you through reading this sentence, which ended with this period. But "you" read this sentence, so "you" destroyed your "self" and created yourself anew. You are nothing over and above your properties, and now you have the property of having just finished reading this sentence. Did I change you? No, you continue to read, imparting meaning to this text, so "you" change "you."

Perspectivism denies the existence of a best or authoritative world view. Different world versions are incommensurable, so interworld comparisons cannot be made, since they would require one to occupy a position outside of both worlds. We are "located in" worlds, and the judgments that we render are constrained by the standards of a specific world version. But Goodman denies that perspectivism implies a radical relativism according to which any possible interpretation of an artwork is as valid as any other: "our grounds for pluralism about worlds do not extend to a like-minded pluralism about works."[20] This claim is either false or misleading. How could it be true, unless individuals (as ordinarily conceived) were somehow single world-constrained? We view objects according to our interests and values, but we can also adopt a variety of different perspectives toward some "thing"[21] seemingly freely. We can annihilate objects by closing our eyes.

Goodman's attempts to illustrate how it is that interpretations of works can be wrong, that is to say, his invocation of examples of individuals applying standards to interpretations of works, calling them "right" and "wrong," are highly unpersuasive, and certainly offer no solace to absolutists, whose bête noire is any thesis which has as a consequence that "Everything is permitted." If perspectivism is correct, then in order to secure the "rightness" of any interpretation it suffices to adopt a perspective (switch to a world) according to which it is right. What Goodman's examples show is that different individuals have different tastes and opinions and that, given some perspective, judgments can be made from it.[22] Since perspectivism is a meta-thesis, it is compatible with any normative theory. So perspectivism obviously does not *imply* a normative theory of radical relativism, since it is equally compatible with its negation. I am assuming here that the levels of theory are fully distinguishable, so even if perspectivism is an inconsistent thesis (as some doubtless believe it to be), it only *implies* every proposition and its negation in its own, what is a "meta-"language. Put simply: perspectivism asserts that for any normative theory, its negation is a possible perspective. It suffices to make correct judgments of value, that one embrace and apply some (any) normative theory, and this seems to be what bothers absolutists.[23]

According to perspectivism, truth claims are appropriately restricted to world versions; it is a linguistic impropriety to apply the standards of one world version to things/persons "located" outside of the relevant world. In other words, there is something confused about applying one's own standards to those who do not accept them. To attempt to apply one's standards to outsiders is to assume truths to have interworld applicability, which perspectivism denies. If perspectivism is correct, then when "an individual" changes his normative theory, "he" switches to another world. To claim that an individual can be mistaken about the application of his own standards would be to suppose that "he," a subsistent entity with essential properties, survives his change in view. This would be to apply the standards of one world to another. Interpretation of an artwork is microcosmic of world-making via conceptualization, since, as with conceptualization, an individual's (conceived of either as a single person's, or the entire human community's, or some subcommunity's) own interpretation is necessarily the right interpretation for him qua interpreter at that time. Does it follow, then, that any other interpretation is necessarily "wrong" for him, since were he to have a different interpretation, he would be someone (thing) else?

That characterization is infelicitous, since saying that an individual's interpretation is necessarily correct for him is not equivalent to saying that all other interpretations would be incorrect for him. It would be nonsensical, rather than false, to ascribe other views to him, since "he" would be a different entity were "he" to hold another view. To the absolutist's dismay, the sufficient condition for an individual's correct interpretation of a work is that he interpret it thus, since his sincere adoption of it constitutes the only justification which an interpretation could have for him.

Viewing individuals as we ordinarily do, a question about transparency can arise. We generally think that it is possible to misapply what one takes to be his own standards. There are two ways of explaining such cases: either the individual doesn't really embrace his avowed standards (this assumes that "actions betray beliefs") or he does, but he has made an error in the application of his standards, which has led to an erroneous interpretation. A recognition of the impossibility of the latter sort of explanation, assuming perspectivism, suffices to defuse the objection, since in the moment of interpretation, the interpreter necessarily views his interpretation as correct: that is *why* it is his interpretation. To claim that an agent has misapplied his own standards is to commit the same error that a "dogmatist" commits in applying his own standards and theories to those who do not share them. This raises the question of the extent to which the radical relativism "implied" by perspectivism is what might be characterized as a "vulgar"[24] relativism.

"Vulgar relativism" asserts both that normative theories are relative to communities (the limiting case being a society of one) and that it is wrong to judge "outsiders," that is, those who are not members of the relevant community, by the standards of theories which they do not affirm. Under one interpretation, this thesis is self-contradictory, since it assumes an absolute value of tolerance, while simultaneously denying absolutism.[25] A more charitable manner in which to interpret this position is as asserting that it is a linguistic impropriety to apply the standards of one community to outsiders, since it constitutes a sort of category mistake. If normative constructs are relative to a given community, then they can only be applied with linguistic propriety to members of that community. Outsiders are not "persons," in the relevant sense, since they are not located within the insider's sphere of morality. To illustrate the point in a simple case, judging outsiders would be to commit the same sort of mistake which one commits in *morally* reprimanding a dog for having harmed a person (assuming here the widely held belief that dogs cannot be held morally responsible). But outsiders, such as dogs, may be treated in any manner in which one wishes (in the absence of other proscriptive beliefs to the contrary). They may be destroyed if they cause harm to the relevant community, in just the manner in which noxious weeds may be extirpated from a garden.

The difference between perspectivism and absolutism is not that the former denies that there are correct or incorrect judgments. The difference lies in their ideas about what truth could possibly amount to.[26] The perspectivist rejects the absolutist's desiderata, believing them to be not only quixotic, but in fact misguided. For a perspectivist, the demands of justification upon an individual are peculiarly easy to satisfy: it suffices that the agent, synchronically individuated, believe his theory to be true, in order for it to be true. "Truth" is always relative to a world version; the notion of "absolute truth" is incoherent. So when the scope of a claim is appropriately specified (e.g., by adding some qualification such as "for me"), then the theory is true. But there is none but the relativized notion of truth, if perspectivism is true.

While an absolutist might allow that "true for X" is a description of a property of X's beliefs, he would insist that there is a further distinguishable type of truth, and X's believing something to be true is certainly not a sufficient condition for its being so. Because a person's sincere assertion of what he takes to be his theory is the sufficient condition for its being true for him, it can only be said to be false by inappropriately applying it in other worlds, to other agents not already accepting it. Perspectivists sometimes characterize absolutists as "dogmatists," when the absolutists apply their own standards and theories to agents who do not accept them. Absolutists project their values and beliefs onto a world, claiming them to be reflective of some exhaustive "World," which is not only a chimerical, but in fact an incoherent notion. But the absolutist is most disturbed by this implication of perspectivism that the conditions for sincerely embracing and correctly applying a theory coincide with the conditions for its being true. That perspectivism has relativism as a consequence is further secured by the fact that the perspective from which standards are said to require any justification at all is itself one abandonable[27] perspective.

The conventions governing some conceptualization about "the world" have become solidified to such a degree that one can no longer raise questions in society about their legitimacy without being thought by others to be insane. There is a range of cases: the conventions governing conceptualizations of what we ordinarily regard as medium-sized objects may be frozen, while those governing the constructs of the latest theories of physics seem to be more or less fluid. In fact, the cases range along another dimension as well, depending on individuals' proximity to or distance from the intersubjectively determined origin of the conceptual sphere of the community. As explained above, "degree of solidification" is finally a function of the community in question. Even if one rejected the extreme view, that basic conceptualizations of what we ordinarily regard as medium-sized objects are radically revisable, different standards of justification could still be supported from different perspectives, but never against one another, if that would require "interworld" comparison. If there are any good arguments for the incommensurability of world versions, they have equally as much force with regard to interworld disputes over justificatory standards.

TWO

Art, Psychiatry, and Intelligence

The largest community to which I belong contains many conventionally delimited communities. These are "institutions," the existence of which is preserved by the larger community's agreement that they exist, and the objects of which are agreed upon by "the experts." Society agrees that "the experts" in an institution are those whose training and experience renders them best qualified to speak ex cathedra of the objects in the domain of that institution. The experts are determined intersubjectively by the entire community of the relevant institution. Their agreement that the experts in a field are "the experts" makes them the experts in that field. Objects in a world are nothing beyond what they are conceived of to be. Institutions seek harmony and stability and eradicate sources of discord and instability. Institutions have a derivative interest, via those whose livelihood depends upon them, in their own continuation. Two types of institutions exhibit an internal tension: those which have mechanisms for self-criticism, and those which revolve around activities which are essentially creative or artistic, generative of new ideas. Institutions which combine both of these features are "self"-destructive.

The institution of art comprises all and only those individuals who constitute the experts as "the experts" and in addition take themselves to have the same objects of discourse. These are the critics, historians, scholars, gallery owners, museum curators, museum goers, and those artists who communicate with the experts. The artworld has an interest in its own perpetuation: critics, gallery owners, and museum curators all derive their means of sustenance from it. But, at the same time, the institution's raison d'être is art, which is essentially deviant. The artist's work is necessarily on the margins of the sphere of comprehensibility of others. This is why what he does counts as original.

Artists are marginal relative to the largest institution, society, to which they belong. If perspectivism is true, then an artist's works depend for their existence upon the artist himself, until "they" are discovered by the artworld. In order to be accepted by the institution of art, an artwork must be comprehensible to the community. But this does not require that it be understood in the very manner in which the artist himself understood it. In fact, that would be surprising, since the reason that the artist is an artist is that he is marginal relative to the larger community. He imparts new meanings to objects agreed upon antecedently to exist. If an artist's meanings are entirely pellucid to others, then they are not new.

Is "creative writing program" oxymoronic? How could you teach someone to make something new?

The question might naturally arise, whether someone else must not on some level "understand" the work produced by an artist. How could a work be radically innovative, given that artists are historically situated? In this view, "newness" is a measure of distance from the origin of the relevant community's sphere of comprehensibility. Relative to the artist's private world, his "new" appropriation of symbols is standard, since he is the absolute in that world. An artist's meanings are "new" only relative to some other, heterogeneously constituted community. If that community happens to contain others relevantly similar to the artist, then they will share something like his own understanding of the work. In contrast to academia, where the experts themselves pass through the very system which they later come to govern, in the artworld the experts typically have gone through a different system. They have been trained in the history of art and art theory. So the experts in the artworld come to their positions through completely different pathways than the artist comes to his vocation as an artist. Indeed, study of art history and theory might hinder the development of one's artistic potential, by inculcating, as it does, ideas of what "art" is supposed to be. Forgers (qua forgers) are technicians, not artists. They are engineers, who devise means to pre-delineated ends.

The sort of "newness" recognized by an institution is predicated upon shared assumptions about the existence of certain objects such as canvas, paint, galleries, in the case of art. Some art objects are just found. Their creators have no relevant connection to the institution, but their works somehow come to be appropriated, despite their not having been created in reaction to the system. Other artists are in a sort of dialogue with the institution.

"Reactive" artists are acknowledged contemporaneously, while "nonreactive" artists, in the few cases where they are discovered, are discovered posthumously. Some "reactive" artists of the twentieth century can be viewed as sort of hybrid "artist-philosophers," since they raise new questions about accepted distinctions. In doing so, they self-referentially exemplify what all artists do, though on a smaller, less obvious scale.

Whether or not what an artist creates comes to be regarded as valuable depends upon a variety of factors, for example, whether or not his works are preserved. The works must be preserved fortuitously, at least at the first juncture, since it is not due to the value which they will only later be deemed to contain. When works are not initially preserved for no or completely arbitrary reasons, then they are preserved for accidental reasons, reasons extraneous to those which in general lead to the preservation of accepted artworks. For example, they might be preserved only due to what a family member regards as their "sentimental value." Works which are preserved out of beliefs about the artistic or aesthetic value which they contain, lie closer to, in fact slightly within, the "sphere of comprehensibility." At least some others have understood. But it is the essence of creativity to be unpredictable. Were some putative act of "creativity" predictable, then it would not be creative, since being creative consists in employing symbols in novel ways, ways not sanctioned by reigning conventions.

Eccentrics flout the conventions of "our fair society," but they are tolerated, to a point. When eccentricity exceeds all limits of comprehensibility, then it effects the expulsion of the individual from the world. Expressed creativity, which is acknowledged as such, can only be at the second and third tiers: the artist either sees different features of the things intersubjectively agreed upon antecedently to exist, or he perceives them tinged by different values than are "normal." Was Duchamp insane?

What could be more insane than to hang a urinal in an art gallery?

The institution of art accepts all of those objects which it perceives of as novel, but in some way ultimately soluble. This requires only that whatever the artist has created be comprehensible via the concepts of the experts, that the object be translatable into a structure comprehensible to the members of the art institution, while at the same time it be perceived by the experts to be "new." What is required is only that some "isomorphism" or translation into an idiom of the object left behind be understood.

It is curious that an institution, which can operate only according to certain fixed conventions, should require novelty from outside in order to continue to exist. The radically other is a challenge to one's own standards, to one's security. The artist challenges the reigning institution's belief in the legitimacy of its own success. The arts provide entertainment for the hoi polloi, but the experts deny that that is what art is about. Scholars and critics must deny that art is about pleasure, otherwise they couldn't be "the experts." Who can measure the pleasure of another? Who can tell another what gives him pleasure? Art critics presumably warrant the payment they receive for rendering judgments upon artworks because they are experts. They can identify what is good and what is bad. But if what constitutes good and bad metamorphoses, their credentials evaporate. This might help explain why some artists completely neglected during their own time can come to be heralded posthumously. If they are radically innovative, then their work is necessarily incomprehensible to nearly everyone, including those who wield power in the artworld. Scholars of art theory and history cannot recognize innovation, since if they could recognize it, either it wouldn't be new, or they would be artists and not scholars. But if they cannot recognize it, then it (and its creator) cannot be acknowledged. Acts of creativity are incomprehensible to most. If they are incomprehensible to all but the artist, they dissipate completely unnoticed. Cases such as that of van Gogh are fully comprehensible in this interpretation.

Artists insist upon doing things their own way. Perhaps artists see or conceive of the world around them deviantly and express these "visions" or "conceptions" through the creation of objects which somehow express "new" aspects. Or do they purposely distance themselves from others, by rendering themselves incomprehensible? You can expel another from your world by refusing to speak to him, by turning your back on him, by closing your eyes. Do artists believe that "man ist, was man ißt"? Perhaps they simply do not understand what "appropriateness" is. Or maybe they just do those things. Are these cases distinguishable?

Sometimes we find ourselves believing in the existence of an object, which provides the basis for a new investigation. Its provenance is irrelevant. The properties of the source of an artwork are irrelevant to our reception of it. We find ourselves confronting the work, and it provides the material for further investigations. The artist's intentions are irrelevant to the identity of a work. Similarly, an author is only the source of a text. He has no other properties. The investigation is about the nature of the text.

No, that's all wrong. This text is a palimpsest. But in this instance I will not hide it from you. I will not annihilate the printed expression of my former view. The reason that "the intentional fallacy" is a fallacy is not that the author's intentions are irrelevant, it is rather that the very notion of some determinate object "the author's *intentions*" is incoherent. Suppose that I had written this explanation over that one. Would my "intentions" have differed? I would have left you a different text. Could you have discovered the hidden layer, effaced by this paragraph? What would you have been looking for? How would you have known when you had found "it"?

No, that's not it. This text is a palimpsest. But I'll not hide it from you. I will not efface the printed expression of my former view. The reason that "the intentional fallacy" is a fallacy is not that the author's *intentions* are irrelevant, it's rather that the very notion of some determinate object "the *author*'s intentions" is incoherent. Suppose that I had written this paragraph over that one. Would "I" have been the same? How could you ever find "me"? You cannot determine the properties of an object without having located it. You must first believe that it exists.

Goodman offers no account about correct reception and interpretation of artworks, not because correct interpretation is prohibitively difficult, but because it is determined by the experts, so it is not possible to specify a priori which criteria will be used, much less which particular interpretation(s) will count as correct. An artwork (as ordinarily conceived), is microcosmic of "the world," since it has no exhaustive interpretation. "The artwork" is never completely interpreted, just as "the world" does not exist. Worlds depend for their existence upon conceptualizers and artworks depend for their existence upon interpreters. A world implodes upon the cessation of conceptualization of its conceptualizer. An artwork ceases to exist when it is no longer interpreted.

Goodman claims that artists can be mistaken about the meanings of their works. But the above interpretation of conceptualizing world inhabitants as essentially comprehensible to one another explains why his view about the artist's "fallibility" does not conflict with perspectivism. The identity of the art object is agreed upon by all disputants over interpretation. Relative to *that* world, the dispute is about the work's quality and what the work means. But there is no reason to think that anything like the artist's own opinion will be the victor, since the artist is an artist because he is deviant. Judgments of rightness and wrongness of interpretations can only be made within worlds, so it is "vulgar" to assume that the artist cannot be wrong. But if judgment is relativized to worlds, then the artist cannot be wrong, so long as he is the sole occupant of the world in question. Relative to that world, the artist is the absolute.

"The artist's intentions" about and the viewer's interpretation of "an artwork" are not really about the same thing unless the community is delimited such as to include both. But artists, critics, and other viewers can and often do disagree. An artist who spurns the opinions of the experts is marginal, alien relative to the institution of art. He is not contemporaneously a member of the reigning institution. He flouts their criteria of excellence. Refusal to accept the experts' answer to the question results in ostracism from them. The person who refuses to accept the outcome of that game, which was a dispute over the properties of an object agreed upon to exist, escapes to another world, appointing himself as the expert. The question was about artistic merit, and the experts provided an answer. The discourse came to an end, a new object and world were created, and a chasm was interposed between the artist and the artworld.

Profoundly innovative artists are incomprehensible to us, but sometimes their works, through sheer historical fortuity, make sense when we look at them. Sometimes societal convention takes time to "catch up." Was van Gogh discovered only posthumously because he was a radical innovator? Or was he a radical innovator because he was discovered posthumously? Are these cases distinguishable? Popular artists are comprehensible to us and only eccentric, rather than fully peripheral. Popular artists attend cocktail parties with critics. Maybe popular artists are radical innovators who have been profoundly misunderstood.

The artist creates the objects to which he attends. He finds himself believing in the existence of an object, a canvas, which serves as the basis for an investigation. He answers the question which he has posed by imparting a new property to it, creating and destroying simultaneously with each brushstroke. Artists change the way others conceive of the world, as Picasso explained when he responded "no matter, it will," to Gertrude Stein's complaint that his portrait of her did not resemble her. Artists manipulate others into seeing things differently. They force a new selection of features and perception of values upon others. They throw an object, which to them has certain essential properties, meaning, out into "the world," where it is appropriated by the interpreting community. The experts sift through the objects which they find, and they create "the wheat" and "the chaff," through the very process by which the artist created his artwork. The experts confer properties upon the works and then try to persuade others that the properties exist.

Supposing for a moment that absolutism is correct, one might think it miraculous that the people who choose to become "the experts" should happen largely to coincide with those who are the experts. Art critics choose to study art history and theory. What better way to ensure that you have refined taste than to become an expert about matters of aesthetic judgment? But to think that one's decision to become an art critic somehow uniquely qualifies one to access to higher-order truths about aesthetics can only be an act of wishful thinking. These sorts of considerations lead even some absolutists to conclude that a relativism about aesthetic values is basically right.

What we conventionally honor with the label "art" are those conceptions/perceptions which are new to us, which make us look at things differently, but which are expressed via accepted media. One way of being deviant is to refuse to play by the rules. Artists who question the very frames institutionally drawn are radical innovators engaging in a "dangerous game." They either succeed in undermining, by shifting, the frame of the community, or they fade away into oblivion. If they change medium, they might be esteemed or further ostracized. (Are these natural concomitants?) To make a new point, Duchamp appropriated a new medium.

Duchamp was impenetrable. Duchamp was opaque. He was insane. He was a philosopher. He was a genius. Duchamp just did those things. Are these cases distinguishable?

Duchamp is incomprehensible. But you make him comprehensible by choosing to occupy some level in speaking about him. You find yourself with this object, Duchamp, and you conduct a discourse about him with others within a world until a new property is applied. Languages are world-constrained and have their own criteria of appropriateness. You can only communicate with someone at some level, in some world, looking at an object which is exhausted by some description. Two psychiatrists have one discourse; two philosophers have another. A philosophical psychiatrist must decide between the two. Duchamp becomes insane, a genius, a philosopher, or an idiot, in a world at the culmination of a discussion. The "real" Duchamp is chimerical, elusive; he is nowhere to be found. If Duchamp remains opaque, you close your eyes and annihilate him. When artists radically change their medium, they have gone too far.

The largest world which I inhabit I share with you and many other people. We call it "society." In society some behavior is deemed completely inappropriate, antisocial, or pathological. The experts on these matters are the psychiatrists. Ordinarily we conceive of the mentally ill as those who are unable to function "normally" in society. The degrees of dysfunctionality vary from minor neuroses, which nearly all people appear to manifest at one time or another, to major disruptive and incapacitating problems.

The important message in Szasz's book is that maybe the day is long past due when we should stop forcing ideas, moral codes, . . . on others for their own good.[1]

Should psychiatrists accept Szasz's claim that it is "wrong to force ideas, moral codes, . . . on others?" Is it a *fact* that we should stop? Perhaps Szasz believes that, supposing that absolutism is correct, it is miraculous that the people who choose to become "the experts" should happen largely to coincide with those who are the experts. Psychiatrists choose to become the experts about "normality" in society. What better way to ensure that one's own concept will be vindicated than to become one of the experts? Szasz might believe that to think that *his decision* to become a psychiatrist somehow uniquely qualifies him to assess the appropriateness of the behavior of others can only be an act of wishful thinking. If perspectivism is correct, then others can only be seduced or converted to new views. Are seduction and conversion means of force? Is Szasz a hypocrite twice over? Does Szasz value a specific form of tolerance more than nonhypocrisy?[2]

One feature which distinguishes moral from artistic deviants seems to be that we believe ourselves to understand the former, and simply regard their behavior as bad, while an aura of mystery surrounds the work of an artist, which we initially do not, but only later come to understand. Deviance is tolerated to the extent that it can be without its harming the community. But harm is not only physical: new ideas and perspectives are destructive of old ideas and traditions. Institutions have an interest in preserving and perpetuating themselves. Those whose livelihood depends upon the existence of such institutions will actively defend them against outsiders.

If you told a psychiatrist that you think that morality is "a vain and chimerical notion," he might notify the police.

Practical reasoning results in policies of action. Theories of practical reasoning prescribe different policies of action depending upon the ends sought. According to purely instrumental theories of practical reasoning, ends are rationally irreproachable. Only according to a noninstrumental theory can people be faulted for their "antisocial" ends, for being "dysfunctional," for not choosing a plan of action which contributes to their ability to interact with others. If perspectivism is correct, then all theories, so theories of practical reasoning, there subsumed, are world-constrained. Given that societies can be delimited in any possible way, depending finally upon the individual, there can be no a priori grounds for preferring one conception over another, unless one already holds certain normative principles, for example, that "it is good to try to get along with most other people." How could one come to believe that, if one did not already?

Are conscious beings necessarily instrumentally rational? If perspectivism is true, then individuals act as though in accordance with their own theories of practical rationality, which are necessarily true for them in the private worlds in which they believe them to be true. When others are incomprehensible to us, sometimes their behavior strikes us as irrational. Sometimes we find their actions ludicrous, for example, if they appear to be seeking a particular goal and go about it in a completely circuitous manner. But according to perspectivism, there is no substantive self, as we ordinarily conceive of it, and such judgments betray the judge's erroneous concretization of the other. Ascriptions of irrationality can only involve application of one's own values to another's situation. But if perspectivism is correct, then no one can fail to be "rational," when "rationality" is appropriately relativized to the individual's world. If we were to see what he sees, and held the theory of practical reasoning which he acts as though in accordance with in the moment of action, then we might prescribe rather than criticize his behavior.

One way of being a skeptic about practical reasoning is to agree with perspectivism, that normative theories are world-constrained, so if the case is fully enough described and the agent's own values are acknowledged, then he could not, with linguistic propriety, be labelled "irrational." Another way of being skeptical about practical reasoning is to think that people just do those things. Whether or not someone's behavior strikes us as irrational depends ultimately upon our interpretation of his enterprise.

If you observed a man spending an entire day at a table, using a pair of tweezers to divide a pile of apparently indistinguishable crystals into two piles, you might think him insane.[3]

What could you infer about his beliefs by observing his actions? You could infer that he finds the enterprise worthwhile; that is why he is engaged in it.

In *The Scientific Image,* Bas van Fraassen claims that belief and acceptance are distinguishable categories and that a scientist's work requires only his being committed to the "empirical adequacy" of the hypotheses which he employs. The distinction must be phenomenological, since it is supposed to be an open question whether a scientist actually believes the theories which serve to guide his actions. Van Fraassen apparently thinks that you can find yourself believing some things, but you can be a scientist even if you never find yourself believing the theories of science. Scientists can use theories the truth of which they have no commitment to. It suffices to be able to use a theory that one believe it to be empirically adequate, that one "accept" the theory.

Harman observes that "belief cannot be distinguished from acceptance because belief is one type of acceptance."[4] But that observation does not impugn van Fraassen's claim, since he never supposed that the categories were mutually exclusive. Van Fraassen might think that acceptance is a volitional or intentional matter, while belief is not. Perhaps finding oneself with a belief concomitantly compels some form of "acceptance." That would explain why belief appears invariably as well to involve pragmatic aspects. Would it be possible to believe something to be true while accepting as a "working hypothesis" that it is false? That might seem to depend upon whether "actions betray beliefs." In fact, acceptance is more specific than belief, and no program of action is compelled by any belief alone. Only in conjunction with other beliefs, desires, and values might one arrive at the acceptance of some program of action. The salient case, willful deception or duplicity, clearly illustrates how belief and action often diverge. When a person knowingly deceives someone else, he is aware that he is uttering a falsehood (or omitting part of the truth), but he believes that doing so will help him achieve some object of his desire. Are policies of action forms of "acceptance"?

It is evident that a belief that the entities apparently referred to in our best-confirmed scientific theories exist does not compel one to be a research scientist. Harman and many other scientific realists are not research scientists. Those who disagree with van Fraassen fail to appreciate the phenomenology involved, as is illustrated in the following example.

Consider what a freshman does in his first chemistry lab. Does he not conduct an experiment without believing the relevant theory behind it? Clearly the student could not *believe the theory* without having assimilated any of its contents. Most majors do not even learn until their senior year that molecules are nothing like the ball and stick models used in their organic chemistry courses. What was the content of their beliefs during their lab sessions sophomore year?

One time you believed that if you poured two clear viscous liquids together, they would miraculously produce a flocculent yellow precipitate. Or did you even believe that before the experiment was over? And supposing that you did, did you also believe that the twelve-step mechanism written on the chalkboard, which explained how the precipitate was formed, actually had some *essential* connection to the mixing of the liquids and the formation of the precipitate? What if your instructor noticed that he had made a mistake and ran up to the board to erase one of the steps and write another one? Which was your belief? What if you poured the liquids together before the instructor wrote anything on the board? How could it be a condition on your execution of the experiment that you believe? Why is it necessary to believe anything other than that the proffered theory is one of an infinite number of possible and adequate theories? But "being a scientist" is not an office to which one is elected or a post to which one is appointed. One trains from freshman year through graduate school and then postdoctoral work in order to become a full-fledged "scientist." When does one first require *belief* in order for us to conclude that he takes his work seriously? Is that the point after which we should call him a "scientist"?

Van Fraassen's point is generalizable: it is impossible to know what another believes until he tells you. (And even then, he must be sincere.) Any action is compatible with, "explainable" by appeal to, an infinite number of adequate stories, involving completely different beliefs, motivations, desires, interests, and values. But this epistemological problem does not imply the impossibility of hypocrisy, only that in any putative case of hypocrisy, we outsiders can never know whether the alleged hypocrite is truly a hypocrite, or whether he holds a set of beliefs and desires which are eccentric in comparison to those of the "simple" scientific realist, who believes his scientific theories to refer to real things in the world no less than his theories of middle-sized objects such as tables and chairs. Such a person need never entertain the "philosophical" question: "Do electrons *really* exist?"

An individual's conceptions are constrained by his own antecedently determined values and interests. He conceptualizes in the manner in which he does by focusing on some things rather than others, and by sanctioning some ways of being while rejecting others. But given the apparent possibility of switching perspectives, of adopting different value theories, these "constraints" would seem to be nominal. According to perspectivism, the things which constitute the worlds in which we act are made through our own symbolization and representation. The possibilities for interpretation are infinite in number, involving (at least) two tiers of "interpretation."[5] The precise number will depend upon how one chooses to differentiate "levels." But in all cases where the individual conceptualizes objects external to himself as having "hidden aspects," there will be at least two tiers. On the more fundamental level, objects are made, and, on a higher-order level, their significance is interpreted via a selection of certain properties as relevant or interesting, at a given time. Some who find perspectivism preposterous are bothered by its blatant denial of the commonsense view that the structure of reality is independent of human minds. We ordinarily think that something is seriously wrong with someone who *sees* purple unicorns. (For the purposes of this example, and in the spirit of perspectivism, assume that "seeing" is defined phenomenologically, so that it is not a contradiction to "see" something nonexistent.)

If you told a psychiatrist that you believed in the existence of eleven-dimensional strings, he might prescribe an antipsychotic depressant.

What is wrong is no more and no less than that the person's reports and behavior do not agree with the concretized conventions governing what we have intersubjectively decided (albeit tacitly) to count as veridical experience. It would suffice for purple unicorns to exist, that the relevant community justifiably believe that they do, since truth conditions are finally justified belief conditions. If perspectivism is true, then, relative to his own private world, the individual is the absolute, so his belief is necessarily veridical. The existence of objects is determined by nothing more and nothing less than prevailing conventions governing realism. The difference between the cases of interpretation of an artwork and description or interpretation of an event (as ordinarily conceived), is not that the symbols in the former case are more replete than those in the latter but, rather, that the conventions governing symbol interpretation in the latter case have been solidified so completely and pervasively, that most people think of "reality" in absolutist terms.

An "event" or "state of affairs" is ordinarily thought to be described by a "fact." Description of "events" by a world version involves interpretation of replete symbols, and "the facts," the interpreted events, are "a matter of habit." On the view under consideration, the manner in which one's experience in the moment is described determines the content of the fact. So, although ordinarily we would expect someone who just "witnessed a car accident" to report that fact, his description might rather focus upon other aspects of his experience, for example, it could involve a finer or cruder level of discrimination than those words permit. He might say that "two pieces of moving metal collided inelastically with a resultant increase in systemically localized entropy." His describing his experience in such ways would render his behavior either completely incomprehensible, or at least inappropriate, relative to the conventions governing intersubjective communication in society. But, from the standards of appropriateness of his own world version, he would still be expressing a fact, describing an event. As suggested above, the idea is perhaps best illustrated by the common case of omission of information in reports of "the facts" in society. While an elliptical description of an event may not explicitly include the utterance of any falsehood, it can mislead through omission. If perspectivism is correct, then every verbal report of any event, as ordinarily conceived, is selective in the way that the common occurrence of misleading omission is. (Strictly speaking, the described event and the original experienced event are disparate objects, so in describing his experience, the agent creates a new object in a new world.)

It is all but impossible to gain an appreciation for the degree to which events are replete, given that we have all been inculcated since birth to attend to some and not other aspects of our environment. But it might be helpful to attempt to imagine what a complete sensory reception, of all possible stimuli to which one could attend at a given time would be like. One way to do this might be to imagine what an integration of several different stimuli would be like and then extrapolate to the harder case. So imagine reading this essay while simultaneously listening to music, taking a bath, and smoking a cigarette. This case is pretty obviously inadequate, since you will most likely switch your focus from one to another aspect of the environment.

The idea is exemplified in music by the form of the fugue. Trained musicians apparently simultaneously attend to the different voices of a fugue, though each is completely independent of the others. To the untrained ear, a five-part fugue is an undifferentiated blast of noise. So the undifferentiated blast of noise is metaphorical for one's unprocessed mass of sense data, which is ordered (by us, the trained musicians) into discrete "events" about which one can discourse and which permit one's functioning in society. The example is not meant to suggest that we have access to some pure sense data, completely independent of all possible theories. Even the "blast of noise" is perceived as noise, so the comparison is apt with regard to the theory-ladenness issue. As in the above case, it is unclear whether the musician is attending simultaneously to the different voices or can simply switch his focus from one to another voice very quickly, in an immeasurably small amount of time. But the example at least begins to suggest the degree to which events are infinitely replete and necessitate a selection and ordering on the part of a conceptualizer.

Some individuals apparently share the common conceptualization of what we ordinarily conceive of as "the world" with us, but focus upon features of it which we do not ordinarily deem worthy of attention. One case is that of an individual who finds incredible significance in the occurrence of "events" which might to others seem coincidental. These people (characterized by psychiatrists as "hypersuggestible" or "paranoid") are, if perspectivism is correct, interpreting symbols, the governing conventions of which to most people appear to be frozen, in novel ways. In some cases, these people could be said to be interpreting "nonaesthetic" symbols "aesthetically," assuming our conventional ideas about this distinction. For example, you might attend to the patterns of the letters on this sheet of paper, rather than reading the text for its content. This would be to consider the letters as aesthetic objects in their own right, not merely as vehicles for the expression of the ideas of this work.

The distinction between aesthetic and nonaesthetic symbols is itself a matter of intersubjective agreement and habit and so such deviant individuals could be said to be artists. Either they are artists each within their own worlds, where the aesthetic/nonaesthetic distinction is differently drawn, or they are artists in society, but they differ from traditional artists in that their media are "events," rather than sounds, paint, or words. But, in either interpretation, these people are imparting an order, a structure to their experiences, devising a theory which is "inappropriate" according to the ordinary standards of society. Was Berkeley psychotic?

If you asked a psychiatrist whether he actually believes that material objects exist, he might say that you have had a "psychotic break with reality."

People whom we call "neurotic" are comprehensible to us. People who are psychotic are incomprehensible to us. People who do not agree with us about the basic ontological occupants of this world are psychotic. Their conceptualizations seem to differ radically from ours, and this is why they are incomprehensible to us. We do not know whether or not they understand us, because they do not communicate with us. If perspectivism is correct, then when we label someone "psychotic" this is tantamount to saying that his values and interests are radically disparate from ours. Had we agreed with him, then he would be right, or "normal." Whether madness is in some sense volitional might depend in part on the agent's interests in being a member of the community. Perhaps his sincere efforts to be a member of the community failed. Or perhaps he prefers the eccentric structure which he imparts to his worlds. Or maybe he just became that way.

Psychiatry is problematic, whether or not perspectivism is correct. First, one's power of judgment, reason, has no subject matter. So it is either sound, to be trusted in all cases, or unsound, not to be trusted at all. Second, if conservatism is true, then a person is justified in believing what he does in the absence of reasons to the contrary. How could another person's testimony provide him with a reason to abandon a belief unless he had antecedently appointed that person the expert? But if he were of sound enough mind to appoint an expert, then why shouldn't he trust his own judgment elsewhere? And, if he appointed the expert, but is of unsound judgment, then why should he accept that appointed expert subsequent to "finding out" that he is of unsound mind? Third, how could a person abandon a belief unless he were persuaded that it was self-contradictory? There is nothing logically contradictory about purple unicorns (or eleven-dimensional strings)!

A conceptualizer must regard himself as a normal conceptualizer, since his willingness even to accept the experts as "the experts" presupposes his belief in his own ability to make judgments. A patient could only be seduced into believing both that he is abnormal and that he is of sound enough judgment to recognize that he is abnormal. Thus the psychiatrist–patient relationship is inherently paradoxical. Is it rational to trust someone whose entire means of sustenance derives from the existence of people whom he has convinced that they are of sound enough judgment to judge that they themselves are of unsound judgment? Doesn't that consideration provide one with an extra reason not to trust him, even if one were predisposed to do so? (Lots of people have bought swampland in Florida. Therefore, some people have sold swampland in Florida.) People who believe that others are "out to get them" are paranoid. But would you trust someone who tried to persuade you that "p and not-p"? Supposing that you believed him to be sincere, could you take him seriously (intellectually) at all?

Belief in the authority of a psychiatrist requires a "leap of faith," since to trust a psychiatrist one must be willing to embrace a paradox. Does not a patient's willingness to believe someone who persuades him that "p and not-p" conclusively demonstrate his own incoherence? This may explain why so many people become dependent upon their therapists. The patient has faith in another person's judgment and has come to view that person as the authority about where he can and cannot apply his own powers of reasoning. In addition to being *conceptually* problematic, psychiatry is *practically* problematic, since many persons who are psychologically disturbed enough to seek professional help are in such a condition due to their prior psychologically abusive relations with people who proved to be untrustworthy and duplicitous.

Do "outsiders" deny that realism is a matter of intersubjective agreement? No, that is impossible, so long as they constitute themselves as the subject of their experiences. They merely select a smaller panel of experts. At the limit, they restrict their community to themselves. They are "the experts." They are the measure of all things. Homo mensura. Ego mensura?

If you told a psychiatrist that every time you shut your eyes you annihilate a world, he might have you committed.

If perspectivism is true, then madmen are artists who flout the conventions of "our fair society." They refuse to accept what the experts have agreed upon to be the facts. They lie outside of our sphere of comprehensibility and are completely opaque to us. But we will never "catch up" to them, because their deviant behavior is fully ephemeral; it is not preserved in material artworks. Their media are events. They divide up things differently than we do. Or else they selectively interpret the environment in exceptionally deviant ways. Or else they value things differently than we do. In fact, all of these collapse into one, since the facts are determined by the experts in a world, and they do not communicate with us and therefore exclude us from their world. They exclude all others from their world, leaving themselves as the experts, so their values completely and exhaustively determine the facts in the worlds which they inhabit alone. They constitute their worlds simultaneously ontologically, selectionally, and valuationally. The difference between the artists whom we honorifically label "artists" and madmen, is that "artists" agree to share at least large crudely constituted worlds with us. They agree with us that extended objects exist. They agree to work in media which will make it possible for the experts of the art institution to retrieve and later understand their work. Their worlds are structured by logic, and they are comprehensible.

One distinction between social deviants and (honorifically labelled) artists may be that the former appear to pose a threat to the security of the institution of the society, while the latter do not. Artists are seemingly innocuous, so long as they are not perceived to step into the territory of "reality." Only within a framework rigidly upheld by the experts is creativity permissible. When art steps out of its legitimate bounds, then "the authorities" intervene. The practice of psychiatry is fully comprehensible in this interpretation. Psychiatry is the community's self-defense against otherness/deviance. Deviants pose a challenge to the structure of the society, and psychiatry serves as a defensive police force. If perspectivism is correct, then the only function which psychiatry could have would be that of making people act like other "normal" members of the community. Institutions have a derivative interest in preserving and perpetuating themselves. Those whose livelihood depends upon the existence of institutions will actively defend them against outsiders.

What this "reconception" of madness illustrates is the extent to which the categories heralded in psychiatry as absolute are a matter of "habit" and convention, dependent upon the delimitation of the "normal" community, not upon any "essential" features of some static thing, "reality," at least if perspectivism is correct. The difference between a perspectivist and an absolutist world lies in how lower-order theories are to be understood. In the former case, "reality" is a matter of intersubjectively inculcated habit and may not itself suffice as a justification for any paternalistic action, without affirmation of specific normative principles such as: It is good for all people to adhere to (abide by) the conventions of "our fair society." But such a view about the arbitrariness of psychiatric categories seems to follow not only from perspectivism, but from any form of (anthropo-) idealism or relativism about value, and also from any view according to which rationality is purely instrumental.

If perspectivism is true, then when a psychiatrist says that someone is "sick," this has a somewhat different meaning than we would ordinarily suppose. Assuming our ordinary views about justification, further marginalization through institutionalization or attempts to indoctrinate through the use of drugs or other forms of "therapy" cannot be justified by appeal to absolutist facts about the structure of "the world." Perhaps some psychiatrists believe that their distinctions are arbitrary, but they value what they take to be "the integrity" of society. The world of society is absolute relative to itself, and psychiatrists are the experts whom we have intersubjectively appointed. One who rejects the judgments of the experts in a world is evicted to another, the world where he has appointed himself the expert.

Also Sprach Zarathustra is a metaphor for madness, since not to speak is to escape to another world, appointing oneself the expert. You can switch worlds by closing your eyes and annihilating the objects currently in view.

Also Sprach Zarathustra is a metaphor for being an artist, since artists are alienated from society, and people who do not understand someone often find him insane. People can only order their experience by the beliefs and values which they understand, those relevantly similar to their own. They naturally impart order to their experience in such a way that it makes sense to them.

Are these cases distinguishable?

One activity of intelligence is the ordering of the data of experience in interesting ways, devising governing hypotheses which "explain," which relate things to other things. The "things" can be anything: marks on paper, pictorial signs, extended objects, ideas, sounds, etc. When previously symbolic signs, such as words, are re-appropriated and granted new significance, then the symbolization can be multilayered and therefore ambiguous.

Intelligence is essentially creative, unpredictable, and so cannot be measured. It is necessarily incomprehensible to most; it is distinguished by this attribute. This activity is a generalized form of what we see in people whom we conventionally and honorifically label "artists." Intelligent people and artists see and do things deviantly; they synthesize features of experience in novel but coherent ways. Intelligent people are hypothesis-mongers, quick to devise theories invoking data from any of a number of levels. They connect observations, facts, or hypotheses together in "deviant" ways, relative to those who do not engage in higher-order hypothesis-making, interpretation. Intelligent people interpret experience in new and interesting and complicated ways which are sometimes incommunicable, since public language is essentially conventional. When ideas are radically innovative, they are completely incommunicable. People who deviate radically from oneself occupy different worlds; they are opaque. Artists, madmen, and geniuses are empirically indistinguishable; they are opaque. They are incomprehensible, so they can be characterized, interpreted, in any number of other ways as well.

There are two kinds of high school drop-outs: idiots and geniuses. Extreme intelligence and extreme obtuseness are indistinguishable from the perspective of the "normal" language user/conceptualizer. This would explain why "stupid" people often think that "intelligent" people are "stupid." Each conceptualizer must regard himself as a normal conceptualizer. What is the difference between madmen and geniuses? From the perspective of most people, they have and share one comprehensible property: the property of being incomprehensible. People who think that Nietzsche is a lunatic find him completely opaque. Their only concept of Nietzsche is as the source of an incomprehensible oeuvre. They expel Nietzsche from their world when they close the book.

Nehamas thinks that Nietzsche is a perspectivist. Harman thinks that Nietzsche is a pragmatist. I believe that Nietzsche is a skeptic, though I'm not really sure. Maybe Nietzsche is a "house of mirrors," in which case I am too, and so are you.

Nietzsche scholars take as their object of study Nietzsche's oeuvre. They all agree that they are talking about the same object. They read the same printed words in their German editions. But they disagree about what the further properties of Nietzsche's oeuvre are. They disagree about the content of the theories or whether there are theories there at all. But since the experts determine the nature of the objects about which they are the experts, this means that Nietzsche has no nature. Each interpreter sees himself, though perhaps unwittingly, in Nietzsche, the "house of mirrors." Nietzsche is microcosmic of "the self," if perspectivism is correct, since they both lack content and continually change. Nietzsche readers either see something interesting, though not always recognizable, and investigate further, or else they close the book, throw a rock into a "house of mirrors," annihilate a world.

The activity of intelligence is indistinguishable from that of philosophy. Intelligence is hypothesis-mongering: putting things together in new ways, superimposing a theory on top of null-order events. The theory is a grid which is laid on top of them. The grid connects things in a world to one another in a pleasing manner. If you are intelligent and have a good memory, you can weave elaborate fantasies, by adducing memory traces and reinterpreting them to fit into a story. Philosophers create grids which they lay on top of things which they find. The grids are philosophical theories which tie things together in new and interesting ways.

The activity of intelligence is indistinguishable from that of philosophy. Intelligent criticism is the exposure of inconsistencies in the views of others. Intelligent criticism reveals to others how their grids are inadequate, how they fail to encompass certain things in the world in, at the level at which, they have been proposed. Assuming the same shared objects of discourse, philosophers illuminate the inconsistencies of theories purported to account for objects at that particular level. This activity, applying logic as a tool for criticizing theories, is general and is the basis for all revision of inter-subjectively inhabited world versions. Logic is the structure common to every language and therefore to every discourse. The law of noncontradiction, "not-(p and not-p)," is a necessary presupposition to any communication. If perspectivism is true, then language makes objects and objects exhaust worlds, so intersubjectively inhabited worlds are logical. The structure of "reality" is logical. The theories devised by finite beings are inevitably inadequate, because they are inflexible grids, and finite people are fallible. The longer a grid is tested, the more likely that its inconsistencies and inadequacies will become evident. Tenable grids strike a balance between precision and generality. If a theory is too precise, differentiates objects to the same degree to which they are differentiated in the world, then it is cumbersome. If a theory is too general, a grid with gaping spaces, then it invites exposure of its inadequacy.

The highest-order hypothesis, covering a given set of data that you come to believe, is irrefutable since nothing at the lower levels can be adduced against it. Your highest order grid becomes your god, once you have been converted or seduced to it, since no possible evidence could falsify it. In order to abandon it, you would have to be converted to another, incompatible grid. So long as your grid displays no internal inconsistencies, there is nothing else which could lead you to abandon it, though, if you become occupied with other matters, you might just forget about it.

Descriptions necessitate selection: retrospective descriptions of actions are omissive, since they involve selection on the part of the speaker. He must decide which features of experience were salient and are relevant to the listener's interests. If he reports irrelevant aspects, then the listener will find his behavior inappropriate or even crazy. People at the null-order level, the level of action, cannot comprehend people at the first-order level. People at the first-order level, reflecting upon the null-order level, cannot comprehend any meta-level. They are like the flatlanders attempting to understand the third dimension. It is opaque; it is incomprehensible. Opacity is multiply interpretable.

In order to be able to tell a story about an assumed determinate set of described events, facts, about their having transpired at the null-order level, one must occupy an external position. It is not merely that temporality imposes a lag between events and descriptions but, further, that one must be able to connect a given set of events together and that requires viewing them from a separate vista. For example, when someone connects two events by telling a story about a causal relation between the two, he must see them in the same plane, but this would be impossible if he were an occupant of that very plane.

In order to be able to tell a story about the facts described at the first-order level, one must be able to see relations between the facts, as expressed propositionally, and this requires viewing them from a separate vista. For example, to see that one's views on abortion and capital punishment are explicable by appeal to a theory about the nature of moral personhood requires that one be able to see the two positions in a different plane from that of the higher-order theory which explains the two.

In order to be able to tell a story about the moral theories which people propose, defend, and act as though in accordance with, one must view them from a different plane. When Protagoras and Harman view the panoply of moralities throughout time and in different places, they have a theory which explains the data: moralities are just the product of people, who bind together in order to further their own (essentially selfish) interests. Absolutists offer other explanations for the heterogeneity: human fallibility and our "dual" nature, our being both rational and emotional animals. Anomalies must be explained away, in order for us to be able to hold on to a grid, to believe in a god.

Different people stop ascending at different levels. Many people in society never ascend past the level of first-order description. They see that something is wrong and they condemn it, but they make no effort to explain their activities in terms of some higher-order normative theory according to which the actions which they view as wrong are wrong. Similarly, some deontologists and teleologists never seriously entertain the metaethical question: "Is there a single true morality?" It is obvious to some that consequentialism is true, the interesting remaining question being which particular form of consequentialism to espouse. Likewise, many scientists have no interests in (philosophical) questions *about* their own enterprise, their interests lie internal to science. They would never seek to devise some higher-order theory about their own activities. Self-reflective understanding is sought by some, but not by others, in all of the various institutions of society. People who are afraid of outsiders may be afraid of being told something about their own activities which they are not equipped to deal with.

THREE

Science and Academic Philosophy

In order to be able to tell a story about science, Kuhn had to occupy a position external to science. He looked down upon science and explained the enterprise by appeal to an elaborate, iconoclastic, and seductive picture. Kuhn called into question the then predominant view of science, favored by Reichenbach, Ramsey, Carnap, Hempel, and other leading philosophers of science in the analytic tradition. Before Kuhn, the received view was that science exemplified the application of human intelligence and industry to empirical phenomena having as results both impressive knowledge and control of the environment. Among the sciences, physics was thought to be the model for all others, exemplifying, so it was thought, excellence in methodology. James contrasts the common view of science, as objective and rational, to what is often regarded as the subjectivistic blathering of the non-scientifically minded in the following noteworthy passage:

> When one turns to the magnificent edifice of the physical sciences, and sees how it was reared; what thousands of disinterested moral lives of men lie buried in its mere foundations; what patience and postponement, what choking down of preference, what submission to the icy laws of outer fact are wrought into its very stones and mortar; how absolutely impersonal it stands in its vast augustness—then how besotted and contemptible seems every little sentimentalist who comes blowing his voluntary smokewreaths, and pretending to decide things from out of his private dream![1]

This is precisely the view of science rejected by Kuhn. Perhaps Kuhn thought that, supposing that absolutism is correct, it is miraculous that "the experts" should happen largely to coincide with those who are the experts. For scientists *choose* to become scientists. What better way to ensure that one is rational and objective than to align oneself with the supremely rational and objective enterprise? But to think that one's decision to become a scientist somehow uniquely qualifies one to access truths about the structure of "the world" can only be wishful thinking.

The Structure of Scientific Revolutions is an account of the scientific enterprise as a specific instance of the above theory of intelligence applied to objects at one level of discourse. The level of discourse is institutionally delimited. Scientists occupy an intersubjective world delimited from society by its activities and objects of study. The experts are those whose training and past experience render them best qualified to speak ex cathedra of the objects of this world. "Paradigms" can serve a variety of functions, depending upon the specific context, so Kuhn's variety of distinguishable uses of the word 'paradigm' is fully comprehensible.

In their most dominant usage, Kuhn's "paradigms" are grids superimposed upon phenomena until it emerges that they are inadequate to account for objects the existence of which is more certain than is that of the grid. Typically outsiders, those who switch to a new domain of study, notice the problems with the old theory and propose replacement grids. They have not been trained to believe that the old grid is true and that objects therefore *must* conform to it. If you believe that a grid is more certain than the things which it is supposed to account for, then you will never devise an alternative schema to account for anomalies, since your grid is your god. You will simply devise explanations of the anomalies. Kuhn characterized the process of getting others to abandon an old grid and accept a new one as "conversion." Was Kuhn a perspectivist in 1962? Or maybe he just despised scientism. Did he change his view?

People whose confidence in the grid that says that science tells you about "the world" is greater than their belief that higher-order theories might be true, find Kuhn ridiculous. Some critics, such as Lakatos, have characterized his theory as "mob psychology." People who deny the existence of indubitable objects are insane. People who assert the existence of nonexistent objects are insane. The people who find Kuhn insane are those who either believe in the existence of objects denied by their interpretation of Kuhn's text, or deny the existence of objects asserted by their interpretation of Kuhn's text. If they do not make an effort to reinterpret Kuhn in a manner pleasing to them, then they shut their eyes and annihilate him, escaping to another world. If you were raised to believe that oil and vinegar are immiscible *because* of the polarity of the constituent molecules, then you might think Kuhn insane. Everyone agrees that Kuhn's sentences are syntactically correct, that he understands how to use language. What some people find disturbing are the contents of his sentences. Their interpretation of Kuhn's sentences leads them to believe that Kuhn is crazy. But Kuhn couldn't have written a story which perfectly accommodated all of his readers, because some of them believe that "p" while others believe that "not-p."

For people who already had the impression that scientists are like religious believers, the way they toil away in their laboratories looking for things which they cannot possibly know exist, certainly not a priori, Kuhn might be the final seduction. Perhaps some other people noted similarities between Morrison and Boyd's *Organic Chemistry* and the bible. Why *do* so many fledgling physicists have posters of Einstein? Kuhn's view is particularly attractive to anyone who already believes that scientism is bad. However, it is much easier to come to believe a theory according to which other people are self-deceived about their own activities than one which implies the same thing about oneself. Most people who like Kuhn are nonscientists and, among philosophers, anti-realists.

Subsequent to the appearance of Kuhn's work, among those who found it brilliant, countless individuals regretted not having themselves been the one to "tell the story," to transmit "the word." They regretted not having taken the time to articulate those very ideas, which had been swimming around in their own heads for years, even decades. They console themselves with the thought that, had events transpired slightly differently, they might have been revolutionaries. They are probably right. If Kuhn hadn't done it, then someone else would have. Maybe Feyerabend would have been more careful, if Kuhn hadn't already done it. But, most people who like *The Structure of Scientific Revolutions* do not ascend to the level at which they might see that it is also a grid placed over objects in a particular world. They want to believe that it is true.

Kuhn seems to have changed his mind. He reneged on most of the radical claims of that work. Did he decide that what he had said was false, that it exaggerated the extent to which science is religious? People don't like other people to talk about them, but when they find out that it already happened, they always want to know what was said. Perhaps Kuhn realized that he found science valuable and surmised that an authorial recantation might prevent vulgar responses from scientists. Or maybe he grew weary of having to deflect "incredulous stares." Are these cases distinguishable?

Kuhn's story reminds us that scientists, though often intelligent, are human beings moved by passions and emotions in their professional just as in their personal endeavors. But of course those observations would be disconcerting only to someone who believed both in absolutism and that the pursuit of knowledge can only be an entirely rational, disinterested, objective enterprise. Although Kuhn's story is highly seductive, it would be a mistake to conclude even from a supposition of its truth, that the scientific enterprise does not lead to knowledge of the world. Nothing follows from the fact that a perspectivist interpretation of science is possible. There are an infinite number of possible stories which "account for" any given set of data.

Did Kuhn know what he was doing? People who do not know what "they" are doing are "self"-deceived. Could Kuhn have written the same story about himself? He wrote the book after having left physics. Could he have stepped away and seen his own grid? Why should that have prevented him from writing the book? That would have been vulgar.

Whether absolutism or perspectivism is correct, science continues to evolve, as scientists either invent or discover and increasingly elaborate scientific theories. Institutions such as science are continually "self"-evolving: they are simultaneously self-perpetuating and self-destructive. The subject matter and therefore ultimately the standards must of necessity evolve in order for the institution to continue to exist. In the institution of art, the subject matter and standards are always separated by a "lag": it takes time for the experts, schooled in history and theory, to learn to understand the newly appropriated symbolization of the deviant source of novelty, whose work necessarily occupies a peripheral position in the sphere of comprehensibility. But there is a less dramatic temporal hiatus between evaluative standards and content in all institutions in which the subject matter evolves. This model aptly explains why some institutions, ostensibly concerned with the production of new ideas, in fact for the most part breed and reward conformity.

Academia is an institution. In order to survive in academia one must produce work that is judged to be accomplished by the experts in the field. There is a tension between the need to apply established standards of excellence and the desideratum that creative work be produced. Academia differs from the artworld, in that what constitutes brilliance is a novel solution to a problem agreed upon by the relevant community to exist. But novel solutions are only solutions if they are comprehensible. Similarly, the institution of "art"-music[2] is such that its performing artists must be contemporaneously comprehensible to the experts. In the artworld, in contrast, the nature of the newly created object is such as to elude nearly all understanding of it. But for both performing artists and those artists who "throw" artworks out into the community, it is necessary only that some translation of the artist's product be comprehensible. So, for example, recording artists' own aural experiences of their live interpretations of works might differ radically from their aural experience of their recordings.

The experts of academic institutions are those esteemed for having accomplished something which has been widely accepted by the community to be laudable. The experts of an academic discipline (the professors) themselves comprise a smaller institution with its own set of intersubjectively appointed experts. The renowned figures in these fields are simultaneously the experts of the experts about that field, in contrast to the artworld, where the experts and the enshrined artists are completely distinct. What happens in some fields is that a very few innovators have come to be regarded as ingenious, while the rest of the community emulates those few. Whether absolutism or perspectivism is correct, we always defer to experts, since it would be impossible to undertake exhaustive investigations of everything of importance to our lives. Professors must defer to the experts of the experts in areas with which they are unfamiliar. More generally, the body of experts, as a whole, assumes and perhaps can only assume the standards of the few currently enshrined individuals to be the standards of excellence, since they are the experts of the subcommunity of the institution comprising its experts.

The inevitable result of this structure is a suppression of novelty. In academic philosophy the presumption is that, among the experts, the work of the few renowned figures, exemplifying excellence, embodies the standards to be applied to the work of students. The standards are applied as though they were objective, despite the fact that they arise purely from the values and interests of a small subset of the experts. Those professors who did not develop internal standards prior to their training, and therefore lack ideas about what other forms excellence might take, find the work of deviant students, which diverges from the familiar and widely received paradigms, opaque. At less prestigious universities, some professors seem altogether unable to assess the merits of objections which they have not encountered in the published works of their professional colleagues. Some professors acknowledge as telling criticisms of widely discussed views only those which have appeared somewhere in print. And then some will suspect plagiarism. But such suspicions merely betray an apparent failure to remember that all experts in academia had to have been students at one time.

As a result of this structure, creative philosophers, those who introduce new ideas or perspectives into the community of discourse, who are recognized during their own lifetime, produce work which is eccentric, relative to the relevant sphere of comprehensibility, rather than work which is fully marginal, as is the work of artists discovered only posthumously. Radical innovators without a name are dismissed as substandard, since they do not exhibit the same virtues which the few have made canonical. Hume and Frege were not recognized as great philosophers during their day. Only posthumously has their work been deemed by the experts to be of striking originality and value.

Given the tension between the desiderata of the production of creative work and the maintenance of institutional stability, how do the experts (of the experts) in academia attain their status? One possibility is that their idiosyncratic interests happen to have contemporaneously intersected with widely discussed problems in the relevant community. This would explain how it is that these individuals did in fact produce genuinely creative work while being nonetheless recognized immediately by the community. These innovators made no attempt to follow those before them, which could only have resulted in tarnished imitations of brilliance. Rather, by a simple historical fortuity, their personal intellectual interests happen to have coincided with fashionable topics of the day, or they produced work which was in some sense "timely."

"The subject" of academic philosophy is determined and exhausted by the interests of the experts, who are interested only in unanswered questions, so it is essentially nonfactual. Philosophy is unique among disciplines in that it is devoid of any diachronically stable subject matter, whether or not perspectivism is correct, so "the core" of the institution of philosophy is more mobile and ephemeral than for any other field.[3] The core is determined by a select renowned few, who espouse positive views and solve currently popular problems. In other areas, the settled facts become a part of the canon of information transmitted to future generations of experts in courses and texts, whereas, in philosophy, "settled facts" are forgotten about or ignored. Once the "settled facts" have left the community, then later generations of philosophers may raise the questions anew. Or could two philosophers of different epochs raise the very same question? Philosophy is quintessentially "self"-destructive, continually posing and answering (thereby dismissing) its own questions.

If perspectivism is correct, then science has no diachronically stable subject matter either, since the meanings of terms and the referents of theories are what the experts take them to be. If perspectivism is correct, then 'electron' refers to disparate things in disparate theories, so scientific theories are necessarily incommensurable. However, if absolutism is true about science and we have epistemic access to "the world," then there are probably at least some cases where the same empirical phenomena might be said (with propriety) to be explicable by appeal to different theories. In philosophy, in contrast, the identity of all referents of all theories is exhaustively determined by the current theory. What is "justice"? What is "virtue"? The experts acknowledge that these concepts have no diachronically agreed upon essence.[4] But even more peculiarly, as compared with other subjects, in philosophy the theoretical concepts lack even any synchronically agreed upon essence. Subjects of discussion in philosophy are open, unanswered questions, about only vaguely determined objects believed by some philosophers, in some sense, to exist.

Answered questions are no longer philosophical problems. They are facts. So philosophy is necessarily "self"-destructive: "it" continually creates and destroys its "self." Philosophy is a model of the self, if perspectivism is correct, because philosophers find themselves with objects about which they pose questions. Philosophy is also microcosmic of all "factual" enterprises, if perspectivism is correct, since in philosophy questions are being answered, so "facts" are being determined, and disputants must somehow persuade others that the properties which they favor are real in order to be victorious. These battles culminate in the expulsion of the former object of study from a world.

Academic philosophy tends toward homogeneity, since standards of competence and interests merge into one: both are determined by the particular values of the experts among the experts. The values of the system are self-perpetuating. Professors only want to interact with students who share their interests, and students seek guidance and direction from professors, whom they often emulate. Another effect is that students who do not share the interests and values of the current group of experts are ostracized by the community and therefore choose not to pursue philosophy professionally, though they might have during other epochs. This is perfectly comprehensible in light of the theory of incomprehensibility under consideration.

Problems which one does not believe to be problems are non-issues, non-things. In order to engage in a dialogue over the properties of an object, one must first believe that it exists, since it is impossible to raise questions *about* nonexistent objects, which have no properties. Lest it be thought that I mean here to suggest that fictional objects have no properties, it may be well to elaborate upon this point a bit, though it will require a short digression.

Fictional objects exist in some worlds, for example, in novels, but among their properties is nonexistence in "the world" which the reader inhabits. In writing fiction, an author takes himself to be creating a thing, a character, which does not live in the actual world. So Prince Myshkin, a fictional character, exists, but 'Prince Myshkin' refers to no existent person (at any time). The person "Prince Myshkin" is nonexistent, but the fictional character Prince Myshkin exists in a novel by Dostoevsky and in the writings and the minds of readers and critics of *The Idiot*.

To return to the matter at issue, it is impossible to conduct investigations *about* things which one does not believe to exist (in any world, real or fictional), because it is impossible to have intuitions *about* non-things. Non-things have no properties. Without an intuition, one has nothing to say, no opinion. It is also impossible to impart a new property to a non-thing; there is nothing to which to pin it. The phenomenon has two facets: students find professors who talk about non-things opaque, and professors find students who ask questions about non-things opaque. People who talk about non-things are opaque, and opacity is impenetrable. A conceptualizer must regard himself as normal, and those who are incomprehensible as, in some sense, abnormal. Opacity is multiply interpretable. Opacity is interpreted as incoherence by people who have reason to believe that they are competent, as all experts do, since they have been elected the experts by the relevant community.

People who talk about non-things babble nonsense. The "utility" of a thing cannot be a reason to believe in its existence, since non-things have no properties, so "its" utility cannot be adduced as evidence for "its" existence. One must be converted or seduced to the belief that the question of whether or not something which he positively believes to be nonexistent exists is worth pursuing. You can seduce someone into believing in the existence of some extended thing by erecting an elaborate façade and persuading him that it is three, rather than two-dimensional. But people can only be converted or seduced to a new philosophical interest, since it requires belief in the existence of a higher-order object, a philosophical "issue," in order to undertake an investigation with the aim of answering some question about it.

The questions of philosophy are "meta" relative to those of the other institutions of society. Philosophers ask questions such as "do molecules exist?" which scientists (qua scientists) find absurd. In their work as scientists, that sort of question is "inappropriate." Using Carnap's distinction between "internal" and "external" questions, the question "do molecules exist?" would be external to the scientific enterprise, in contrast to an internal question such as, "does tetrakis(2-chloroacrylonitrile) copper (I) tetrafluoroborate catalyze diels-alder reactions?" Philosophy is alienated from society, since its intersubjective world comprises conceptualizers who agree about some objects, their subjects of discussion, which other people in society, executing their tasks in their respective occupations, do not believe to be objects at all. They call them "non-issues." They are right, when these characterizations are viewed as relativized to the world version of the larger community, society. Those who espouse "the death of philosophy" reject as otiose, or at least undesirable, the discussion of external, meta-level, questions. They answer the external question: "are external questions worthwhile?" in the negative.

Philosophy is "inappropriate." Philosophers live at the margins of society, asking questions at the meta-level, isolating themselves from that community, refusing to work. They spend their lives creating and annihilating their objects of study. Philosophy is a sort of refusal to play "the game" of society. Ordinary language philosophy assumes that ordinary language refers to existent objects and that analysis of usage can illuminate interesting features of those objects. Ordinary language philosophers accept the language of the society which they spurn. Ordinary language philosophers are like defenders of scientific realism, in that they stand outside of another enterprise, praising it, while at the same time declining to participate in it. They find themselves with ordinary beliefs and commence their philosophical investigations from them. Ordinary language philosophy is ironic, when one remembers that philosophers are alien vis-à-vis the world of society. To accept the language is to accept the game, isn't it? Are ordinary language philosophers hypocrites? Do actions betray beliefs?

Some people in society believe that the questions that philosophers spend their time discussing do not have any answers, since the criteria for what would constitute an answer are themselves utterly moot. Some philosophers believe that questions about possible worlds and mereology do not have any answers, since the criteria for what would constitute an answer are themselves utterly moot. Some think that metaphysicians create pictures; they are artists who create new worlds by erecting elaborate palaces using their thoughts as media. But pictures cannot be true or false, only aesthetically pleasing or repugnant. Of course, if perspectivism is true, then new pictures create new worlds, since worlds comprise all and only their objects, so metaphysicians create new worlds. The facts are exhaustively determined by the experts of a world, so if a metaphysician creates a picture which he shares with no one, then it is nonetheless a "true" or "right" world for him: everything which he thinks about it is true. People who deny the existence of objects in his world find him opaque, since they think he talks about non-things, babbles nonsense.

Metaphysicians form their own subcommunities of people who believe that questions such as whether the sum of two objects itself comprises another object can be answered, given other features of their pictures. The only constraint which applies absolutely, relative to the world versions of metaphysicians, is logical consistency. In fact, consistency is an "absolute" value relative to the world versions of philosophy. This is hardly surprising, since logic is a presupposition to all discourse, it being presupposed by every intersubjectively shared language. But, in contrast to other fields, the only diachronically stable presupposition of philosophy is logic, whether or not perspectivism is correct. Every higher-order hypothesis is amenable to examination and criticism, according to some philosopher. Every question is permitted. Nonetheless, so long as a metaphysician's system is consistent, it is philosophically irreproachable.

Metaphysical systems are divine, since no lower-order data can refute them. Metaphysicians' theories are pictures in the sense that they are interpretations of substrata, even when they deny, as perspectivism does, the coherence of a notion of "substratum." Metaphysicians' pictures lie, structurally speaking, below all other types of theories. No amount of digging through other theories could afford an answer to a metaphysical question. But these pictures lie, theoretically speaking, above, since they are immune from attack by any facts from any less abstract level. The less a metaphysician says about his system, the less chance that he will emit a contradiction. When a metaphysician espouses a self-contradictory theory, then he will not win converts to his theory. But he can continue to believe in his system, since he only says things in an effort to persuade others to come to believe something which he already antecedently believed. A metaphysician can bask in the splendor of his own world without any danger of subversion. So long as he says nothing, he can say nothing falsificatory. Some find such systems and the people who spend their time discussing them insane. But why might one think that questions about mereology are any less answerable than questions about objects' existence, or any other philosophical question, for that matter?

The tendency of academic philosophy toward homogenization, given the nature of philosophical interests, manifests itself most dramatically in the twentieth-century phenomenon of the split between the analytic and continental philosophical communities. An apparently unbridgeable chasm now separates these communities, both of which amazingly enough grew out of the same Cartesian tradition. Continental philosophers do not understand analytic philosophers, who argue about "counterfactual conditionals," "rigid designators," "tropes," etc. But this makes sense, since if "counterfactual conditional" refers to no object in any of the worlds which one inhabits, then one cannot have an interest in determining "its" properties. Non-things have no properties. They must be talked into existence before battles over their properties can be waged. Continental philosophers believe that analytic philosophers engage in meaningless enterprises, try to answer pseudo-questions about non-things. Do analytic philosophers misunderstand continental philosophers? They seem to believe them to be engaging in meaningless enterprises, babbling nonsense, trying to answer pseudo-questions about non-things.

A student who wrote the equivalent of an analytic philosophy paper for a professor in France or Germany would probably be criticized for writing about trivial, "merely verbal" issues. (Note that, if perspectivism is correct, then "merely verbal" issues exhaust all issues.) A student who submitted a continental philosophy essay would probably be judged by the vast majority of analytic philosophers to be incoherent, or at least confused. It is plausibly due to the stringency of the standards (most evidently, the standard of "meaningfulness") and the narrowness of the interests of the influential figures in one of these geographically separated communities during the early part of this century, that a marked homogenization of these communities came about, and they now appear to be irrevocably alienated from one another. The standards and interests of philosophy are self-perpetuating, so when the community is delimited narrowly, as was the case during the reign of the logical positivists, a marked homogenization should be expected to ensue. The case of logical positivism is illustrative of a few general phenomena, so let us examine it in some detail.

Perhaps partly in reaction to the excesses of nineteenth century idealism, logical positivists assiduously but unsuccessfully attempted to reform philosophy. The positivists certainly had an effect upon the shape of anglophonic philosophy during this century, but it wasn't the one that they had envisioned. The failure of Carnap's project of formulating an inductive logic was only symptomatic of fundamental problems with the positivists' program. By now, it has come to be widely acknowledged that the verifiability criterion of meaningfulness is meaningless, by that standard itself, since it cannot be empirically verified or falsified. The facts about the scientific facts are themselves obviously meta-scientific. If 'metaphysical' refers to that which is not confirmable by the methods of science, then meta-scientific hypotheses are "metaphysical." In order more fully to appreciate the extent to which the positivists were literally blind to the nature of their own commitments, it will be useful briefly to review some of the more important metaphysical presuppositions of the scientific enterprise.

The logical positivists did not think that people should not organize experience intelligently using meta-theories: scientists themselves organize experience intelligently by devising meta-hypotheses that connect lower-order data in interesting ways. But, even ignoring the problem of the theory-ladenness of any putative data, the positivists completely failed to appreciate the degree to which scientists require pragmatic criteria in order to be able to devise and choose between competing hypotheses. One version of the problem of the underdetermination of theory by data is that, for any set of data, an infinite number of adequate hypotheses will account for them. Some antecedently stipulated criteria of hypothesis choice must be assumed in order to opt (nonarbitrarily) for one over another hypothesis. Since those pragmatic criteria cannot themselves be empirically verified, the entire mechanism of science itself presupposes countless answers to what the positivists themselves derogatorily characterized as "Scheinprobleme."

Indeed, at the most fundamental level, the very notion of "evidence" presupposes that one can be warranted in believing in the truth of some hypotheses. So the most basic question for the positivists would be: Why think that there is a true higher-order theory at all? A story can always be told; an explanation can always be offered. Is any story better than none? Is any explanation better than none? Did the positivists believe that being able to tell a certain kind of story about something suffices to make it true?

If a hypothesis, H, connecting a group of facts together, is true, then the hypothesis "H or these facts are unrelated" is also true. Coming to believe H means changing from believing that the hypothesis was a possible story, which could be told, to a belief that it actually "accounts for" the phenomena and is, therefore, true. How could one come to believe that the first disjunct is more likely to be true than the second? What could persuade someone to think that the story which can be told is true? Belief in hypotheses that "account for" seemingly unrelated data is a sort of wishful thinking. Why should wanting there to be a true story make it the case that there is? Why should wanting there to be a simple explanation make it the case that, when "found," it will be true? People who devise elaborate fantasies in order to "make sense" of their experience, to "account for" all of the details of every interaction which they have with every person who passes them on the street, are "paranoid." You must first believe that there is some story which will be true when told, in order to believe that some criteria would warrant you in believing such a story when it is in fact proposed.

"H or these facts are unrelated" is a simple and all-encompassing hypothesis which "accounts for" all data of your experience. Why not stop there? How could one distinguish between epistemic and pragmatic criteria for belief unless one already knew in which specific cases the first disjunct of this general hypothesis was true? In order to know that, it seems that one would need a higher-order hypothesis such as, "hypotheses with these features are always more likely to be true than is "these facts are unrelated.'" But which criteria might those be? Simplicity? How might one come to know that S, "simple hypotheses are more likely to be true than complex ones?"

For the purpose of illuminating the substantively metaphysical presuppositions of logical positivism, I shall assume for the moment that the principle sanctioning "inference to the best explanation" is sound. This issue will be treated at greater length below, in conjunction with a general discussion of wishful thinking and ampliative inference to higher-order hypotheses. For now, suppose that one may justifiably "infer" to "the best explanation," that the best explanation of a set of phenomena is more likely to be true than no explanation, and that the fruitfulness or simplicity of a hypothesis makes it good.

What constitutes "fruitfulness"? What is "simplicity"? Even supposing that one had some applicable notion of simplicity, why think that the universe is simple in *that* way? If perspectivism is correct, then the objects of the world versions of science are exhaustively constituted by the experts, scientists. But let us assume for the moment that the positivists were not perspectivists.

If something like Ockham's razor is a principle of rationality, then to say that simple hypotheses are more likely to be true than those which are not is to say that it is as *though* a rational creature created the universe. But, that "a rational creature created the universe" is a better explanation than none. A belief in simplicity as an epistemic criterion and a principle sanctioning "inference to the best explanation" is stronger than a mere belief in the existence of a God. It is a belief in a scrutable God, a God whose ideas and values are relevantly similar to our own. Supposing that God believes that it is good to be rational, why assume that he shares our ideas about what "rationality" is? Even supposing that the almighty hypothesis-monger, whose believing a hypothesis to be true makes it true, existed and his values coincided with ours, why assume that he would "decorate" the universe parsimoniously? Is God a miser? If you were going to decorate your apartment and knew that you had no budgetary constraints whatsoever, wouldn't you do it as luxuriously as possible? And even if you restrained yourself, believing perhaps that what is good is "moderation in all things," wouldn't you still have an infinite number of choices about how to select and combine fabrics and colors? You would even have an infinite number of possibilities for basic furniture!

Ignoring those problems, let us soberly suppose that there were a workable and relevant criterion of simplicity, and that S were a sound principle. Then that criterion would lead ultimately to the simplest hypothesis of all: "All is one," since that meta-hypothesis covers every case of "H or these facts are unrelated." Given two hypotheses, H_a and H_b, the truth of the schema "H or these facts are unrelated" implies the possibility of some higher-order hypothesis H^1, such that, "H^1 or H_a and H_b are unrelated" is true. But the criterion of hypothesis simplicity would lead in every case to the conclusion that H^n, the higher-order hypothesis, is true, since it is obviously simpler and therefore warrants belief more than the hypothesis that the two lower-level hypotheses are essentially unrelated or coincidental. Every higher-order hypothesis would need to be connected to all other hypotheses, according to S, and so ultimately H^∞ would be reached:[5] "All is one." A commitment to simplicity as a criterion for hypothesis choice seems to imply that the highest-order hypothesis devised is the one which warrants belief. If the positivists accepted the (meta-)hypothesis, S, that given the choice "H or these facts are unrelated," H is always the better hypothesis, then they would be led to the parmenidean principle. But if they did not accept it, then they would never be able to count any empirical data as confirmatory of any scientific hypothesis and therefore would have to dismiss all as meaningless, by their own verifiability principle. So it seems that the logical positivists, in advocating the scientific enterprise, would be committed to the hypothesis that "All is one," too. The only way to avoid this conclusion would be to insist that the hypotheses leading up to H^∞ be real possibilities, that they be hypotheses actually proposed by scientists. Scientists (qua scientists) stop at the level of "scientific" hypotheses.

The positivists thought that their "verifiability principle" excluded "metaphysical" hypotheses, but it excludes everything in the absence of either some pre-delimited, question-begging criterion of what can constitute evidence, or else an arbitrarily stipulated community of hypothesis-mongers. Simple observations of events do not confirm so-called "scientific" hypotheses, like H, any more than they confirm the hypothesis that "these facts are unrelated." A commitment to simplicity as an epistemic criterion includes the idea that the world *is* how we want it to be. Homo mensura. Homo faber. The positivists delimited the relevant community so as to include scientists and not philosophers. But scientists do not devise meta-scientific hypotheses, so the highest-order hypothesis which "we" could devise, assuming that community, determines what will be sanctioned as a scientific hypothesis. That community seemed to the positivists to act in accordance with something like the hypothetico-deductive "method" of hypothesis testing, which broadly distinguishes empirical or confirmable from non-confirmable hypotheses, but cannot itself be confirmed and so is also meaningless by their criterion.

Without having antecedently affirmed "homo mensura," scientific realism is completely indefensible. But, even then, the "success argument," that the success of science warrants belief in science, is circular, since the criteria of success are determined by the current state of the scientific enterprise, and the state of the scientific enterprise is "successful" when evaluated by appeal to scientific criteria for success. Coherentists deny that circularity is vicious, but a coherentist theory of justification would not alone suffice to defend the supremacy of a scientific world view. A defense of the claim that a scientific world view should be exhaustive still requires an extra normative stipulation to that effect, since there are many other human (e.g., "aesthetic" or "moral") ways of viewing things. The logical positivists delimited the relevant community in a particular way, namely, by excluding all nonscientists.

The positivists claimed that meta-level speculation was illegitimate, but that claim is itself a "meta"-meta-level hypothesis. While the statements of science are not themselves explicitly "metaphysical," the entire mechanism of science rests upon a complex metaphysical apparatus, and so a commitment to science implicitly commits one to that apparatus. A commitment to science like the positivists' is profoundly metaphysical, not only because the entire mechanism underlying the enterprise is, but, further, because science cannot be used to defend the claim that "science is the perspective of choice," that a scientific outlook exhausts reasonable outlooks. Were the positivists unable to see what they were doing? Nothing precludes one's opting for a scientific world view, but it is simply and obviously delusive to claim that such an outlook is preferable in virtue of its avoidance of metaphysics. Did the positivists really believe what they said? Or were they perspectivists who valued scientific more than nonscientific views? Are these cases distinguishable?

What is prima facie remarkable about the logical positivist movement is not that it terminated abruptly, but that it should ever have had any success at all. How did the positivists persuade others to believe them? How did they divert their attention? Individual conceptualizers make sense of their own experiences. Why would anyone accept logical positivism who did not already believe it? The positivists stipulated rigid constraints on how order could reasonably be imparted to experience. They promulgated their procrustean criterion perhaps in part in order to be able to uphold stringent standards which could be intersubjectively agreed upon: "No act of intuition can be said to reveal a truth about any matter of fact unless it issues in verifiable propositions."[6] Apparently blind to the irony of their own words, some positivists even went so far as to preach "the death of philosophy," acknowledging that their own enterprise was worthless by their own lights, though failing to see that their own assessment of what they were doing presupposed its legitimacy.

The verificationist criterion undoubtedly had a stifling effect upon philosophy. The people attracted to philosophy were "scientists," insofar as they shared the basic outlook of scientists. From the vista of the positivists, those who wanted to engage in metaphysical discourse were opaque. Because interests are determinant, either overtly or covertly, of criteria of competence, those who dissent are culled from the academic community, since they call into question the expertise of the experts. People who talk about non-things are insane. People who are insane are irrational. To eliminate an irritant it suffices to close one's eyes and annihilate a world. It is plausible that logical positivism ostracized from academic philosophy the "deviants," those with other beliefs, values, and perspectives, those interested in what the positivists believed to be "Scheinprobleme." Deviants were removed from academia at an early stage so that dissent was muted, since it is simple for experts to dismiss nonexperts who disagree with them as confused or even crazy. Any possible question can be entertained by philosophers, but personal interests exhaustively determine the subject matter of philosophy. So the community became even more homogenized than would be expected during an arbitrarily selected episode of history, due to the positivists' extremely narrow interests.

The positivists and those alienated from academic philosophy during that period were incomprehensible to one another. Those who would erect new castles, or who believed that subjective experience should be the starting point of philosophical reflection, as did Descartes, were excluded from academic philosophy during this period, and the mechanism of academia ensured that the interests and values of the early positivists were perpetuated. Plato, Aristotle, Kant, and many others would have been ostracized by the academic philosophical community during the reigning period of logical positivism. It does not necessarily follow that the positivists were to be faulted for this. Their view was that philosophy was like science in that it aimed for truth and knowledge and therefore should share the values and methods of science. Or maybe they just didn't value pluralism. Are these cases distinguishable?

If "religious" views are those which cannot be arrived at via sound reasoning, then the positivists' commitment to science was deeply religious. No sound argument could lead one from the premise that "metaphysics is nonsense" to the conclusion that the methods and values of science exhaust all acceptable forms of discourse about "the world," since that "the world" should be delimited and exhausted by science is itself a "meta"-physical hypothesis. One would have to be converted or seduced to a position like the positivists', since no facts can be displayed to settle the question. Furthermore, the motivating premise actually undermines the very enterprise that the positivists believed it to support.

The logical positivists instantiate a general tendency on the part of people to fail to recognize the presuppositions of their own enterprises, even when they contradict their explicitly avowed values and interests. The case illustrates, in particular, the considerable extent to which philosophers can be blind to their own presuppositions, even when they blatantly conflict with policies which they explicitly advocate. It also exemplifies the general phenomenon of homogenization, which occurs in academia, though perhaps less obviously, all of the time. And finally, logical positivism offers a concrete example through which to understand the particularly dramatic tendency of academic philosophy toward homogenization, given the intimate connection between standards of competence and interests and the human tendency to explain the incomprehensibility of others.

Although logical positivism commenced in the "Vienna Circle," its most vocal exponents relocated in the United States and can quite plausibly be seen as ultimately responsible for the state of analytic philosophy in this country during this century. Moreover, A. J. Ayer, whose influential *Language, Truth and Logic* has been used in countless introductory courses in philosophy in English universities, undoubtedly played a role in the analytization of academic anglophonic philosophy.

In saying that philosophy is concerned with each of the sciences, in a manner which we shall indicate, we mean also to rule out the supposition that philosophy can be ranged alongside the existing sciences, as a special department of speculative knowledge. Those who make this supposition cherish the belief that there are some things in the world which are possible objects of speculative knowledge and yet lie beyond the scope of empirical science. But this belief is a delusion. There is no field of experience which cannot, in principle, be brought under some form of scientific law, and no type of speculative knowledge about the world which it is, in principle, beyond the power of science to give.[7]

It is difficult to imagine how teaching that *Language, Truth and Logic* exemplifies philosophical excellence might have any more tangible effect than to dissuade nonscientistic students from pursuing philosophy professionally.

     Society stipulates that the experts in an institution are those whose background, training and knowledge qualifies them to speak ex cathedra of the objects of that domain. But in philosophy there are no diachronically stable objects. While many professors defer to the experts (the enshrined figures) among the community of experts (the professors), they of course regard themselves as experts within the larger institution comprising students and professors. But since the activities of philosophy, hypothesis-mongering and criticism using logic, are indistinguishable from those of intelligence, this is to assume that they are more intelligent than their students. Such a probabilistic conjecture may or may not be warranted in any particular case. But in all cases the nature of the professor–student relationship is inherently paradoxical. In order to accept a professor's negative evaluation of his work, a student must antecedently have accepted the professor as an expert. But the student must simultaneously presuppose the soundness of his own judgment in appointing the experts the experts. Philosophical writing is also the application of reason to issues, so if a student judges his own work to be good and this is denied by a professor, then the student has some reason for thinking that his appointment of the experts might also have been of unsound judgment. Sometimes logic is mistaken for "sour grapes."

Despite his disagreement with Carnap on a number of issues, Quine shares much of the scientistic outlook of the positivists. Indeed, one of the most common allusions to Quine is his own allusion to a metaphor, "Neurath's boat," from an outspoken proponent of logical positivism, Otto Neurath:

> Naturalism does not repudiate epistemology, but assimilates it to empirical psychology. Science itself tells us that our information about the world is limited to irritations of our surfaces, and then the episte-mological question is in turn a question within science: the question how we human animals can have managed to arrive at science from such limited information. Our scientific epistemologist pursues this inquiry and comes out with an account that has a good deal to do with the learning of language and with the neurology of perception. He talks of how men posit bodies and hypothetical particles, but he does not mean to suggest that the things thus posited do not exist. Evolu-tion and natural selection will doubtless figure in this account, and he will feel free to apply physics if he sees a way.
>
> The naturalistic philosopher begins his reasoning within the inher-ited world theory as a going concern. He tentatively believes all of it, but believes also that some unidentified portions are wrong. He tries to improve, clarify, and understand the system from within. He is the busy sailor adrift on Neurath's boat.[8]

There is no question that Quine, whose writings are suffused with admi-ration for his mentor and friend, Carnap, perpetuated the spirit of positivism, through his seductive advocation of a preeminently scientific and formalistic outlook. Although the formal program of logical positivism was abandoned, the spirit of the movement has dominated the Anglo-American philosophi-cal community, throughout this century. Now, looking back, we can see how such beautiful prose and persuasive rhetoric could have brought thousands of philosophers to hail science as "the answer." Now, looking back, we can see the diaphanous screen which many mistook for the front side of a beau-tiful castle.

During this century, many self-proclaimed "scientifically minded" phi-losophers have pursued projects relating to the formalization of natural lan-guages, either for their own sake or in the service of making the language of science more precise, despite the fact that a moment's reflection reveals that those projects exhibit the very sort of incoherence as that of the program of their mentors, as I shall now explain.

In theorizing *about* a formal system, all proof is informal. So, if formalization is a general desideratum, it would seem that formalization of the metatheory should be undertaken, for any or all of the reasons that the original formalization was. Any argument to the effect that formalization is, at this point, undesirable would apply, mutatis mutandis, to the starting point. One is led to either an infinite progression of formal languages talking about formal languages or a finite progression ending in an informal account of the formal languages devised. The former is not a real possibility for finite beings; the latter is real but seemingly self-defeating.

Formalization aims at an uninterpreted language, syntax sans semantics. However, this is evidently unattainable, since so long as one has some consciousness of a symbol, one is interpreting it. The very distinction between semantics and syntax presupposed by advocates of formalism is arguably incoherent, given the nature of intentionality, since it is impossible to entertain a symbol thoroughly devoid of meaning.

Moreover, despite the fact that formalization is undertaken in order to obtain a well-behaved language, free from ambiguity and vagueness, the final theory and all of the results pertaining to it, expressed in the metalanguage, do not and, in the end, cannot escape the features which were to have been avoided via formalization. The resultant formal theory is itself fashioned from informal tools, since simplifying "classical abstraction" can only commence from the perspective of informal language, and all metatheorems are expressed in "crude" informal language and can only be proven by informal proof. Through "formalization," ambiguities in natural language will translate into either ambiguities in formal language or simplifying abstractions, which altogether change the subject of discussion.

These fundamental problems with formalism somehow eluded the "scientifically minded" followers of Quine, whose formal logic textbooks were studied assiduously by the graduate students who went on to become "the experts" of academic philosophy. There is little doubt that Quine's many rhetorically persuasive manifestos, such as illustrated in the above cited exhortation to "naturalism," were the ultimate motivating source of many projects for the naturalization of epistemology pursued during this century, which, though not internally inconsistent, as was the positivists' program, nor obviously quixotic in the manner of formalistic programs, would seemingly require a solution of the "is-ought" problem in order to be successful. Of course, if perspectivism is correct, then there is no "is-ought" problem, and the fact-value dichotomy is chimerical.

Given that historically philosophers have often been quite critical of the accepted dogmas of society, the degree to which scientism has dominated analytic philosophy during this century still might seem surprising. But the scientistic bent of analytic philosophers is comprehensible, given that the positivists did somehow manage to dominate the Anglo-American philosophical community for a substantial period of time, that institutions tend toward conservatism and homogenization, and that the subject of academic philosophy is exhausted by the interests of the experts. Moreover, the positivists provided a structure for future philosophical projects and a framework in which to order experience consonant with the widely lauded developments of science during the early part of the twentieth century. This suggests a further purely psychological explanation for the pervasiveness of the scientistic outlook of philosophers in the analytic tradition, relating to the familiar human phenomenon of wanting to side with "the winning team."

The prodigious technological success of science is incontestable. Scientists have developed truly impressive means to prediction and control of our environment, and the number of remarkable gadgets invented during this century which have affected the lives of all members of society is staggering. In the midst of all of this technology, it is understandable why philosophers, appreciative of the contributions of science to their own lives, would want to align themselves with that enterprise. So both the technological success and the ground breaking theoretical developments of science provide further explanation of the somewhat puzzling phenomenon of the radical homogenization of philosophy during this century. It is virtually indisputable in the world of society that people derive satisfaction and even a sense of purpose from being associated with "winning" causes and teams. Professional philosophers, though often intelligent, are nonetheless human beings.

A second episode in academic philosophy which illustrates how very narrow interests can come entirely to dominate the academic philosophical community is that of the "West Coast semantics" of the seventies. During this period, when discussion of a very narrow range of issues relating to technical questions in linguistics became popular in analytic philosophy, a large number of professors were tenured due to their having contributed to the solution of the then fashionable problems. In the ensuing years, professors who received tenure during that period had to convince students that their philosophical approaches and issues were interesting and valuable. They had some success, as is evidenced by the relative preponderance from 1970–1990 of doctoral dissertations treating very specialized issues in the philosophy of language.

The need of individuals to justify to themselves their own positions as experts, may well explain the phenomenon, but homogenization and narrow specialization is further ensured by the human tendency toward developing habits of thought, since one's interests can be strengthened and even decisively determined through intensive work in an area. A simple sociological hypothesis can also be adduced to explain the phenomenon of homogenization in academia in general: people in academia are forced to specialize narrowly for a period of time in order to survive, to succeed in their field. But, by the time they have secured their positions, their major interests are often fully determined. For example, scientists often emerge from their arduous training with a robust set of intellectual interests all of which are internal to science. This is not to insinuate that something is wrong with that, but to point out that it is a result of our tendency to develop habits of thought, conjoined with our finitude.

It is impossible for a finite being to be interested in everything. Finitude necessitates selection, and the nature of academia, conjoined with the massive and ever-increasing volume of available information, necessitates specialization. In science, mastery of even a small specialty of a single area, for example, plasma physics or organo-metallic chemistry, can easily exhaust all of the time that even an extremely gifted individual can reasonably invest in professional activities (i.e., assuming that he has other nonprofessional interests). In academic philosophy, only rare individuals manage to keep up-to-date with the current debates of more than one area of specialization.

The journals have reached the point where they publish only very thoroughly defended theses, which are, therefore, of necessity quite narrow. The state of philosophical journals can also be understood by the particularly dramatic tendency of academic philosophy toward homogenization given the intermingling of interests with standards of competence. The "best" journals have the most stringent standards, but those standards are determined by the work of those figures deemed to be exemplary in the field, the experts among the entire body of experts. In fact, the celebrated figures in an area are often members of the board of editors of one or more journals. Professional survival all but mandates that one engage in currently fashionable debates, at least until one receives tenure. But by the time that one has produced enough narrow journal article-type work to receive tenure, one's interests may well be determined, since interests tend toward further specialization and self-perpetuation.

A further possible contributing sociological factor might be that the majority of active members of academia are men, often married, who have personal responsibilities (to their families) to succeed professionally, in order to be able to provide needed financial support. This would explain why many contemporary philosophers follow the path of least resistance, by producing work which exemplifies and further perpetuates the reigning standards and interests of the community as a whole and therefore is more likely to ensure professional success than would the sort of "gambling" involved in remaining faithful to one's own first inclinations.

The respectability of any philosophical work can be boosted through the invocation of important ideas from a work previously widely accepted to be revolutionary. And in fact, the tendency of interests toward specialization in contemporary philosophy can be further illuminated by appeal to the Kuhnian framework, especially the idea of "normal science." According to Kuhn, subsequent to a scientific revolution an entire corpus of small projects are generated, projects which provide vast numbers of scientists with directed activities, the accomplishment of which secures their gainful employment and professional success.

Kuhn's model is quite apt for philosophy, since whether or not perspectivism is correct, "philosophical revolutions" of necessity involve radical paradigm shifts, insofar as they direct the entire community's interests toward those of the "revolutionaries," and the introduction of incommensurable world views, since philosophy does not build upon itself diachronically. As explained above, this is because there are no diachronically stable philosophical facts, since once a question is definitively settled, it no longer belongs in philosophy. The interests of philosophers exhaust the subject matter of philosophy, and philosophers are interested in unsettled questions. Philosophers engage precisely in the enterprise of raising questions about putative facts, or raising altogether new questions. However, "philosophical revolutions," such as logical positivism, ordinary language philosophy, "West Coast semantics," Kuhnian philosophy of science, provide a new framework, a temporary origin, a foundation, which, relativized to the community at that time, provides an absolute set of philosophical "facts" from which to work.

The phenomenon of logical positivism is rendered altogether comprehensible by appeal to Kuhn's picture, since it is plausible that philosophers in the Anglo-American community were ripe for an "answer," as people in general seem to be, as the pre-revolution community must be in order for a revolution to succeed, and the positivists provided one. In general, as a Kuhnian reading would predict, breakthroughs by renowned philosophers generate entire industries of activity for vast numbers of other philosophers. For example, when "possible worlds semantics" was discovered as a new approach, countless books applying this idea to specific problems and other areas in philosophy appeared. Similarly, the "causal theory of reference" led to the appearance of a plethora of books applying the insights of a few renowned figures to many other areas of philosophy. When a "new way" is discovered and gains favor among influential figures, then hordes of followers jump on the bandwagon (believing the experts) and begin elaborating the new theory, applying it to old problems in new ways, in the manner of the "worker bees" of normal science.

The acolytes of groundbreaking figures in philosophy, whether they be graduate students or junior faculty members, can secure professional success through a willingness to work out the details of their mentors' newly introduced and widely lauded theories, since the experts of the experts assess the merits of their work and naturally find that which builds upon their own discoveries interesting and valuable. The acolytes of famous philosophers become themselves experts, but acolytes never come to enjoy the status of their mentors, though they may, if charismatic, acquire a few acolytes of their own. Many graduate students have no clear sense of direction and will enthusiastically follow the advice of an expert in selecting a dissertation topic.

Revolutionary work in philosophy has a polarizing effect upon the community. People have strong feelings one way or the other about it: admiration or revulsion. Kuhn was either brilliant or insane. But, either response demands reaction, since if the work is brilliant, then it should be applied elsewhere, and if it is insane, then it should be decisively refuted, especially in view of the fact that some poor deluded souls have mistakenly found it brilliant. How many professors have received tenure for their detailed book-length criticisms of *A Theory of Justice?*

In general, philosophical revolutions are not supplanted by replacement revolutionary theories, since there is no set of empirical phenomena "to be explained," such as binds interparadigm scientists together. Nothing that happens to string theory will change the density of water from 1.0 g/cm^3. Of course, in Kuhn's view, successive theories only illusorily replace one another, since the constructs of different theories are in fact incommensurable. But in philosophy, the working hypotheses, "facts," are so near the surface that there is not even an illusion of diachronic commensurability. When a single gust of wind blows through, the entire house of cards collapses to the floor. But when the horizon is thus cleared, philosophers' interests tend to change to entirely different questions and subjects of discussion. How many philosophers under the age of forty have read any work by Strawson, Ryle, or Sellars?

If a revolutionary theory is in another domain altogether from their own areas of specialization, philosophers may seize the opportunity to elaborate interesting connections between previously believed to be disconnected topics.[9] Kuhn's *The Structure of Scientific Revolutions* itself generated an enormous industry, but that industry transcended all disciplinary boundaries and had its greatest effects in the social sciences, perhaps in part because of social scientists' eagerness to elevate their own enterprises by emphasizing the weaknesses of the natural sciences, which have always in some sense put them to shame.

Similarly, since the appearance of Foot's highly influential article, "The Problem of Abortion and the Doctrine of Double Effect," a veritable "trolley problem" industry has erupted. Within the milieu of the analytic philosophical community, this is a widely accepted way to approach moral philosophy. Some students coming to philosophy from "the outside," taking a philosophy course for the first time, find this methodology ludicrous. They wonder why anyone would suppose that thinking about fat men in caves, child-crushing machines, and senior citizens picnicking on trolley tracks would have any relevance whatsoever to some interesting philosophical issue. Nonetheless, within the paradigm of contemporary moral philosophy, this is a highly respected approach to moral problems, perhaps accruing some of its respectability through transfer, from Rawls, whose *A Theory of Justice* introduced the widely lauded idea of "reflective equilibrium" into the community. Moral phenomenology can be viewed as an application of Rawls' idea to a new realm, and Rawls' work has received far-reaching acclaim. Rawls' work, another salient example of a philosophical revolution, has generated manifold industries and led to the writing of hundreds of interpretive, elaborative, and critical books.

A further example of the application of revolutionary work is the predilection (which has only recently diminished) of analytic philosophers for formalization of statements clearly expressible in natural language. When the experts of the experts have evinced their favor of some technique or their interest in some issue, that suffices for countless aspirant experts to adopt the technique or develop that interest. In spite of the fact that it is undeniable that given any statement either it is unequivocal, and therefore formalization is an otiose expenditure of time, or it is equivocal, in which case disputes over its meaning will translate directly into disputes about how precisely to formalize it, many philosophers of the past, in the wake of the wide favor which formal logic gained during the early part of the twentieth century, due to the accomplishments of Frege, Russell, Hilbert, and Gödel, availed themselves of formal techniques in their discussions. In the eyes of some, formal logic became a kind of ammunition, to be brandished against "soft-brained" subjectivists. Now, looking back, we can see the manifest absurdity of thinking that formalization can solve philosophical problems (given the problems described above). Our recognition of the painfully obvious fact that decisions about *how* to formalize can only commence from intuitions, themselves evidently subjective, allows us to see that the use of a highly technical apparatus in philosophy was really nothing more than a kind of security blanket. Philosophers, like all people, take refuge in and derive satisfaction from knowing that they are competent *at something,* that they have a subject matter, that they are experts at something, that there is a framework, a locatable origin, that they are skilled laborers engaged in important building projects. But students who encounter professors who insist upon speaking in tongues are always ostracized and sometimes, ironically enough, even bullied into believing that *they* are philosophically incompetent. Of course, students who can be persuaded by experts to believe that "p and not-p" are incoherent.

One notable disanalogy between "normal philosophy" and Kuhn's "normal science" is that the research projects engendered by scientific revolutions are seemingly interminable, since, for example, the number of significant digits of a physical constant can be potentially endlessly determined. There will always be something for a normal scientist to do, since he builds on established facts, which, when quantitative, can be made increasingly precise, the terminus, $n = \infty$, being unattainable for finite beings. In philosophy, however, revolutions dissipate rapidly through time, leaving no traces behind, since the sorts of problems solved by "normal" philosophers begin to lose their interest to others, once they become too narrow. Although many a philosopher has received tenure for having written a book applying or elaborating the "causal theory of reference," when this work becomes too recondite, people just ignore or forget about it. They decide to pursue more intuitively interesting issues and questions. Still, it is indisputable that professional success can be secured through a form of devotion to an expert of the experts, a willingness to do "normal" philosophy.

Philosophers who offer courses on highly recondite issues relating to the details of their detailed elaborations of their mentors' work are largely opaque to undergraduate students, who obviously have not followed the development of the issues from their origin in a philosophical revolution. This underscores the earlier explanation for the degree to which philosophy has undergone homogenization during this century. One can only be interested in objects which one believes to exist. Non-issues are non-objects and have no properties about which to have intuitions. It is very difficult to write a paper about some "thing" with which one shares no world, about which one can have no opinion.

A further, less obvious, disanalogy to the sciences is that the expert/acolyte relationship in philosophy can be paradoxical, since the activities of philosophy are the activities of intelligence, so in appointing the experts, one presumes oneself to be of sound judgment. But then shouldn't one also be able to choose a good dissertation topic? In the sciences, a professorial thesis advisor must direct his graduate students, since they couldn't possibly know which "wheels" have and have not already been invented. But in philosophy there are no diachronically stable "wheels." A good topic in philosophy is precisely a topic about which a philosopher has concern and intuitions. It would be very difficult to write about something without having any intuitions about "it." How could you build a façade out of air? Non-things have no properties.

Subsequent to philosophical revolutions, among those who find the work brilliant, countless individuals regret not having themselves been the one to "tell the story," to transmit "the word." They regret not having taken the time to articulate those very ideas that had been swimming around in their own heads for years, even decades. They console themselves with the thought that, had events transpired slightly differently, they might have been revolutionaries. They are probably right. If Kuhn hadn't done it, then someone else would have. Maybe Feyerabend would have been more careful, if Kuhn hadn't already done it. The details of a Kuhnian reading of contemporary philosophy could be multiplied endlessly, but that would make this work normal.

Philosophy constitutes/structures worlds by asking questions that change worlds, by creating new facts.

FOUR

Metaphilosophy

Philosophy, though always "self"-destructive, is "suicidal" when it sanctions the adoption of a view according to which philosophical questions are to be decried. This is what happened most flagrantly in the case of logical positivism and somewhat less obviously with Hume:

> If we take in our hand any volume; of divinity or school metaphysics, for instance; let us ask,
> *"Does it contain any abstract reasoning concerning quantity or number?*
> No.
> *Does it contain any experimental reasoning concerning matter of fact and existence?*
> No.
> Commit it then to the flames: For it can contain nothing but sophistry and illusion.[1]

As always with such seemingly self-referential statements, it is not obvious whether the author is being ironic and actually appreciates the degree to which his own hypothesis is in fact a meta-level hypothesis and therefore "metaphysical." The early Wittgenstein blithely confessed (in the *Tractatus*) that his own account of philosophy as nonsense was itself nonsense. These writers, Hume and Wittgenstein, like the logical positivists, are in some sense disdainful of "metaphysical" speculation. There are a variety of possible explanations for such an attitude. One is a belief that there is something intrinsically misguided about meta-level speculation. This would seem to be an impossible position to defend, at least unhypocritically, if all propositions are selective higher-order descriptions of replete null-order events. Another explanation might be the realization that beliefs are essentially religious and that the views of finite beings upon close examination will inevitably give way. It is unclear why, if the latter is Hume's reason, he should be bothered by the existence of "school metaphysicians," since they provide skeptics with the grist for their mills, which otherwise might lie dormant.

Perhaps Hume is concerned about the well-being of other, more impressionable philosophers. Maybe Hume wants to prevent others from being converted or seduced to substantive philosophical positions, other than his, that "Metaphysical speculation is illegitimate." The irony of Hume is that he seduces his readers to the belief that "only *abstract reasoning concerning quantity or number or experimental reasoning concerning matters of fact and existence* is legitimate." Hume seduces his readers to this piece of "sophistry and illusion."

Similarly, genealogical stories, such as Nietzsche offers about many of our moral concepts, often have the effect of persuading the reader that what he uncritically accepted as immutable truths are in fact historically conditioned, arbitrary, and utterly fortuitous. Had events transpired differently, our moral concepts might be quite different from those which we currently embrace. But people who are disturbed by genealogies, who believe them to debunk concepts or unmask false idols, fail to appreciate that the contexts of discovery and justification are logically distinct and that it should come as no surprise that a story can be told about some concept, since a story can be told about anything. A story's being told does not suffice to make it true, and, more importantly, even a story's being true would not suffice to debunk a concept. The concept or enterprise might be just as good or valuable as ever. To think that the possibility of telling a story suffices to debunk a concept would be a form of nihilism, since for any concept a story about its origins can be constructed. How could the underdetermination of theory by data refute absolutism?

People who find *Zur Genealogie der Moral* and *Morgenröte* shocking fall prey to both the seductiveness of Nietzsche's writing and the rhetorical efficacy of the genealogical method. Part of the reason why genealogies have this effect upon people is undoubtedly the human tendency to believe one's latest stories. Every person conducts himself as though temporal subsequence were epistemically relevant. (Recall that if perspectivism is correct, then one's current theories are necessarily true, when appropriately relativized.) Every person finds his latest, up-dated theories to be the best, and a genealogy gives the appearance of offering new, previously unavailable information. In assimilating the new information, it seems reasonable to change one's view of the phenomenon in question, and the immediately obvious change is toward a skepticism about the validity of the concept. Once one has appreciated the arbitrariness of the origins of something, it seems prima facie reasonable to conclude that it has no justification. But what happens in these cases is not that a former justification is lost. What happens is that the formerly unjustified concept is only now seen to lack justification and suggested necessarily to lack a justification. Accidentally discovered concepts might have been their contraries.

The grand irony of Socrates is that his questions seduce people to the belief that their own beliefs require justification, while simultaneously persuading them that no justification is available. The supreme irony of Nietzsche and Socrates is that they seduce people to the belief that beliefs require justification. But that new belief itself becomes and can only be an article of faith.

Philosophy constitutes/structures worlds by asking questions that change worlds, by creating new facts. It is an as of yet unsettled fact whether perspectivism or absolutism is correct.

      Since perspectivism is a meta-thesis, which therefore has no implications for action, the difference between absolutism and perspectivism lies only in the interpretation of facets of "the world," for example, why the experts are "the experts." If perspectivism is correct, then most people in society do not know what they are doing, since they take themselves to be finding out facts about "the world," not creating them. Most people are deceived about their own enterprises. If absolutism is true, then intersubjective communities are nonetheless delimited by language users, who disagree about some of the facts about the objects which they agree to exist. "The facts" are still determined by the outcomes of disputes. But this is interpreted in absolutist terms as having "located" the facts.

The process, of either creating or discovering "the facts," appears to be identical in the two cases: intersubjective agreement is taken as criterional for truth. We always defer to the experts, whether absolutism or perspectivism is true, because the experts have access to "reality." But if perspectivism is true, the experts are the most "powerful," the better proselytizers or seducers, in the domain in question. They have succeeded in determining the "essential" properties of the objects of that world. A world is absolute vis-à-vis itself. It is built from choices about properties made according to individual conceptualizers' values. How does this differ from absolutism? "Facts are biased" means that some details are selected as important, while others are ignored. But "focusing upon different details" is what is going on in both cases, right?

Perspectivism can be self-affirming, once one has adopted the thesis, since the putative problems to which the thesis might lead are easily solved. Perspectivism could also be self-destructive, since it can sanction the adoption of a view according to which perspectivism is preposterous. Perspectivism is compatible with any lower-order theory.

Consider, for example, the semantic paradox associated with the assertion of perspectivism. To assert perspectivism is to assert that truths are world-constrained and, therefore, in principle abandonable. According to perspectivism, that perspectivism is true is only one possible perspective or interpretation among an infinity of others. But a perspectivist can easily sanction some world version according to which paradox is innocuous or irrelevant to judgments about what sorts of views are reasonable to accept. The perspectivist is not even constrained by the ordinary (commonsense) minimal rational constraints of consistency and nonhypocrisy, since these are constraints within abandonable world versions and depend upon our ordinary concept of a substantive self, which is in some sense a deceptive interpretation anyway, if perspectivism is correct. Perspectivism is divine.

What sorts of arguments can be offered for adopting perspectivism? As in the case of belief in God, the benefits of belief are great: a single "leap of faith" leads to the (dis)solution of all of one's metaphysical problems. It suffices retrospectively to justify the "leap of faith" to perspectivism that one adopt a world view according to which "leaps of faith" are justified. The only remaining question/problem is how to persuade oneself to believe it.

The epistemological problem is quite general and multileveled. At the most basic level, it seems impossible univocally to support higher-order level theories by lower-order data. The underdetermination of theory by data is a problem at every level of theorizing. Every higher-order theory is underdetermined by the data at the next lower level. So for any two putative data, whether they be facts or hypotheses or meta-level hypotheses, it is an open question whether or not they are related to one another in some necessary way and, if so, in which particular way. Every higher-order theory is devised by some person in order to connect lower-order data together in an "orderly" way. Does assent to any higher-order theory then involve inductive ascent, a "leap of faith," wishful thinking?

Ordinarily the problem of the underdetermination of theory by data is recognized as such at one level: the level of hypotheses, under the assumption that the description of facts is itself unproblematic. That alone is a serious problem. But it is important to recognize that the problem of the underdetermination of theory by data comprises three distinct forms:

1. The problem of selection and description of data. (This includes the question of which level and degree of precision is appropriate and which objects to talk about (if absolutism is correct).)

2. The traditional problem of induction: "H or these data are unrelated."

3. "H_1 or H_2": which of two adequate hypotheses should be selected.

There are prima facie two distinguishable problems subsumed under the first form: relevance and choice of level. Which features of an experience are relevant, and in which idiom should they be described? Linguistic reports can themselves be viewed as higher-order hypotheses, fully underdetermined by "the data," themselves what I shall call "replete."

The meanings I intend by "discrete" and "replete" may be best conveyed through metaphorical examples. Nuggets of metal can be piled up, so as to make it impossible to tell, by sight alone, how many are present. But each nugget of the pile is nonetheless a distinct entity from all the rest; it is "discrete." The content of a cauldron of molten metal, however, is "replete," in the sense that it has no nonarbitrarily distinguishable parts.

When I claim that "the data" of our experience are "replete," I am not making a claim about the ultimate constitution of the universe. I am not proposing, for example, that there are no natural kinds. I am emphatically *not* presuming an answer to the question whether perspectivism or absolutism is true. I mean only to point out that our use of language superimposes upon reality a structure. This does not necessarily mean, as metaphysical idealists claim, that the structure of reality is mind-dependent. It means only that our theories of the world are mind-dependent, an obvious point to some, but one that is nonetheless worth pausing to mention here.

For example, consider our use of a kind term such as *paper*. The category of "paper" subsumes a certain class of things, which we have deemed it useful to group together. It excludes, among many other things, wooden planks, chalkboards, and etch-a-sketch toys. We might have chosen to group those things together with paper, along with everything else upon which words can be written. We would then have christened those things with a name, perhaps: "writables." My claim about the "repleteness" of the data of our experience is not that there are no natural kinds, but that we have no obvious way of distinguishing such kinds from those which we happen to find interesting and important. I do not pretend to know whether or not our theories "carve reality at the joints," nor, for that matter, whether "reality" has any "joints" at all.

Not only can any event, state of affairs, be described in terms of completely different objects, but, if absolutism is true, the same object can be described in an infinite number of distinct ways. The first form of the problem is similar to "the new riddle of induction," but should nonetheless be distinguished, since they pose distinct problems at different levels of discourse. Due to the repleteness of events, there is a problem of selection, how faithfully to report "an event" or "state of affairs" in language. If you ask me what I am doing, should I report that I am writing this essay, or that I am typing, or that I am sitting in a black chair, or that I am thinking, or *what?* (What do you *want* me to say?)

Then, even when we look at the same object, the problem reemerges: Should I report that this bottle contains a 5% solution of acetic acid, or vinegar? If I say the former, my dinner companion may decide not to pour it on his salad. (But maybe I thought that he knew chemistry!) The first-order verbally articulated data are "mensongères," insofar as they necessitate the speaker's adopting a stance, choosing a language of discourse, selecting a level of description. Verbal reports confer necessary properties upon "events" and "states of affairs": the very identity of an event or state of affairs is determined by the manner in which the speaker articulates, or an intersubjective community agrees to tell the story. (These cases need not be distinguished, since the limiting case of an intersubjective community is the individual.) Because of the theory-ladenness of data, the two problems can merge into one, or the choice of level can be viewed as a form of the problem of relevance. Although the milieu in which a discussion is conducted includes a context of appropriateness, at the next level up, two competing descriptions can come into conflict with one another, if the canons of appropriateness are world-constrained and devising meta-hypotheses requires one to adopt a position external to the world from which the data to be combined, connected, "accounted for" by the meta-hypothesis, can be viewed.

A profound recognition of the all-pervasiveness of this problem might well persuade one to think that perspectivism must be correct. But the problem could equally well provide grounds for skepticism. Indeed, the problem as articulated by Goodman appears to point to skepticism, since it implies that perspectivism and absolutism are both necessarily underdetermined by any conceivable data. Furthermore, if most people believe that the world is absolutistic, then "absolutistic" is more projectible than "perspectival" and Goodman's position would seem to be rather ironic and even seemingly self-contradictory. (Then again, perhaps "Goodman mensura." Goodman mensura?!) *Do* most people believe the world to be absolutistic? I shall return to this issue below. For now, simply bear in mind that if canons of appropriateness are world-constrained, then what was inappropriate in one world, at the lower level, need no longer be upon ascension.

Turning to the second form of the problem of the underdetermination of theory by data, we have the traditional "problem of induction," how one might be justified in connecting separate data (even ignoring the first problem) together. In the above discussion of the presuppositions of logical positivism, it was suggested that the problem of induction is an instance of the general problem how, for any hypothesis H, one might be justified in affirming H as opposed to X, that "these facts (hypotheses) are unrelated or only coincidentally related." Thus viewed, the problem of induction is merely a form of the more general problem of the underdetermination of theory by data. Before the meta-level dispute over the truth of a hypothesis, H, is settled, it is an open question which of the disjuncts of "H or these facts are unrelated" is true. But any putative principle of induction would have to be justified either by induction itself, in which case the justification would be circular, or by deduction, which is impossible.

Third, there is what might be called the "doxastic" problem. Even if the problem of selection and the traditional "problem of induction" are somehow solved, a further problem can remain, namely, whether one is justified in preferring one over another of two hypotheses each of which adequately "accounts for" the data. A skeptical problem is the version of "H_1 or H_2" in which the competing hypotheses are "it is as though X" and "X." Another distinguishable skeptical version of this problem involves van Fraassen's alternatives for all scientific hypotheses, H: "H is true" or "H is empirically adequate."

Goodman's "new riddle of induction" is a hybrid problem, between the first and the third forms of the problem of the underdetermination of theory by data (listed above), in a context of quasi-scientific hypothesis testing.[2] Goodman considers the predicate "grue," that is, "green before the year 2000 or blue after the year 2000" and asks: Which hypothesis, that "emeralds are green" or "emeralds are grue" is confirmed by the discovery of emeralds which are green today? His answer is that some predicates are "projectible," while others are not. But, "projectibility" is and can only be a function of the language and community in question. Appropriately relativized, any predicate can be seen as "projectible." The problem is all-pervasive, transcending, above and below, the bounds of the context of scientific hypothesis testing.

In the case of the unsettled fact in question, the third form of the problem is encountered: there are two rival hypotheses available, perspectivism and the negation of perspectivism, absolutism, which have indistinguishable implications, so no facts from any lower level can compel one to believe one or the other alternative. Because every instance of the third form of the problem of the underdetermination theory by data implicitly involves the first two forms as well, a solution to the third problem would have to simultaneously include a solution to the other two problems.

One proposed solution to these problems, taken together, is "explanationism." The status of this response to one form of the third version of the problem is central to a debate between scientific realists and constructive empiricists, who, despite their disagreements, agree that the problems of selection and induction are not troublesome. Even if the problem of induction is dismissed, even if universal generalizations about a given set of agreed-upon data can be warranted, the further question remains whether belief in empirically adequate universal generalizations requires or somehow commits one to belief in scientific laws. Van Fraassen denies that even a full-fledged commitment to science necessitates a belief in the (approximate) literal truth of its theories and, there subsumed, its laws. Since defenses of scientific realism rely heavily upon "inference to the best explanation," which looks to be the only candidate for solving the problems introduced above and, accordingly, the unsettled question at hand, a closer look at this debate may be helpful.

Van Fraassen claims that commitment to a principle of "inference to the best explanation" is incoherent because it sanctions inference extending beyond conditionalization. Conditionalization is the up-dating of one's subjective probabilities of beliefs in light of new information, in accordance with the following principle:

$$P_f(X) = P_i(X \& E)/P_i(E)$$

where P = probability; f = final; i = initial
X = the event to transpire
E = new evidence

Commitment to ampliative rules of inference, that is, rules leading to changes in view beyond conditionalization, can subject one to a "dutch book." A "dutch book" is a set of bets which guarantees that the bettor will lose money, no matter what the outcome is. No one thinks that rationality has essentially and exhaustively to do literally with gambling behavior, so "dutch book" may be metaphorical for inference leading to belief in falsehoods or contradictions. Thus construed, it becomes immediately obvious that the best manner in which to minimize irrationality would be to refuse to assent to any proposition that might possibly be false. Does this imply that it is irrational to believe anything other than tautologies? The "danger" of misidentification of tautologies would remain. So perhaps it would be best to suspend judgment altogether. There are a few other, less drastic ways to dismiss van Fraassen's rejection of "inference to the best explanation" (hereafter, IBE). I shall review all of the obvious ways.

First, one might reject the suggestion that the principle of conditionalization is exhaustive of considerations relevant to rationality. There are a couple of different ways of doing that, the most extreme of which may be to deny that it is rational to regard oneself as a diachronically identical entity, in the relevant sense. Perspectivism denies that persons, as ordinarily conceived, have diachronic essences. In that view, what we ordinarily regard as persons in fact comprise sets of successive distinct individuals. Assuming such a view of personal identity, the principle of conditionalization would be irrelevant, since the individual whose prior probabilities were changed would become a new individual upon that change, and so it would be impossible for him to fail to obey the principle, since "adjusted probabilities" would and could only coincide with prior probabilities.

Alternatively, one might deny that the principle is exhaustively determinant of rationality even for individuals as ordinarily conceived, that is, diachronically identical (in the relevant sense, viz., as loci of rationality, etc.). There may be other factors, beyond whether one has violated the principle of conditionalization, relevant to overall assessments of rationality. It might be that, although it is irrational to exceed conditionalization, after due consideration of other factors, one's overall view still is not irrational. Harman observes that "one can sometimes rationally adopt incoherent commitments."[3] In fact, the principle of conditionalization itself asserts very little, only that, given the assumption that one values money (read: prefers not to believe falsehoods), it would be irrational to modify one's probabilities in ways which deviate from simple conditionalization. So, to claim that other factors might be relevant to an assessment of overall rationality does not impugn the principle. With respect to the principle itself and alone, it would always be irrational to modify one's view in violation of it. But Harman's point seems to be that the charge of incoherence is itself not at all serious. In order to see why that is so, we should consider Harman's own interpretation of "dutch book."

Above, I construed "dutch books" in terms of commitments leading to belief in falsehoods or contradictions. If, contrary to that reading, the incoherence involved in "dutch books" consists in one's commitment to the belief both that each of a set of things would be good for oneself and that the whole set together would not be good for oneself, then it is not clear that "dutch books" are to be avoided. The familiar phenomenon of diminishing marginal utility in fact leads directly to nonmereological "dutch book"-type conclusions. Moreover, in cases where the goods in question are qualitatively disparate, it may be that individual goods would conflict with one another due to a variety of factors. Perhaps some goods are valuable only when not combined with others. To offer only one of an infinity of examples, one might think that it would be a good thing to learn to play any of the following instruments: piano, saxophone, french horn, violin, cello, guitar, harp, flute, timpani, but that to do all would not be good and might even be thoroughly frustrating, since it would guarantee that one remain a dilettante at all. While it is true that, given infinite time and energy, one could pursue all possible projects of value, people are finite. If "dutch books" involve this sort of "incoherence," then people are necessarily incoherent, but they couldn't be otherwise, and the charge lacks any force against ampliative rules of inference.

If the putative incoherence is an intransitivity of preferences, then a similar response is available: it may be that only certain sequences of goods are desirable. This would explain why, viewed synchronically, a person with intransitive preferences looks incoherent.

Another manner in which to dismiss van Fraassen's rejection of IBE is to call into question the principle of conditionalization itself. Are the arguments leading to the principle of conditionalization themselves decisive? If not, then the simplest manner in which to avoid this sort of irrationality would be to reject the principle of conditionalization, since then it would be impossible to violate it. Does anyone really believe the principle of conditionalization? If "*ought* implies *can*," and one cannot abide by something nonexistent, then it cannot be the case that one should. Harman facetiously remarks that "The argument for the basic principles of probability is that if one's probabilities do not satisfy these axioms, they are incoherent."[4] Even if the arguments are decisive, is belief in the principle of conditionalization itself rationally compelled?

Supposing that it is, the cases purportedly illustrative of the incoherence of commitment to that rule can themselves be described variously, as Harman has suggested.[5] The principle of conditionalization is actually compatible with a commitment to "inference to the best explanation," when the goodness of an explanation's tendency to lead to belief in true hypotheses is "built into" one's determination of prior subjective probabilities.

Finally, returning to the most general strategy, alluded to above, in order decisively to dismiss van Fraassen's rejection of IBE, one might attempt to show that his arguments implicitly commit him to a rejection of any instance of inference as irrational, involving a sort of "leap of faith." If van Fraassenian reasons apply to every case of belief, then they would hardly discredit a commitment to IBE, in particular. Indeed, the general conclusion to derive from van Fraassen's remarks about IBE seems prima facie to be that it is irrational to commit oneself. The best manner in which to maximize rationality is to commit oneself to no hypothesis, no plan of action, in order to avoid the possibility of "dutch books" altogether. If that is impossible, then there must be something wrong with a notion of rationality which requires it.

If Harman is right, then enumerative induction is best regarded as a special case of "inference to the best explanation" whereby "one infers, from the fact that a certain hypothesis would explain the evidence, to the truth of that hypothesis."[6] Harman's thesis is compatible with a thoroughgoing skepticism about induction since he claims that "either enumerative induction is not always warranted, or enumerative induction is always warranted but is an uninteresting special case of the more general inference to the best explanation."[7] If enumerative induction is *never* warranted, then it is *not always* warranted. But it is difficult to see how one might affirm the second disjunct, without having first determined that conservative coherentism (itself a higher-order hypothesis) is true. That "enumerative induction is always warranted" looks to be an assertion of the necessary, inherent, justification of any inference on the part of an agent. So Harman delineates two alternatives: skepticism or conservative coherentism. Again, a coherentist can circularly defend his position. But to get to a coherentist position to begin with requires a "leap of faith" by anyone who does not already believe (cf. "the paradox of morality").

In the final analysis, van Fraassen's arguments also seem to imply one of the two possible views delineated by Harman. First, it might be best to be a skeptic, since if it is irrational to accept rules of ampliative inference, then it is irrational to assent to any proposition, if, as the first version of the problem of the underdetermination of theory by data suggests, every proposition involves ascent, assent to a selective description of a replete state of affairs. One chooses one's representation of the facts in choosing a level of description. If the process were inferential, then one might say that it accorded with the general rule: "When it seems as though X, then infer X." In that case, if one held any positive views, then it would seem that he is irrational, according to van Fraassen, since any positive view leaves open the possibility of error, relative to some world version's criteria of appropriateness. Of course, if perspectivism is correct, then the agent cannot be wrong, when the case is appropriately relativized to his quasi-solipsistic world. But "the agent" can be wrong, relative to the larger worlds, for example, the largest, quasi-absolutistic world, which he occupies whenever he disagrees with the other members (in particular "the experts") of the relevant community. But I am assuming throughout this discussion that van Fraassen is not a perspectivist.

Does van Fraassen's view then embody a reductio ad absurdum? Only if radical skepticism is wrongheaded (e.g., impossible). Van Fraassen claims that belief in laws of nature is not rationally compelled, and it would seem that he must admit the reasonableness of general skepticism for the same sorts of reasons. Van Fraassen's arguments against IBE seem to apply either categorically, to every case of belief, or to none, since, as explained above, assent to any proposition can be viewed as an "inference to the best explanation." Do we in fact conclude that "X" from the fact that "it seems as though X"? One can only believe what one believes to be true. Is every coming to believe a "change," though perhaps imperceptibly quick, from believing that "it is as though X," to a belief that "X"? But then, why don't van Fraassen's arguments against ampliative rules of inference commit him, contrary to his own belief, to a skepticism about belief in the existence of all things, which seem of necessity to be "inferred" ampliatively? What is his point?

In *The Scientific Image*, van Fraassen compares scientific realists to religious believers. Is this comparison supposed to make us think that scientific realists differ from anyone else holding any positive view? Scientific realists find themselves with beliefs in the existence of the entities apparently referred to in the best confirmed theories of science. But, if you did not already believe, how could an argument convert you? How might a conclusion seduce you? How could an argument bring something into existence in a world devoid of it? How could an argument cause an object to pop into a world ex nihilo? In order to be seduced you must find the façade, not witness its assembly in front of a vast empty space. Is this van Fraassen's point? It is impossible to argue van Fraassen into a world inhabited by things which he does not already believe to exist, because it is impossible to argue anyone into a world inhabited by things which he does not already believe to exist. In his discussion of Aquinas' "Five Ways,"[8] van Fraassen chides scientific realists who claim to believe *because of* the available arguments for realism. But *nowhere* does van Fraassen call belief in scientific realism (or God), tout court, irrational. The suggestion seems to be that the retrospective rationalizations of scientific realists are both deceptive and superfluous. Perhaps van Fraassen's position, then, is simply that arguments cannot effect conversion and those who think that they can are confused, deluded. Of course, that position is compatible with Harman's as well. So what are these philosophers arguing about?

Both Harman and van Fraassen seem to have skeptical leanings. Constructive empiricism can be viewed as a reaction to skepticism about science in the sense that it tries to offer a less metaphysical account of science. One reason for trying to do so would be that science (tout ensemble) is indefensible, but has practical value and is therefore good. Anything *less indefensible* than scientific realism (e.g., constructive empiricism), but which nonetheless accounts for the practice of science, would then be preferable. On the other hand, scientific realists such as Harman may think that science is ultimately indefensible, if justification is construed in a strong, Cartesian sense, but no more so than any other putatively factual enterprise. Belief in scientific entities is *no less defensible* than beliefs about tables and chairs. Harman touts pragmatism and conservative coherentism as our best approaches to epistemology.

Once again, the question arises whether van Fraassen should not, in order to be consistent, be equally skeptical about "observables," the ordinary objects which we believe to exist when we leave the room, and the back and front sides of which we can never view simultaneously. But van Fraassen does not think that the beliefs with which we find ourselves require justification anymore than Harman does. Does van Fraassen advocate relativism? He writes that:

> Just because rationality is a concept of permission rather than compulsion, and it does not place us under the sway of substantive rules, it may be tempting to think that 'anything goes'. But this is not so. . . . belief in laws of nature does not 'go'. It is true that if some philosophers believe in the reality of laws they are not ipso facto irrational. But it does not follow that they are in a position to persuade us or even give us good reason to follow suit.[9]

This is reminiscent of the perspectivist's claim that his thesis does not imply a radical relativism according to which any possible interpretation is as valid as any other. And again, the observation is apt precisely and only because it is true that a higher-order level theory has no implications for any lower-order level theory. Van Fraassen asserts that "it is rational to believe anything that one is not rationally compelled to disbelieve."[10] In his view, namely, epistemological voluntarism, nothing is compelled and apparently everything but commitment to ampliative rules (or contradictions?) is rationally permitted. Again, on one reading, a "dutch book" *is* none other than a set of beliefs which leads one to contradictions. If van Fraassen means something else by "dutch book," he would presumably also repudiate belief in contradictions, although it is not immediately obvious in what sense any

individual could meaningfully be said to embrace contradictions synchronically. Likewise, mutatis mutandis, for IBE, as we shall see.

Embracing a higher-order theory of epistemological voluntarism implies
that one is not obliged to endorse any other person's views. But it would suffice to sanction alternative views, that one adopt other types of pragmatic and
epistemic criteria or that one adopt different specific standards for the application of pragmatic and epistemic criteria, and those are, in van Fraassen's
view, rational possibilities.[11]

The dispute between Harman and van Fraassen seems ultimately to revolve around their views about the distinction, or lack thereof, between pragmatic and epistemic reasons for belief. Pragmatists such as Harman claim that
all epistemic reasons are also pragmatic, though not all pragmatic reasons need
be epistemic. Van Fraassen, in contrast, sees pragmatic reasons as irrelevant
to epistemological warrant for belief in the truth of scientific theories, though
they can provide warrant for acceptance of theories, that is, for using the theories in research programs. But, according to van Fraassen's meta-level view,
to embrace Harmanian categories would be a rational possibility. Even if one
does not reject his arguments in one of the manners outlined above, van
Fraassen's repudiation of IBE and other rules of ampliation loses its sting in
light of his epistemological voluntarism.

In my view, this dispute provides an interesting example of philosophers
arguing past one another. Scientific realists and anti-realists occupy different
justificatory worlds and as such do and can only talk past one another. The
case is completely analogous to "debates" between atheists and theists, who
cannot possibly be talking *about* the same entity, since the former group denies that the word 'God' refers to anything at all.

Upon closer analysis of this debate, the underdetermination of theory by
data appears to be relevant in its first form, as presented above. One might
wonder, for example, how anyone could possibly "be committed" to a rule
of ampliation. It would hardly be worth van Fraassen's time to argue to the
conclusion that those committed to rules of ampliation are irrational, if there
never could be such a person. What could evidence such a commitment?
Would the fact that your actions appear to coincide with those of someone
thus committed, show that you are thus committed? Is it an erroneous characterization of someone's behavior to say that he is committed to IBE if he
himself does not claim to be so committed? The answer to these questions

might appear to depend upon the answer to the question of whether or not "actions betray beliefs."

Harman ingeniously observes that the very ascription of subjective probabilities to the allegedly incoherent wielder of IBE in fact presupposes IBE, since they are derivable only via principles which one can be said implicitly to follow, that is, which one is inferred to follow.[12] If van Fraassen is right, that scientists need not be committed to the truth of the theories which guide their actions, then it would seem to follow also, mutatis mutandis, that no one is committed, implicitly or otherwise, to the truth of any philosophical theory devised by any philosopher simply because he can explain or account for behavior using that theory. Are all (higher-order) hypotheses selective misrepresentations of human action? Is my talking about these "stories" itself equally falsificatory? Either Harman's observation is apt, in which case van Fraassen's repudiation of IBE is self-contradictory, or Harman's observation is inapt, but no one is ever "committed" to IBE, so van Fraassen's adversaries are straw men, and people who believe themselves to be committed to IBE are self-deceived. In that case, van Fraassen's discussion of Aquinas' "Five Ways" should, as intimated above, properly be viewed as a criticism of self-deception. Does van Fraassen argue for his position or does he display it? Does Harman argue for his position? Perhaps Harman thinks that he can seduce those who believe that arguments can effect conversion.

"Inference to the best explanation" is a codification of wishful thinking, either because stories including descriptions of its putative use involve self-deceptive interpretations of a person's processes of coming to believe, or because its actual use involves inductive ascent to a possibly true story, devised by some person who wants there to be a (simple, interesting, etc.) true story. If beliefs are propositional attitudes, then beliefs are higher-order hypotheses connecting null-order data, events, or states of affairs together. But if beliefs are higher-order hypotheses, then they are, as are all other hypotheses, always underdetermined by the lower-order data which they subsume. In this sense, then, all beliefs could be said to be "religious," since they necessarily involve ascent, a "leap of faith," wishful thinking.

"Inference to the best explanation" is a codification of wishful thinking because "projectibility" is a function only of the community, and the selection of admissible pragmatic and epistemic criteria will sanction the adoption of whichever view one favors, for whatever reason. Suppose that good explanations are simple and that IBE is warranted. Is absolutism or perspectivism the simpler hypothesis? Absolutists answer "absolutism" and perspectivists "perspectivism." "Absolutism or perspectivism" is an unsettled question precisely for those who lack the relevant criteria for discriminating between these hypotheses. But if "the choice" has already been made, then the criteria are irrelevant, superfluous.

Philosophy constitutes/structures worlds by asking questions that change worlds, by creating new facts. It is an as of yet unsettled fact whether perspectivism or absolutism is correct. It is an as of yet unsettled fact whether whether perspectivism or absolutism is correct is a fact.

One manner in which to construe perspectivism is as a thesis about language. Our language differentiates things into categories which are useful to us, but these categories are variable. For example, if we are interested in subtle nuances of color, we might distinguish mint julep from janitorial green. If not, we might be satisfied with categories which do not distinguish between these colors. But according to perspectivism, all distinctions are like this, ultimately conventional, artifactual. It is incontestable that before computers were invented, there was no way to talk about "the nature" of computers, because they were nonexistent. But perspectivism asserts that our language picks out "the nature" of all things only insofar as we decide to count certain features as essential. When we decide that an organism's DNA is essential to it, then and only then does it become so. Some scientific realists view what has transpired as a successive accretion of information leading toward a complete true account of the world. We are no longer ignorant about DNA; our knowledge of the world has increased. The implicit assumption is that wherever we are is preferable to where we were yesterday. Is temporal subsequence an epistemic relevance?

The conventionality of language obviously affects all discourse and, therefore, all discourse about putatively factual issues. Whether or not a statement is true is commonsensically thought to depend upon whether or not, in the domain in question, the linguistic expression corresponds to, represents the facts already assumed in the world. But this suggests that, as perspectivists are wont to emphasize, the notion of "absolute truth" makes no sense, because truth can only be relative to a given world version, that is, at a certain level, with respect to a certain language. Matters of fact are internal to practices which we have adopted and find ourselves believing and engaging in. Could perspectivism then be a necessary truth, given our finitude and the nature of language?

I have offered an explication of the perspectivist notion of "world" and "conceptualizer" according to which "the world" can never be captured by any conceptualizer scrutable to me. If God exists, then "perspectivism" is nonetheless an attractive thesis about finite first-person experience and what societies could be (a disjoint set of individual conceptualizers). Societies and conceptualizers would not be affected one way or another by the existence of "the world," an absolutistic world capturable by God. Thus construed, perspectivism is compatible with a thesis about the inscrutability and irrelevance of God.

Let "perspectivism" be the general, radical thesis about the nonexistence of "the world" and "*perspectivism*" the phenomenological thesis about the experience of finite conceptualizers, who cannot capture "the world." *Perspectivism* implies that descriptions of events are selective, since language is public, symbolic, and therefore discrete, and differentiates objects from one another using only crude categories. But even if perspectivism is not true, *perspectivism* is nonetheless a plausible theory about first-person experience for "the world" construed as the largest world to which an individual (as ordinarily conceived) belongs. So, whether or not perspectivism is true, *perspectivism* provides a model for the first person experience of any individual who participates in at least one intersubjectively inhabited world. Either "the world" is absolutist, or "the world" is quasi-absolutist, the largest world to which an individual belongs. In either case, the individual's own descriptions of events in "the world" are necessarily selective. So, to reiterate, from the point of view of a finite subject, a perspectival is indistinguishable from an absolutistic world.

This suggests that, if language is the creation of finite beings, then descriptions are necessarily fictionally omissive, "mensongères," since they relate only to objects in the larger, more crudely discriminating worlds that one inhabits, whether or not perspectivism is correct. Does this not imply that analytic philosophy of language rests upon a mistake, a false quasi-tractarian picture of the connection between reality and language? It is obvious to some that since language is conventional and, therefore, originally completely metaphorical, a close study of language cannot reveal substantive truths about the world any more than a close study of moral phenomenology can reveal truths of (normative) or about (metaethical) morality. Philosophy of language in this century has focused upon analysis of English usage, but only the most parochial philosopher could think that anything interesting about reality might follow from facts about English. Languages and moralities comprise wildly heterogeneous sets. Studies of language can tell us about the creators of language, and studies of moral phenomenology can tell us about how different people feel about moral issues. Of course, historically, philosophy has been written in language. Could this be why Socrates thought that "the subject" of philosophy is "the self"?

To sum up, the underdetermination of theory by data pervades all discourse about anything, since it is a problem even at the first level of description. Since every higher-order hypothesis is in language, the problem is a fortiori a problem at the "meta-" and "meta-meta-" levels.

As we have seen, explanationism only "solves" the problem of the underdetermination of data flagrantly tendentiously. "Inference to the best explanation" is a codification of wishful thinking because the selection of admissible pragmatic and epistemic criteria will sanction the adoption of whichever view one favors, for whatever reason. Suppose that good explanations are simple and that IBE is warranted. Is absolutism or perspectivism a simpler hypothesis? Absolutists answer "absolutism" and perspectivists "perspectivism." "Absolutism or perspectivism" is an unsettled question precisely for those who lack the relevant criteria for discriminating between the two hypotheses. But if "the choice" has already been made, then the criteria are irrelevant, superfluous.

Because of the underdetermination of every higher-order theory by the data which it accounts for, "the facts" about the facts cannot be displayed, so one can only be converted or seduced to them, since the data never compel one possibility over another. According to Goodman, the facts are a matter of "habit," not "fiat."[13] What does he mean? Perhaps Goodman means that although our concepts and categories are purely our own constructions, we are inculcated to regard them as absolutist. We are trained to view the world as absolute, as independent of us and, accordingly, of all human conception. So it is not the case that people are *literally* "power brokers," self-consciously engaged in battles to make their own values reign supreme. People *really be-*

lieve that they are engaged in factual disputes, in the ordinary sense of those words. Well, except maybe some philosophers, those who have come to a perspectivist understanding of the world, or at least of their own enterprises.

The early Wittgenstein seems prima facie not to have been a perspectivist, since he clearly delimits the factual from the nonfactual. Although his own enterprise lies beyond that which he asserts can be meaningfully articulated, the enterprise of science does not. Such a reading locates the *Tractatus* in "the death of philosophy" tradition, given his prefatory remarks:

> scheint mir die Wahrheit der hier mitgeteilten Gedanken unantastbar und definitiv. Ich bin also der Meinung, die Probleme im Wesentlichen endgültig gelöst zu haben.
>
> [the truth of the thoughts communicated here seems to me unassailable and definitive. I am, therefore, of the opinion that the problems have in essentials been finally solved.]

It is difficult to say what transpired in *Philosophische Untersuchungen*, but it is possible that Wittgenstein came to a general perspectival understanding of the world. It is also possible that he became profoundly skeptical. Perspectivists and skeptics are empirically indistinguishable.

There is no denying that perspectivism is a very appealing thesis, philosophically speaking, especially when one reflects upon the following sorts of ideas:

> *How would my experiences be any different, even if there were an absolute?*

I would still be the absolute relative to all of my worlds, which would in turn be only a tiny part of "the world."

> *But what lies outside of my experience is irrelevant to me; it has no effect; how could it?*

I can only be affected by the objects which I find myself believing to exist in worlds which I occupy.

I can annihilate anything by closing my eyes.

Death is unproblematic, since it is a conceptual truth that "the world" (= all of one's worlds) ends upon death, which is no more and no less than irrevocable cessation of consciousness.

What goes on after I cease to exist can have no effect upon me, because "I" no longer exist. And this is true for every moment:

"I" never survive any of my experiences; I change; I become something(one) else, so guilt over "my" past is misdirected, irrational.

You are reading this work. So you have unanswered questions. You want to know what "the meaning" of this work is. You are imparting properties to this text as you read it, by interpreting, by destroying and reconstructing it. You are posing new questions and answering them continuously throughout your reading, just as you do in every act of conceptualization. You want to find out more about "the properties" of the only vaguely determined object. You want to make your conception of the object richer. You want to annihilate the world you currently occupy with it and create a new one. You are "the expert" in this world: you pose the questions, which means that you assume which are the fundamental facts, and you impart the properties. You seek to answer the questions about the "essential" properties in the same way that all philosophers seek the answers to the questions which they pose. So you are microcosmic of philosophy, since your identity is determined by what you choose to do, just as the identity of philosophy is determined by the questions it decides to pose. You determine the properties which answer the questions, just as philosophers settle their disputes by the standards which they accept as applicable. When you stop looking, you have no further interest in the question. When they stop discussing the question, they are no longer interested in it; it has become a non-issue or a fact. You do something else; you find another object more fully to determine. They find another question to answer. And this process continues until the cessation of consciousness, the implosion of the self, the final, irrevocable self-destruction. When you decide to close your eyes and ask no further questions, then you are dead. When philosophy poses no further questions, it self-destructs in a final implosive act.

Two types of intelligence are in conflict: constructive, synthetic, hypothesis-mongering intelligence; and destructive, analytic, critical intelligence (which applies logic as its tool, assuming that consistency is required). Although they require one another, since synthesis requires parts to synthesize, and analysis requires a whole to analyze, the two conjoined can lead to the impossibility of diachronically held positive views. Combined in one person this is continual "self"-destruction and creation, continual "change in view." Combined in one discipline, this is philosophy. Philosophy is a model for "the self," if perspectivism is correct, since it changes its subject through both asking new questions and reflecting upon itself. Philosophers discourse "meta" relative to society, but they are also members of that community, and many others as well. So when questions are resolved in philosophy, facts are concomitantly determined in society. Is this why Plato wanted the "philosopher-kings" to rule? Or was he stating the fact that they do? Are these cases distinguishable?

Philosophers ask questions "meta," or external to the practices of society, and problems arise when one attempts to ask questions about the truth of meta-theories, for example, whether the correspondence theory of truth is true. Is scientific realism true? This question cannot be answered by appeal to any facts about science, since anti-realism and realism are themselves adequate hypotheses, at least to some philosophers. Do two objects combine to form a third? How could such an issue be resolved?

Some philosophers believe that epistemological issues are prior to metaphysical issues, in the sense that questions about how such disputes might be resolved must themselves first be resolved. But how are epistemological issues to be resolved? It cannot be by appeal to facts, metaphysical or otherwise, if the epistemologist is correct in thinking that the metaphysical facts cannot be determined without first answering the epistemological questions. This sort of foundationalist view, which ranks issues hierarchically, leads directly to skepticism, since it both necessitates and precludes the possibility of answering epistemological questions. In the absence of some sort of indubitable but potentially ampliative structure, the epistemologist cannot proceed. In response to this problem with foundationalism, some philosophers adopt a coherentist approach, rather than capitulating to skepticism. The motivating intuition seems to be something like "*ought* implies *can.*" If it is impossible to give a foundationalist grounding for knowledge, then it cannot be the case that we ought to.

One possible disadvantage of coherentist views is their apparent need of an interworld version notion of truth. In order to be able to assess the overall coherence of one's view, it must be possible to compare truth claims from disparate domains. Perspectivism denies that this makes sense. The standards of truth are different for science than for art criticism. But in order to make judgments of overall coherence, it would seem necessary to compare these enterprises. Although a deflationary theory of truth circumvents the problem on one level, by making truth primitive, and thereby vacuously equating the truths of different domains, the problem reemerges in the form of questions about the value of truths from different domains. The pragmatist response is to redefine truth in terms of utility (or some other practical construct). Truth then becomes a notion relating to human lives, and human beings interact in a variety of communities, so they will presumably be capable of evaluating truths from disparate domains, since these evaluations will be in the same currency.

If pragmatists are right, then it would seem that agents who are constrained by their own evaluations of the utility of various enterprises and facts to their own lives, are in some sense committed to "ego mensura." Perhaps, then, agents can only attempt to effect changes by seducing or indoctrinating others to their own views, in order that they might achieve a greater satisfaction or utility. This idea coheres with one possible interpretation of Nietzsche's concept of "der Wille zur Macht," if agents are necessarily constrained in their judgments by their own values, and since they cannot get others to agree with them by displaying the facts. Although it is possible to be a "martyr" of sorts, namely, by sacrificing one's own immediate wants and desires for someone else more important or for a greater cause, the agent is nonetheless constrained by his own powers of judgment about "importance" and "greatness," and so does not in these sorts of cases sacrifice all of his own values. In other words, pragmatism seems to imply the truth, in at least one sense, of egoism. Pragmatism and perspectivism, on this reading, are both forms of anti-realism, which deny that questions can be answered by appeal to "the way things are" independent of the agents who judge them so. But perspectivism denies that there is a way which things are (beyond what we take them to be), while pragmatism may be a slightly different reaction to skepticism.

It is an indeed interesting question, whether to deny that things, ordinarily conceived, have essential properties is the same as to deny that we have access to things as they "really" are. But since this is a philosophical question, it turns upon itself, leading to an infinite spiral of philosophical inquiries. Could this then be a vindication of skepticism, en fin de compte? The perspectivist thinks not, since in his view, language is a human construction, and therefore the very questions raised by philosophers (or "anyone else") are themselves creations. Philosophers create their objects of discourse. Before philosophers pose those questions they do not exist, so there can be no fact of the matter, if facts are world-bound, as perspectivists think. "Knowledge" is and can only be what epistemologists take it to be. Epistemological questions are external questions, which need answer to no facts in any other world version, so in what sense could it be possible to be wrong about what knowledge is? To ask a question is to presuppose a certain level of discourse. But in philosophy there are no standards for the resolution of debates other than those created by the interests and values of individual philosophers. Philosophy is quintessentially "inappropriate."

Every "external" question is a philosophical question, but even the rejection of external questions as otiose is a philosophical stand. Is any person who asks an external question a philosopher? Since any question can be viewed in a variety of ways, does this imply that every person asks external questions (though perhaps often unwittingly)? Or, perhaps external questions are impossible, since they presuppose some absolute notion of externality? A rejection of external questions as "illegitimate" looks suspicious, since its articulation betrays its own identity as an answer to an external question, namely, whether or not external questions are legitimate. Both acceptance of and rejection of the distinction between internal and external questions answers a meta-level question. People do apparently make decisions whether to participate in the disputes within an intersubjectively inhabited world, or not. But skeptics continually call into question the standards of dispute resolution proposed and accepted by philosophers.

It is impossible to fail to pose questions, so when a philosopher is ostracized by the current professional community, he escapes to another world, appointing himself the expert. Only an individual can abandon an interest, close his eyes, annihilate a world. In submitting to the authority of the experts, the individual himself takes a philosophical stand. No authority can compel any other individual's beliefs about his subject matter of expertise, since the individual himself must decide to accept the other as an expert before he becomes the expert in a world inhabited by both of them.

Perspectivism seems to agree with "nonphilosophers," that "philosophy of (science, art, ethics, mind, language, etc.)" issues are not factual issues, since they exceed the bounds of the domain of the objects about which questions are being posed. Skeptics and metaphilosophers are then concerned a fortiori with nonfactual issues, since they transcend the bounds of an already nonfactual domain. But perspectivism further asserts that no issue is a factual issue in the ordinary sense. Perspectivism is a fundamentally paradoxical thesis, because it asserts, apparently as a fact, that there are no facts in the ordinary sense. But the ordinary sense of fact would seem to be and have to be what we take it to be, according to the thesis itself. There is and could be nothing further beyond the appearance. If we construe the concept of "fact" in a certain manner, then that is what it is. Is perspectivism self-contradictory?

An explication of perspectivism requires the use of ordinary, quasi-absolutistic categories, the perspectivist will own, but this shows nothing more than that our discourses and practices are pervaded by quasi-absolutistic concepts. Yet this leads to an interesting problem for the perspectivist, since a willingness even to entertain the question "perspectivism or absolutism" commits one to either answer's comprehensibility. Surely if perspectivism asserts something, then it denies its contrary and its contrary must therefore "make sense" as well. But then perspectivists are wrong, since they take themselves to be espousing a comprehensible view. Don't they? Or are perspectivists knowingly babbling nonsense? If perspectivism is true, then it is false, since its being true presupposes the meaninglessness of its being false, that is, absolutism, which they reject as nonsensical. Does this mean that perspectivists are incoherent? Is this just a version of "the paradox"?

In any case, it might reasonably be wondered how, if absolutism is true, one would ever *know* when he had located "the truth." Would it be signalled by some sort of feeling of satisfaction? But if there could be no way of knowing when one knows, then isn't the quest in some sense misguided, similar to Ponce de Léon's search for "la fontaine de la jeunesse?" Perspectivism asserts the futility of searching further for absolutist foundations, since it denies that there might be any, by denying that the question of foundations even makes sense. Perspectivism terminates the frustrating quest for foundations quixotically "sought" by skeptics. Uncertainty is uncomfortable and perspectivism provides a simple, satisfying certainty: the question of absolutistic foundations is nonsensical, incoherent. Perspectivism may be therapeutic to discouraged foundationalists previously unable to escape the spectres of skepticism. And perspectivism has no normative implications, so perspectivists who continue to conduct epistemological investigations will be empirically indistinguishable from absolutists, though they will regard their own enterprises differently.

Perspectivists recognize that the conditions for the truth of absolutism and the existence of God are the same, since absolutism is in their view tantamount to the claim that "the world" is capturable, but only a conceptualizer incomprehensible to us could capture "the world" and himself simultaneously. Most absolutistic atheists do not seem to appreciate that belief in metaphysical absolutism is tantamount to belief in a god. But the denial of metaphysical absolutism is a positive denial of the existence of a fixed point, some "archimedean point" independent of us. There subsumed is a denial of the existence of God as the metaphysical absolute and a denial that it is reasonable to ask foundational questions. Perspectivism seems to imply not only that no dispute has a terminus, but also that inquiry about the question of the existence of the noumenon or about some absolute world, or about God (they are interchangeable) has reached its terminus. In ending inquiry, the perspectivist has opted for atheism, which exalts another god, though differently clad. Some perspectivists might regard themselves as having been liberated from the oppressive shackles of absolutism, having come at last to appreciate the meaning of the prophetic proclamation of Nietzsche's madman: "Gott ist tod!" But, in fact, perspectivism serves as no more and no less than an intellectual panacea, providing the very type of foundation which the absolutist's metaphysics would have provided, were he able to elude the banes of skepticism about foundations. This world view is grounded on the supposition that *there is no external fixed point.*

Perspectivism is a deceptive thesis since it claims that absolutism is incoherent, but this is supposed to follow from our finitude. How could our finitude imply perspectivism, unless we had antecedently stipulated "homo mensura"? If God exists, then he can capture himself and "the world," but he remains nonexistent to me, until he pops into a world which I inhabit, until I find myself believing in the existence of that opaque, impenetrable, incomprehensible, object. It is the existence or nonexistence of God which determines whether perspectivism or absolutism is true, but relative to all of the worlds which I inhabit, I am the absolute, just as you are, relative to yours. This phenomenological datum cannot refute the existence of God.

In order for the absolute, God, to be able to preserve "the world," that is, all possible worlds of all possible conceptualizers, he would have to be able to capture himself. God must then be completely opaque, utterly incomprehensible to me. God might exist, while *perspectivism* about us is correct, but in order to believe in God one would have to believe in something incomprehensible, since nothing which conceptualizes as the pure conceptualizer does, imparting properties in the manner in which we do, can capture "the world." Do perspectivists mean that you cannot believe in God because you cannot ascribe properties to him? Is that true? Cannot one find oneself with a belief in God? An affirmation of perspectivism is a denial of the existence of God, who alone might preserve the existence of the world versions from which we escape. But how could you annihilate something which never existed in any world which you inhabit? To deny the existence of God, you must find yourself believing in his nonexistence. You must find yourself believing *that God does not exist.* How could one come to that belief? You might think that his putative attributes, omnipotence, omnibenevolence, and omniscience are mutually incompatible, either logically or metaphysically. But how could you know what the incomprehensible cannot be? Leibniz offered the necessary and sufficient theodicy: if God exists, then we, in our finitude, could never fathom his inscrutable ways.

FIVE

Skepticism

If perspectivism were true, then one would have to be either indoctrinated or seduced to belief in any thesis which one did not already believe, so you would have to come to the belief that you could trust your indoctrinator. But this requires your being able to accept that your own powers of judgment are inadequate alone to locate the truth, since previously you have failed to "see the light." So you must both believe in your own powers of judgment, enough to trust them in selecting the guide as a guide, and disbelieve them insofar as they have never before led you to the "truth." Unsurprisingly, debriefing from absolutism would be nearly impossible to effect by oneself, because the absolutist has come to depend upon and trust authorities. To come to believe that he is wrong requires his being able to believe not only that the authorities were wrong and tricked him into believing in absolute truths, but also that he himself was tricked. No one likes to play the fool. It is equally difficult for perspectivists to debrief absolutists, since they must somehow convince the individual both that the absolutists are wrong and that they themselves are right. But if the individual absolutist was wrong in the first instance, and was led into absolutism through the wiles of the authorities, then why should he trust his powers of judgment now? If the absolutist believes the debriefers, that his own powers of judgment are not to be trusted, then he should not believe the debriefers, since his own powers of judgment are not to be trusted. Given this dilemma, the simplest, most painless solution is to retain the original commitment to absolutism.

Many powers of psychological coercion have been used on the absolutist. The other absolutists all reinforce his belief that his view is correct. When everyone believes the same thing, then you start to sound insane when you disagree. To reject the judgment of an entire intersubjective community for his own requires a sort of arrogance on the part of the individual. How could he be so brash, so presumptuous, as to think that he is right and everyone else is wrong? In a cult, exposure to outsiders is often proscribed, and not without reason. Interaction with outsiders might cause a cult member to realize that the seeming unanimity of his intersubjective community is illusory, merely a product of the homogeneous constitution of that sheltered group, comprising individuals who have already been persuaded by the cult leader to believe.

If absolutism were true, then you would have to be either indoctrinated or seduced to belief in any thesis which you did not already believe, so you would have to come to the belief that you could trust your indoctrinator. But this requires your being able to accept that your own powers of judgment are inadequate alone to locate the truth, since previously you have failed to "see the light." So you must both believe in your own powers of judgment, enough to trust them in selecting the guide as a guide, and disbelieve them insofar as they have never before led you to the "truth." Unsurprisingly, "debriefing" from perspectivism to absolutism would be nearly impossible to effect by oneself. To come to believe that one is wrong requires one's being able to believe not only that one has been holding a false theory, but also that one has been tricked. No one likes to play the fool. It would be equally difficult for absolutists to "debrief" perspectivists, since they must somehow convince the individual both that the perspectivists are wrong and that they themselves are right. But if the individual perspectivist was wrong in the first instance, and was led into perspectivism through the wiles of perspectivists, then why should he trust his powers of judgment now? If one believes the "debriefers," that his own powers of judgment are not to be trusted, then he should not believe the "debriefers," since his own powers of judgment are not to be trusted. Given this dilemma, the simplest, most painless solution is to retain the original commitment to perspectivism.

Many powers of psychological coercion have been used on the perspectivist. The other perspectivists all reinforce his belief that his view is correct. When everyone believes the same thing, then you start to sound insane when you disagree. To reject the judgment of an entire intersubjective community for his own requires a sort of arrogance on the part of the individual. How could he be so brash, so presumptuous, as to think that he is right and everyone else is wrong? In a cult, exposure to outsiders is often proscribed, and not without reason. Interaction with outsiders might cause a cult member to realize that the seeming unanimity of his intersubjective community is illusory, merely a product of the homogeneous constitution of that sheltered group, comprising individuals who have already been persuaded by the cult leader to believe.

How could you come to believe perspectivism? You would need to be persuaded both that your powers of judgment were wrong, up to this point in your life, and that *now* you are able to "see the light." If you never arrived at a perspectival understanding of the world before, why should you believe that you should trust your powers of judgment in accepting perspectivism as espoused by another, *now?* Is temporal subsequence an epistemic relevance? If your powers of judgment are sound enough to be able to recognize that another's view is tenable, then doesn't that show that your powers of judgment, which never led you to perspectivism, simultaneously vindicate your current view? Should you believe both perspectivism and absolutism? How could you believe that "p and not-p"? Or maybe you should withhold judgment altogether. Did you ever really *believe* absolutism? Or has someone persuaded you to think that you did, that you might have been playing the fool? Perhaps you think that since "perspectivism or absolutism" is an exhaustive disjunction, you must be committed to one or the other thesis. But if you never entertained the question, then it didn't exist for you, so you could have no opinion about it. If *"ought* implies *can,"* then it cannot be the case that you should have had an opinion about it, if you didn't know that it was a question. Now that you know that it is a question, are you required to opt for one or the other alternative? Or could you reserve judgment, recognizing that the lower-order data favor neither alternative? Could you not rationally believe "perspectivism or absolutism" without knowing which disjunct is true? Can you not rationally believe that it is an as of yet unsettled fact whether perspectivism or absolutism is correct? If you have some queries about language and reality, you might even ascend once again to the belief that it is an as of yet unsettled fact whether whether perspectivism or absolutism is correct is a fact. . . .

Perspectivism is religious, since perspectivists accept as an article of faith, "homo mensura," itself indefensible. Lower-order data favor neither absolutism nor perspectivism. Only the interpretation of data differs according to whether absolutism or perspectivism is true. Perspectivism has the notable appeal of conferring upon its adherents the property of not being self-deceived about their own actions as the vast majority of other people are. One achieves a sort of satisfaction, in knowing that one knows what others do not. But no one can argue you to perspectivism; you must find yourself believing it. While there is little doubt that reflecting upon "ego mensura" can be a liberating and even gratifying experience, to conclude from one's finitude that "the world" does not exist can be no more than wishful thinking.

Philosophy constitutes/structures worlds by asking questions that change worlds, by creating new facts. It is an as of yet unsettled fact whether perspectivism or absolutism is correct. It is an as of yet unsettled fact whether whether perspectivism or absolutism is correct is a fact. We are in the process of settling these matters.

Harman has been a metaethical relativist for as long as he can remember.[1] He found himself believing that there is no absolute morality, that people construct moralities relative to their interests. How could Harman abandon this belief? If you found out that something had eleven dimensions, you might close your eyes and annihilate it. But no argument could cause an absolute morality to pop into a world. Nothing at the lower levels is relevant. Any position in normative ethics is compatible with metaethical relativism. In order to change his view, Harman would have to be converted to a belief in absolutism, or somehow made to forget his belief in relativism. But he has a good memory.

Lewis advocates modal realism and says that "the price is right."[2] But does *Lewis* believe that there is a plurality of worlds *because* they were a bargain? Non-things have no properties. Non-things have no price. You cannot go shopping for non-things. Who would pay something for nothing? Lewis found himself with this belief and then worked out some more of the properties of those worlds and devised arguments to convince us that there are good reasons to believe. But Lewis cannot argue you into belief, because it would be absurd to pay something for nothing. You might pay to keep something. You might pay an enormous amount to keep something. You might even prefer to sacrifice your own or another person's life rather than forsake a deeply cherished belief. But *no one* would give money to someone for something which he did not already believe to exist. A blundering fool might pay an exorbitant sum for something of little or even no value. But *no one* would pay something for nothing.

The views of finite beings will necessarily contain errors upon sufficient elaboration and close examination. Does the requirement of logical consistency have nihilism as a consequence? Only if good views are exhausted by eternal verities. No view of any finite being can withstand "the test of time," since no finite being is infallible. The more fully a view is articulated, the greater the chance that errors will be detected. Critical intelligence is despised since it destroys the positive views of others, by exposing their inconsistencies. Popper's methodological falsificationism is microcosmic of intelligent criticism of others' views. So Popper's view is microcosmic of philosophy vis-à-vis society and of skepticism vis-à-vis metaphysics.

Skeptics ask questions about existent objects, beliefs, employing a magnifying glass, logic, to examine structures and eventually detect cracks. When a crack, an inconsistency, is detected, then the belief shatters and the residual dust blows out of a world, leaving no traces behind. A skeptic claims that he is looking for truth and knowledge but, by what is ordinarily thought to be a reasonable view of induction, he has evidence that he can demolish any positive thesis. Is he a liar? Is the skeptic a liar and a hypocrite? Does he believe in perspectivism? The skeptic, when probed, will deny that he believes that any amount of putatively inductive evidence could compel him to believe that he will *never* find truth or knowledge.

Skepticism keeps formulating a new question, changing the topic of discussion. Every object adduced as evidence for settling an open question itself introduces the opportunity for a new question. So skepticism is an interminable discourse, a ceaseless posing of questions. Skeptics call into question distinctions, borders, and boundaries; they seem to want to say that they are all arbitrary, that they do not reflect facets of reality. Skeptics keep pointing out to us that *we* make the boundaries, *we* draw the lines; they search out and destroy "false gods," dogmas, by exposing them as the substanceless façades which they always seem to turn out to be. It might be thought that skeptics are indistinguishable from perspectivists, since they ceaselessly pose new questions. But, although it is true that skeptics seem to act *as though* they believe that discourse can never come to an end, so do absolutists who believe themselves not yet to know the answers to all questions of interest to them. If perspectivism asserts only that discourse can never end, and skeptics assert that discourse can never end, then skeptics are perspectivists. But skeptics will not say that discourse can never end. Skeptics leave open the possibility that discourse might come to an end. Do they believe it?

Perspectivism and skepticism are indistinguishable only if the perspectivism is vulgar. The skeptic insists that he does not know the answer to the question whether perspectivism or absolutism is correct. No, more: he does not even know whether or not he knows the answer to this question, . . . ad infinitum. What could possibly answer those questions? How could any finite being answer those questions? Skeptics even withhold judgment on the question: "Do actions betray beliefs?" But, supposing that the question were answered in the affirmative, any action could be a manifestation of any belief, appropriately conjoined with some other beliefs and desires.

Adoption of perspectivism provides immediate justification of all of one's lower-order theories, since theories of justification are world constrained and necessarily true, appropriately relativized to individual conceptualizers. "*Ought*" implies *can*" and "*is*" implies *ought*" merge into one for a world relativized to its conceptualizer. This conservatism is a feature common to pragmatic theories of truth and coherentist theories of justification. Pragmatists see themselves as "facing up" to the problem of foundations by honestly admitting that we do and can only take practical value as criterional for truth. They, like perspectivists, seem to believe themselves to have been liberated from the delusive and interminable quest for foundations which have no even in principle recognizable form. Pragmatism about truth, coherentism about justification, and perspectivism about "the world" all involve a sort of complacency about what can be required of a person, and could be regarded as phases in "the death of philosophy" tradition.

The conservative "solution" to skepticism "proves" too much, since it can be brandished at any level of one's belief system. Some claim that Descartes' doubt was hyperbolic and unjustified. Others claim that a doubt that the gratuitous torture of innocent children is absolutely wrong is unjustified. Others claim that a doubt about the existence of an omniscient, omnipotent, omnibenevolent creator of the universe is unjustified. Still others would say that doubt about the reports of one's government officials, about the "facts" taught in school, about what the newspapers report, about . . . Pragmatism and conservative coherentism are forms of capitulation to relativism, a willingness to assert and embrace "homo mensura," appointing as the experts whomever one likes. Conservative coherentism rejects skepticism by reformulating it: doubt is only justified if one believes there to be some reason for it. Conservatism is divine.

Of course, skeptics are finite, so, how does any of this differ from skepticism? Skepticism is stepping back and assessing beliefs, analyzing the structure of beliefs, networks of beliefs, and arguments up close until an inconsistency emerges. But being a skeptic does not require calling everything into question simultaneously. That would be a conceptual impossibility. A conceptualizer must find himself believing in the existence of an object in order to be able to ask a question about it. People misunderstand Descartes' method of radical doubt when they interpret him as suggesting that one ought to call everything into question simultaneously. They wonder what Descartes might have meant. But Descartes himself explicitly acknowledges that there are some things that he cannot *really* doubt:

> Comment est-ce que je pourrais nier que ces mains et ce corps-ci soient à moi? si ce n'est peut-être que je me compare à ces insensés, de qui le cerveau est tellement troublé et offusqué par les noires vapeurs de la bile, qu'ils assurent constamment qu'ils sont des rois, lorsqu'ils sont très pauvres, qu'ils sont vêtus d'or et de pourpre, lorsqu'ils sont tout nus, ou s'imaginent être des cruches ou avoir un corps de verre. Mais quoi ce sont des fous, et je ne serais pas moins extravagant si je me réglais sur leurs exemples.[3]

> [How could I deny that these hands and this body are mine? Unless, I were to compare myself to those who are out of their minds, whose brains are so clouded and troubled by the black vapors of bile that they continually assert that they are kings when they are very poor, that they are dressed in gold and purple when they are naked, or else they imagine themselves to be clay pitchers or have bodies made of glass. But they are madmen, and I would be no less absurd if I conducted myself in their manner.]

Then again, what could distinguish methodological from real doubt?

Pragmatism effectively denies the reality of both the fact/value and the practical/theoretical dichotomies. All wisdom is *practical* wisdom. These denials have some plausibility when one considers questions such as: How could something be theoretical wisdom? How could any intended object fail to affect the self? Pragmatism asserts that every genuine effect is a practical effect: everything entertained effects change of one's self. Since theory and practice merge into one, the ultimate philosophical question for pragmatists is "What is the good life?" Can pragmatism be summarized by the injunction: "Don't worry; be happy," or, perhaps, "Don't worry; do your work"? In claiming to be a "solution" to skepticism, does pragmatism presuppose that one's "work" shouldn't be the very sorts of investigations in which skeptics have traditionally engaged?

A question is a created object, so skeptics seem to be believers, since they seem to believe that questions are genuine issues, which can only be annihilated by refusing to attend to them. Skeptics seem to believe that things must be talked into existence, except for questions. Questions presuppose logic, so skeptics also seem to believe in reason. The only thing which survives the skeptic's scrutiny is logic. Nothing is sacred in philosophy, except logic. Every question is permitted, but no one can do what is impossible. No one can *question* logic. Even for skeptics, logic is and can only be an article of faith. It cannot be questioned, because the questioning itself would presuppose the object. It is impossible to derive a contradiction from a tautology. Every question is permitted, but no one can question logic. No one can do what is impossible. To attempt to transcend logic, is to go too far.

Gilbert Harman argues in *Change in View* (Chapter Two) that logic is not of any special relevance to reasoning. But the conception of logic to which he refers involves principles such as modus tollens and modus ponens. Counterfactual and subjunctive conditionals clearly provide examples of the insufficiency of logic to reasoning in natural language, but, in arguing for any conclusion, Harman would seem to be implicitly committed to the law of noncontradiction and the law of the excluded middle for all meaningful propositions of the language in which he is arguing, at that level of discourse. Of course, Harman does not explicitly claim that the laws of noncontradiction and the excluded middle are *irrelevant* to reasoning. In any case, Harman's notion of "reasoning" is a type of practical reasoning, the principles for change in view (assuming that a change in view is a type of action and that practical reasoning eventuates in policies of action). This is why the discovery of an inconsistency may or may not warrant some change in view which rectifies the inconsistency. Since one may have other more pressing concerns than a desire to be consistent, one might prefer to eat lunch (as Harman is fond of pointing out) before worrying about how to render his belief set consistent.

Does Harman believe that *anything* is "specially relevant" to reasoning? A full-fledged skepticism about practical reasoning is compatible with Harman's view, since if people "just do those things," then nothing could compel belief one way or another. One wonders whether Harman's evasiveness about the normative/descriptive dichotomy is not also symptomatic of a skepticism about practical reasoning. His espousal of conservatism then would still be comprehensible, since to say that conservatism is unwarranted would be to expect people to do the impossible. If "*ought* implies *can*," then the negation of nonconservatism, conservatism, would have to be permissible. Everything necessary is permissible.

Skeptics seem to believe that the process of questioning is valuable. Do skeptics never question the "value of valuing"? Or maybe they do, but never conclude that valuing is valueless? Perhaps their antecedent values unerringly predispose them to believe that valuing is always valuable. Do they then believe in an absolute value? Is this their god?

Leben könnte kein Volk, das nicht erst schätzen.[4]

[No people could live without first valuing.]

The *impossibility* spoken of by the author suggests that, as with the idea of questioning logic, there is a conceptual problem involved with the idea of questioning "the value of valuing." Indeed, "the value of valuing" is presupposed by any question, just as logic is, but not because the question cannot be formulated without it. Rather, *the possibility of an answer* requires one to be able to adopt a stance. It is a part of the concept of questioning, a part of *that game*, that one be capable of answering a question, which necessarily presupposes the ability to favor one over another perspective. To refuse to ask questions would be to shut one's eyes, to annihilate all worlds. So long as one is conscious, one cannot fail to look at objects as the starting points for further investigations. In this interpretation, to say that questioning the "value of valuing" is "gefährlich," dangerous, as Nietzsche does, is to say that it is life-annihilating.

For example, sometimes skeptics ask and answer questions about arguments. They find problems with, inconsistencies in, arguments offered in support of positive views. They ask: "Is this a good argument?" If it is fallacious, they answer: "No." All questions are questions "about values," since the possibility of an answer presupposes one's willingness to prefer one answer to another, but no fact can be displayed which might compel you to prefer one to the other, since you always have the option of calling the question itself into question. If conscious life is questioning, through experience, attending to objects and more richly developing one's concepts of them, then questioning the "value of valuing" could terminate all discourse. It would be suicide. For the skeptic, that would be a rejection of the law of noncontradiction, "not-(p and not-p)," or the law of the excluded middle, "p or not-p," with respect to all meaningful statements of a given language, at a given level of discourse.

Why have so many philosophers preached "the death of philosophy"? They conceive of philosophy in a particular way, then they undermine that concept, and conclude that "Philosophy is dead." They assume that 'philosophy' (in their idiolect) refers to some static thing diachronically. But philosophy is devoid of subject matter. Preachers of "the death of philosophy" mistake one set of garments for an "essential" being. Philosophy has no diachronic essence, since it comprises and is exhausted by the interests of philosophers. Is conservatism a form of complacent submission, a denial that issues are issues, a sort of apathy? A full-fledged belief in "the death of philosophy" would seem to lead ultimately to apathy, the terminus of philosophy for a philosopher, the end of discourse, if "full acceptance ends inquiry."[5]

Those who claim that "Philosophy is dead" unwittingly recreate philosophy, since philosophy is whatever the relevant community takes it to be. For the synchronic philosophical community there are some philosophical "facts"; they are absolute, relative to the world version of that group of philosophers. For logical positivists, it was a fact that science is good and leads to knowledge of the world. For ordinary language philosophers, it was a fact that an analysis of language can reveal interesting facts about the world. For philosophers of language in the seventies it was a fact that there was a problem of reference. When philosophers forget that those facts, which must of necessity be assumed in order to undertake investigations in order to philosophize at all, were themselves hypotheses, themselves susceptible of criticism, then they fall prey to the erroneous concretization of philosophy. The concretization of philosophy is the preamble to the mourning of the death of philosophy. Philosophy is seductive insofar as it leads philosophers to believe theories, which they or someone else will eventually unmask as constructed façades. When a philosopher unmasks a façade which he himself has come to believe exhausts the content of philosophy, then he mourns and sometimes even preaches "the death of philosophy."

We have no reason, some claim, to doubt the existence of the external world. This sort of rejection of skepticism is no more and no less than an assertion of the metaphysical foundation sought by the absolutist. Although it is admitted to be fallible and revisable, in the moment it serves as the absolute. But of course the foundation which the absolutist seeks could only be "held" in the moment, in reflection upon his beliefs. Perspectivism, pragmatism and coherentism all embody a commitment at some level or another to a form of conservatism which denies the fact/value and the descriptive/normative "dogmas." Because according to all of these views, one's current state is authoritative, they lead ultimately to the unobjectionable conclusion: "It is what it is." Conservative coherentism implies that if you think that "*is* implies *ought*" is wrong, then you are right. It implies that if you think that skepticism is right, then you are right. It implies that if you think that coherentism is wrong, then you are right. It implies that you are right. You are who you are. Wie wird man, was man ist? Man wird, was man ißt. Coherentism is divine.

Of course, coherentists are only infallibilists when relativized to the moment. Coherentists can with linguistic propriety judge (retrospectively) their own beliefs to have been wrong, unless they are diachronic infallibilists. But, as with perspectivists, coherentists cannot be wrong in the moment. Since philosophy has no diachronically stable content, fallibilist coherentism is microcosmic of philosophy. Coherentism can even sanction the adoption of a view according to which it is itself false, just as a philosopher can adopt a philosophical position according to which "Philosophy is dead."

"The facts" about the facts are themselves unsettled facts, so the terminus can never be attained, since it will always be an open question to the skeptic whether the putative fact, which constitutes the final story about "the world," is a fact. This is why "the world" does not exist for finite beings, according to skeptics, because we cannot capture it. If we were to capture "it," that would raise a new question, and "the world" would have escaped us once more. Skepticism is microcosmic of philosophy, since philosophy also depends for its existence upon the ceaseless posing of new questions and therefore also presupposes logic. Resolved questions are no longer part of "the subject" of philosophy. Philosophy is essentially creative, since it has to create its questions in order to survive. It must confer subject matter upon itself. Intelligence cannot operate on a void. Philosophy is "self"-destructive since it continually calls into question its own standards and interests, but its interests constitute, exhaust its "self." Philosophy is suicidal when it sanctions philosophical views according to which philosophy is absurd, and one should cease asking questions.

The skeptic can call into question the value of skepticism and thereby self-destruct. Full acceptance of the claim that skepticism has no value ends further inquiry and delimits the world as it is. When objects are frozen in their place, then no debate over foundations in that world can be undertaken. Nonskeptics are believers in the essential nature of the objects thus frozen. But skeptics are believers too, since their article of faith permits them continually to call into question the nature of objects. But if "religious" views involve ascent to higher-order hypotheses, that is, exceeding the data which the hypotheses cover, then, because of the underdetermination of all higher-order theories by data, the only "view" which is not religious is the lack of any view, the complete cessation of consciousness.

"Inference to the best explanation" is a codification of wishful thinking, either because stories including descriptions of its putative use involve self-deceptive interpretations of a person's processes of coming to believe, or because its actual use involves inductive ascent to a possibly true story, devised by some person who wants there to be a (simple, interesting, etc.) true story. If beliefs are propositional attitudes, then beliefs are higher-order hypotheses connecting null-order data, events, or states of affairs together. But if beliefs are higher-order hypotheses, then beliefs are, as are all other hypotheses, always underdetermined by data. In this sense, then, all beliefs could be said to be "religious," since they necessarily involve ascent, a "leap of faith," wishful thinking.

You can only be converted to perspectivism, if you already believe in absolutism. You can only be converted to absolutism, if you already believe in perspectivism. You can only be converted or seduced to absolutism or perspectivism, if you don't already believe, since these are meta-theses, which have no implications observable in the world, and all higher-order theories are underdetermined by lower-order data. Furthermore, the facts cannot be displayed, because "the fact" doesn't exist until "the experts" agree upon it. But "the experts" in philosophy are philosophers, so if they are entertaining a question, then it is still open. Philosophers qua philosophers are concerned only with open questions, so there are no diachronically stable philosophical "facts." A fact only becomes a fact when the experts have agreed, but in philosophy this coincides with its expulsion from the domain of philosophy. Is this perhaps what Wittgenstein meant in the *Tractatus?* Then did he change his view in *Philosophische Untersuchungen,* having recognized that the distinction between philosophy and nonphilosophy portrayed in the *Tractatus* was finally arbitrary? Was Wittgenstein a perspectivist? Or was he a skeptic? Or was he a conservative coherentist? Are these cases distinguishable?

You can only be converted or seduced to perspectivism or absolutism, if you don't already believe, since no argument can compel your belief in one or the other thesis. Every change in view involves a "leap of faith," a change from believing the possibility to the truth of a story. You can only be converted or seduced to perspectivism, if you don't already believe it. But in saying this, I do not mean to suggest that it differs in this way from any other positive philosophical thesis.

Skeptics assert neither "ego mensura" nor "homo mensura." But in deciding whether or not an argument is sound, the skeptic is nonetheless constrained by, dependent upon, his own powers of judgment. Is the skeptic then implicitly committed to "ego mensura"? Does skepticism involve a sort of practical irrationality, hypocrisy, or incoherence about the way to lead one's life? Do "actions betray beliefs"? The skeptic denies that an answer to that question would settle anything and, further, retorts: "How could one fail to pose questions about found objects?"

Questions in philosophy die by being transformed into "facts" in worlds or being abandoned because they are no longer interesting. But only individual conceptualizers have interests, and only individual conceptualizers can close their eyes. So there *is* one sense in which "Ego mensura" is a conceptual truth for skeptics and nonskeptics alike. It is impossible to escape from one's own values, since the very attempt to repudiate all of them involves holding on to at least one of them. Complete self-abnegation is a conceptual impossibility. Doesn't calling into question a belief require simultaneously holding onto another, *that the matter warrants investigation?* But then, how do fallibilist coherentists and skeptics differ from one another? Could this be why Socrates thought that "the subject" of philosophy is "the self"?

Do you know whether or not fallibilist coherentists and skeptics are distinguishable?

Philosophy constitutes/structures worlds by asking questions that change worlds, by creating new facts. It is an as of yet unsettled fact whether perspectivism or absolutism is correct. It is an as of yet unsettled fact whether whether perspectivism or absolutism is correct is a fact. We are in the process of settling these matters.

Whether or not perspectivism is correct, interests and standards of competence coincide, either overtly or covertly in philosophy, since both the subject matter and the criteria of excellence are exhaustively determined by the values of the experts. People are dismissed as wrongheaded and misguided for being interested in the "wrong" things. The positivists made extravagant claims about what the limits of philosophy should be, claims that betrayed their failure to recognize their own commitments to the legitimacy of their own philosophical enterprise and of criticism, using logic. In one of the great ironies and most remarkable episodes of profound self-delusion in the history of philosophy, "scientifically minded" philosophers came to view and persuaded others to regard themselves as rational, "tough," and "hardheaded," in contrast to their "soft-brained" adversaries. Countless numbers of burgeoning philosophers have been seduced into believing that their own beliefs can be superseded by the claims of science. But this belief is, and can only be, an article of faith.

In this century, philosophers have tended toward specialization as all professions within society have, but the parallels do not stop there. Institutional philosophy is microcosmic of society. The experts are the professors, and a select group of experts, those who have become renowned for their contributions to the field, determine the current topics of discussion. In society, the experts are the bureaucrats and administrators and the select group of experts are the psychiatrists. Similar dynamics are involved in these two institutions.

In society, psychiatrists prescribe the limits of acceptable behavior. Psychopathology is deviance from the norms agreed upon by the psychiatric community. The standards of the community are self-perpetuating because the authorities are a product of the system, which inculcates its own standards into new students. Students who disagree with the prevailing standards are easy to dismiss as pathological, by those who hold the standards to reflect truths about what "normality" is. Perhaps some of the administrators had doubts at one point or another about the standards. Some revision in the institution's standards has taken place, but this is plausibly due to pervasive changes in society rather than in response to internally generated criticism. For example, homosexuality is no longer thought to be pathological, as it was for many years by psychiatric professionals.

Medical students are so busy with their rigorous training schedules that they have little time to spend pondering external questions. Raising criticisms about the system impedes students' progress in two ways: it diverts their attention from the work which they need to be doing in order to make satisfactory progress, and it causes them to call into question their own motivations for embarking upon such a career. If one disagrees strongly with the values of the system, then it may be impossible to finish. The effect is that those who successfully complete these programs have undergone a rigorous indoctrinatory training procedure, which has left them exhausted, with little energy left to question the system, even if they can still remember what their concerns once were, and supposing that their own value systems have not in the process unrecognizably metamorphosed. The training procedure is both arduous and lengthy, spanning more than a decade.

Both society and academic philosophy exalt and perpetuate the values of a select few and train the students who will become the future experts to adopt the same standards. These systems have efficient mechanisms for ensuring the self-perpetuation of standards, since students who vehemently disagree either leave or are cast out of the community. This has the effect of reinforcing the experts' beliefs that they are in fact employing objective standards, since little dissent ever arises in any context, so there is seldom any reason for an individual to undertake a self-critical examination of the standards. The professors and psychiatrists are experts due to their having exhibited agreement with the prevailing standards, through their having produced acceptable work, so it would be extraordinary that they should be the ones to call the standards into question. But students who do call them into question are easy to dismiss as substandard, confused, or misguided.

If perspectivism is correct, then people choose to impose their values upon the relevant community when they embark upon careers which will lead to their becoming the experts in a domain. This means that institutions will tend toward conservatism, since those who disagree strongly with the values of a system will most often opt for other careers, when available, where their interests and values are already shared by the experts of the community, rather than attempting a revision from below. Revision of standards from below is all but impossible to effect, since institutions have built-in mechanisms for removing dissidents, since failure to agree with the experts automatically evidences incompetence.

Since it is of the nature of a system to protect itself against outsiders, in order to preserve itself, it is fully comprehensible why those in positions of authority would try to eliminate deviants. They are acting out of what they perceive, on some level, to be their duty. Not only do institutions depend on the continual reaffirmation of their own standards, but the individuals whose livelihood is justified in terms of those standards (viz., because their work exemplifies the values deemed worthy by those standards) also have interests at stake. To permit other radically disparate standards to infiltrate the system could lead to the revision or even abandonment of the standards of excellence by which the individual secured his own position. The suppression of novelty is a twofold form of self-defense: both the individual and the system require and actively seek protection.

Social reformers attempt to revise the value system of society, by raising questions about the system in intelligent ways, which is very bothersome to bureaucrats, since they cannot in all cases simply be dismissed as psychopathological. In many cases the criticisms are simply ignored, seemingly willfully forgotten, because either they are too unsettling to the individual, or the individual regards himself as upholding the values which all "good people" embrace, the values of the institution, which now constitutes his society. To eliminate an irritant it suffices to close one's eyes and annihilate a world. Outsiders are the enemies of institutions.

The tendency among graduate students in philosophy is to orient interests toward those of their mentors, and this is facilitated by their attending seminars and reading their publications. Students' eagerness to "learn" from their mentors manifests itself in other ways as well. For example, some even imitate the writing styles of their professors. Of course, since the experts determine the standards of excellence in the field, if one is interested in professional success, as nearly all students are, then it behooves one to develop the appropriate tools for attaining that goal. Contemporary training in philosophy involves no attempt to connect the problems discussed in seminars to issues in society or in the student's personal life, so it is understandable why questions revolving around the legitimacy of the standards and values of the experts seldom arise. Furthermore, in order to be taken seriously one must have antecedently demonstrated his ability to excel by the rules of the reigning regime. But, even then, nothing prevents the experts from believing that a deviant student has suffered irreparable brain damage since the last time that they approved of his work.

Very few tenured professors in academia are skeptics. But this is hardly surprising, since skeptics are to academic philosophy what social reformers are to society. Skeptics and social reformers do not know when to leave well enough alone. Skeptics poke holes in the pretty systems of metaphysicians and other defenders of positive theses. They expose their weaknesses and flaws. Skeptics do not typically believe in the existence of the things which philosophers discuss and so have a difficult time preventing themselves from switching levels, from changing the subject of discussion to the very existence of the things the properties of which are in dispute.

The dearth of skeptics in academia is explicable by a highly plausible sociological hypothesis: Professors were all students and had to have survived the system in order to achieve their positions. Skeptical students force professors to address questions which they have always ignored, either because they never surfaced, or because they were too unsettling to entertain seriously. But deviant students are easily dismissed as incompetent, since criteria of competence and interests are both determined by the values of the experts. Moreover, in contrast to other areas, where the subject matter is essentially factual, that is, comprising what are intersubjectively agreed upon by the community to be facts, in philosophy there are no facts about which to be an expert, since the subject matter of philosophy is exhausted by open questions.

In other fields, the experts are always in a superior position vis-à-vis their students, since their training has given them a knowledge of the subject matter which the students, having never studied the material before, cannot possibly have. Students' questions in these areas are about the facts, which the experts are experts about, and therefore the experts can answer these questions authoritatively and with confidence. Even in the rare instance where an expert makes a factual blunder, it is simple to cover it up and thereby circumvent embarrassment, in order to avoid the student's calling into question the expert's competence. In philosophy, in contrast, no amount of familiarity with the more "factual" elements of the discipline, for example, historical details about the dates and what are currently taken to be the canonical interpretations of the philosophers of the past, can prepare an expert to respond to skeptical students' questions, which always simultaneously call into question the expert's logical or intellectual capacities. If a philosophy professor contradicts himself, and this is pointed out by a student, there may be no quick and easy way to recover, to regain composure, without simply admitting the blunder. But to admit the blunder is to admit to some degree of incompetence, since in philosophy competence is exhausted by intelligence. In analytic philosophy, competence has come to be thought to be virtually exhausted by critical intelligence, logical acumen.

It is comprehensible why professors who are challenged by skeptical students sometimes become unnerved and even perceive themselves to be antagonized: They are human beings. In some cases students come to realize that it is futile and counterproductive to point out problems with a professor's views, since his reaction may be an inordinate discomfort or simply a curt dismissal, a refusal altogether to take the criticism seriously. And of course all of this holds, mutatis mutandis, between junior and senior faculty members as well. Senior faculty members may believe themselves to have a reputation at stake and so may actively seek to protect it. But if a student encounters enough experts like these, he may decide that his temperament predisposes him to conflicts with members of that community and will likely preclude any possibility of professional success. The problem is a serious one for skeptics, since it is impossible to know a priori what kinds of criticism will be welcomed or perceived as bothersome by any particular professor. It is also impossible to divine any particular person's highest-order hypothesis. But, according to skeptics, nothing is sacred in philosophy except logic. Different people have different abilities to handle criticism and, perhaps more importantly, different feelings about the relation between their own opinion of themselves and the opinions of others. People who believe the lies which others tell about "them" are "self"-deceived.

Skeptics heat the empty flasks, beliefs, under pressure, until their star cracks cause them to explode, leaving no traces behind. They say that they do not know whether the flasks are empty or not. But there is always a hairline fracture, and no contents are ever recovered. Skeptics detect inconsistencies which thereby undermine systems, since the fundamental, indeed the only, constraint on philosophical theories is consistency. Skeptics are always lurking around corners ready to leap out at philosophers who emit contradictions. Many philosophers, though themselves critical of others' views, find it very difficult to accept trenchant criticism of their own work with any semblance of equanimity. When the criticism is too devastating these philosophers simply ignore it, because it is too unsettling to their world view. As we have seen, the theories which philosophers embrace can acquire a sacred status. In some cases, as explained above, inordinately defensive philosophers merely betray their concern that their professional reputation could be damaged, if they are revealed to have made egregious errors of reasoning. In *Gödel, Escher, Bach,* Hofstadter says that conscious intelligence is the ability "to leap out of systems." What would he do if someone unravelled his braid?

Many people do not like philosophers. They think that they do not know when to leave well enough alone. Sometimes they find them incomprehensible, think them insane. Philosophers keep pushing the boundaries, insisting that "non-issues" are in fact issues. Some philosophers do not like skeptics. They think that they do not know when to leave well enough alone. In Kierkegaard's view, religious faith can take any possible form. He offers two incompatible views in *Fear and Trembling* and *Concluding Unscientific Postscript.* He illustrates what he takes to be the fundamentally subjective nature of religious faith by offering these incompatible models (one involves paradox and the other certainty) and ascribing them to pseudonymous authors. According to Kierkegaard, the object of religious faith can take any form. It can be a single truth, belief in a simple hypothesis. Throughout history pagans have been loathed by religious believers. Skeptics are no exception to this general rule.

Skeptics are the enemies of metaphysicians. Skeptics are troublemakers. Skeptics are rabble-rousers. Skeptics are party poopers. (Why invite someone with darts to a party with balloons?) Skeptics are self-indulgent. Skeptics are insolent. Skeptics like to make fun of other people. Skeptics want to show everyone how clever they are. Or maybe they just do those things. Are these cases distinguishable?

Skeptics and metaphilosophers keep pushing the boundaries, insisting that "non-issues" are in fact issues. Every question leads to another in diametrically opposed directions. Metaphilosophers give accounts about philosophy which are ever-expanding. They must continually expand, because they can never catch up to themselves, though they need to, in order to be adequate, because metaphilosophers are philosophers too. But metaphilosophers do not seem able to talk about themselves. They are too elusive, slipping away behind new properties into new worlds. They do not seem able to capture themselves. Only ancestors can be captured.

Are all (higher-order) theories selective misrepresentations of human action? Is my talking about these stories itself equally falsificatory? Is assent to any hypothesis necessarily a case of wishful thinking? Is that why Socrates never wrote? Or was Socrates a skeptic? Are these cases distinguishable? If Socrates was a skeptic, and "knowledge is virtue," then no one is virtuous, according to Socrates. If Socrates was a skeptic, and "knowledge is virtue," and *ought* implies *can*," then no one is vicious, according to Socrates. Was Socrates "jenseits von gut und böse"?

One way to be a skeptic might be to undermine every positive view which one espoused, continually to contradict oneself. Was Nietzsche a skeptic? Or was he a perspectivist? Or did he think that language is purely conventional or necessarily falsificatory? Are these cases distinguishable?

SIX

Homilies and Diatribes

In each world the objects of discourse are agreed upon by all members of the community. They disagree about the "essential" properties, relativized to that world, of the objects of discussion. "Essential" properties are stipulated within a world. Disagreements are battles over what those properties should be. The culmination of these battles coincides with the destruction of an old and the creation of a new world. It suffices that the experts of a community agree that some properties be "essential" in order for them to be essential. Individuals attempt to make properties which they value essential to objects of a world. If perspectivism is true, then in order to convince people that the properties which you deem valuable should be accepted as "essential" you must either convert or seduce them. They have to be converted, through indoctrination, or seduced, through deception, because there are no facts to show them. The facts are being settled, that is, determined, in these disputes.

"Conversion" is the culmination of a process, "indoctrination," by which individuals come to a change in view which they did not, in any sense, willfully seek. The most obvious examples of indoctrination are training procedures which involve repeated and intensive exposure to ideas to be assimilated or attitudes to be adopted. These procedures effect a change in belief or attitude (typically both) about some individual(s) or thing(s). In religious cults the change takes the form of a "realization" that some specific individual is "the messiah" or a deity. But any case in which an agent neither foresees nor intends that his following someone else's prescriptions for action will lead to the change in attitude or belief that it does effect, is a case of indoctrination. One such type of change in view is to come to believe that something, formerly not believed to exist, in fact exists. Although "conversion" might to some connote a change from one to another positive view, it can also be used to describe the process by which one changes from an agnostic to a positive position. "Conversion," in the most general sense, is a change to a positive view about something. To believe something not to exist is a positive view which is not the same as not to believe that something exists.

A few salient features of this phenomenon warrant mention here. First of all, the indoctrinator/proselyte relationship is one of faith, since the proselyte must somehow come to the belief that he can trust the indoctrinator, which simultaneously requires his being able to accept that his own powers of judgment have until now failed to locate the truth, since previously he has failed to "see the light." He must both believe in his own powers of judgment, enough to trust them in selecting the guide as a guide, and disbelieve them insofar as they have previously led him astray. When the guide is thought of as serendipitously encountered, then the two ideas are not so problematic, since the proselyte can believe that his powers of judgment are sound and that he never before encountered the transmitter of "the word," who, being messianic, is of course unique. If people were able to discover "the word" on their own, then there would be no sense to the notion of "messiah."

Unsurprisingly, debriefing is nearly impossible to effect by an individual himself, because he occupies a world of the indoctrinator's creation. He has come to depend upon him as an authority and to trust him. To come to believe that he is wrong requires his being able to believe not only that the indoctrinator is wrong and that he in some sense "tricked" the proselyte into believing, but also that the proselyte himself was tricked. No one likes to play the fool. But, it is equally difficult for outsiders to debrief cult members, since they must somehow convince the individual both that the "guide" is not to be trusted and that they, the debriefers, are. But if he was wrong in the first instance, and was led into the cult through the wiles of the cult leader, then why should he trust his powers of judgment now? If he believes the debriefers, that his own powers of judgment are not to be trusted, then he should not believe the debriefers, since his own powers of judgment are not to be trusted. Given this dilemma, the simplest, least painful solution is to retain his ardent commitment to the cult.

Many powers of psychological coercion have been used and continue to operate upon the individual. The other cult members all reinforce his belief that his is the true religion and that this is "the way." When everyone believes the same thing, then it sounds insane when one individual disagrees. To challenge the received view of an entire intersubjective community by oneself requires a sort of arrogance on the part of the individual. How could a person be so presumptuous as to think that he is right and all of the others are wrong? In a cult, exposure to outsiders is often proscribed, and not without reason. Interaction with outsiders might cause a cult member to realize that the seeming unanimity of his intersubjective community is illusory, merely a product of the homogeneous constitution of that sheltered group, comprising individuals who have already been persuaded by the cult leader to believe. Of course the cult leader won't tell the proselytes that; he says that outsiders are besotted, sullied, beclouded, lost.

Another interesting feature is the means by which individuals may become dependent upon their indoctrinator, through being placed in positions of weakness and discomfort antecedent to their being "saved." This "discomfort" can be purely emotional or cognitive, but probably usually involves both, for example, being in a state of uncertainty or ignorance, which seems generally to have the effect of producing anxiety in people. When the proselyte surrenders his powers of judgment to his indoctrinator, by accepting what he says on faith, he simultaneously becomes dependent upon him for access to the truth, "the word," since only the source of "the word" can know when the facts have changed, as they are discovered. In order to change his view, he would have to reconcile himself with the fact that he had wasted his time and energy prostrating himself before a mere mortal. That would undoubtedly be very difficult.

Initiation to a cult often requires a large sacrifice. But contrary to what some might think, the main reason for this is not to obtain the object of sacrifice. The sacrifice has the psychological effect of reinforcing the proselyte's commitment to the cause. It would be very difficult, take an enormous amount of courage, for a person to be able to acknowledge that he had squandered years of his life for someone who had lured him through a beautiful forest down a long narrow path, which terminates abruptly at a desert.

"Seduction" is the process by which a person is persuaded to believe something which he did not formerly believe to be true, for example, that something exists, or that something has some property, through the construction of a façade which suggests in some effective but deceptive sense that something more lies behind the appearance than "meets the eye." For example, a suggestible person can be lead to infer an object's existence through a type of wishful thinking. He wants it to be the case that the façade is the real appearance of something substantive and diachronically stable. Although "seduction" might to some connote the process by which Emma Bovary, Johannes' Cordelia, and many other women have been lured into disreputable actions (judged by the standards of their society), it can also be used to describe any process leading to a change in attitude or belief the effectiveness of which depends upon the use of a façade, which exploits the agent's suggestibility and vulnerability to wishful thinking. The most obvious example of seduction in contemporary society is of course advertising. Advertisements often involve people with no essential connection to the products which they advertise. Yet their glamour or respectability or athletic prowess, or other qualities increase consumers' vulnerability to buy, by causing them to suppose, perhaps, that the connections are substantive, more than the beautiful models' or the successful athletes' having been paid an enormous amount of money to say that they use the products being advertised. This example misleadingly suggests that all seducers are self-consciously aware of what they are doing. If one believes in the existence of something, one may nonetheless construct a façade with the aim of persuading another to believe, on the grounds that the end justifies the means and that it might be otherwise quite difficult to bring the other person to the belief, which, being true, should be acknowledged by all. This might be true for some advertisers, since they might believe that a product is good, but that the best way to get people to use it would be by building such a façade, which they themselves can see through, but which is justified by the end.

Seduction and indoctrination are most effective upon individuals who are in some sense dissatisfied with their current view (including about themselves), who are looking for "an answer." Cult leaders and advertisers are often keen psychologists, capable of detecting human frailties and exploiting them to their own benefit. But, given the sorts of dynamics involved in indoctrination and seduction, it is understandable why people tend toward a conservatism in their belief systems. No one likes to play the fool. It is much easier to believe that what one has believed for a long time to be the truth is in fact the truth, than it is to come to believe that one has been continually indoctrinated and seduced by authorities who manipulated one into believing a bunch of lies.

In order to persuade you to believe me, I must divert your attention from the fact that I too am employing a grid. If you already had this vague idea, that "might makes right," this might be just the theory you've been waiting for. Did you ever notice how philosophers often uncharitably characterize the positions of their adversaries, so that anyone who finds those views attractive is left feeling slightly embarrassed? (Nietzsche and Quine have a particular talent for this.) This theory might explain other puzzling aspects of your experience too, like how *that* person ever got tenure. Perhaps you also have noticed that essays with arguments are impotent. Maybe you have the impression that moral philosophers are sometimes profoundly hypocritical. My theory would explain why there is absolutely no correlation between being a decent person and being a successful philosopher.

Did the thought ever cross your mind that some of the most influential figures in contemporary philosophy share salient characteristics with television evangelists? Didn't you ever wonder why the most widely renowned philosophers at any given time always disagree? If the experts were the experts in virtue of their superior rationality, shouldn't their views display some convergence? Has the thought never crossed your mind that the great historical works of philosophy, those that have stood "the test of time" and have generated entire interpretive industries, have an incredibly low argument to assertion quotient? Furthermore, the arguments of those works are typically poor, sometimes even patently fallacious. Isn't it somewhat curious that the most ardent followers of the famous philosophers of this century studied with them personally? If you find my grid pleasing and it "accounts for" features of your experience, you might find yourself believing it. If not, you'll close your eyes and annihilate me, escaping to another world.

AUTHOR UNKNOWN

My Private Fantasy

The respectability of any philosophical work can be boosted through the invocation of important ideas from a work previously widely accepted to be revolutionary. And, in fact, the tendency of interests in contemporary philosophy toward specialization can be illuminated by appeal to the Kuhnian framework, especially the idea of "normal science." According to Kuhn, subsequent to a scientific revolution, an entire corpus of small projects are generated, projects which provide vast numbers of scientists with directed activities, the accomplishment of which secures their gainful employment and professional success.

Kuhn's model is quite apt for philosophy since, whether or not perspectivism is correct, normal philosophical revolutions of necessity involve paradigm shifts, insofar as they direct the community's interests toward those of the normal revolutionaries, and the introduction of incommensurable world views, since philosophy does not build upon itself diachronically. As explained above, this is because there are no diachronically stable "philosophical facts," since once a question is definitively settled, it no longer belongs in philosophy. The interests of philosophers exhaust the subject matter of philosophy, and philosophers are interested in unsettled questions. Philosophers engage precisely in the enterprise of raising questions about putative facts, or posing altogether new questions. However, normal philosophical revolutions, such as logical positivism, ordinary language philosophy, West coast semantics, and Kuhnian philosophy of science, provide a new framework, a temporary origin, a foundation which, relativized to the community at that time, provides an absolute set of philosophical "facts" from which to work.

Philosophers who offer courses on highly recondite issues relating to the details of their detailed elaborations of their mentors' work are largely opaque to undergraduate students, who obviously have not followed the development

145

of the issues from their origin in a normal philosophical revolution. This under-scores the above explanation for the degree to which philosophy has under-gone homogenization during this century. One can only have interests in de-termining the properties of objects which one believes to exist. Non-issues are non-objects and have no properties about which to have intuitions. It is very difficult to write a paper about some "thing" with which one shares no world, about which one can have no opinion.

In philosophy, normal revolutions dissipate rapidly through time, leaving no traces behind, since the sorts of problems solved by philosophers begin to lose their interest to others, once they become too narrow. Although many a normal philosopher has received tenure for having written a book applying or elaborating the "causal theory of reference," when this work becomes too abstruse, people just ignore or forget about it. They decide to pursue more intuitively interesting issues and questions.

Some expert/acolyte relationships are paradoxical, since the activities of philosophy are the activities of intelligence, so in appointing the experts, one presumes oneself to be of sound judgment. But sometimes an expert assigns his acolyte a dissertation topic. If the acolyte is of sound enough judg-ment to appoint an expert, then shouldn't he also be able to choose a good dissertation topic? In the sciences, a professorial thesis advisor must direct his graduate students, since they couldn't possibly know which "wheels" have and have not already been invented. But in philosophy there are no dia-chronically stable "wheels." Has someone persuaded you otherwise? Why is it so difficult to write a dissertation about objects which occupy no world which one inhabits? Because non-things have no properties. It is impossible to have intuitions about non-things. Without an intuition, one has no opinion, nothing to say. Did someone ever try to trick you into believing that you were stupid because you did not have an opinion about something which *he* believed to exist? Did he succeed? Then he was right, because he persuaded you to be-lieve that "p and not-p." How could *you* have an intuition about the occupants of *his* private fantasy, unless you were him? But you are who you are, and you're not who you're not. Could this be why Socrates thought that "the sub-ject" of philosophy is "the self"?

A good topic in philosophy is precisely a topic about which a philosopher has concern and intuitions. It would be very difficult to write about something without having any intuitions about "it." How could you build a façade out of air? Some experts try to persuade their students that they are stupid for lacking intuitions about objects of the expert's own world version. When they succeed, they are right, since no one could have an intuition about the contents of another person's private fantasy, because non-things have no properties. Were you ever bullied into believing that *you* were stupid because you lacked intuitions, had no opinion, about the objects which another person believes to exist? Why should *you* have an opinion about the contents of *his* private fantasy? How could you? If anything is true, doesn't 'ought' imply 'can'? If he persuades you to talk, then you might say something false, and then you'll confirm your and his belief that *he* is the expert. But, of course, acolytes who believe that "p and not-p" are incoherent, so experts rarely derive any genuine satisfaction from being fawned after by them. Unless, of course, *they* are incoherent.

Others can point out problems with your views, if you blunder and emit contradictions, but what should you say if someone tells you that your arguments aren't persuasive? Of course, he'll be right, if he means that you didn't cause an object to pop into his world, but if anything is true, doesn't "*ought imply can*"? If you don't find my writing persuasive, what do you want me to do? Apologize for not being you? Then you're incoherent, because you want me to deny one of the conjuncts of the following tautology: "I am who I am, and I'm not who I'm not."

If I contradict myself through the course of this work, then you may criticize me. In order to avoid embarrassment, you might first try to make sure that I wasn't making jeux de mots, speaking in doubles entendres, or "level hopping." But *you* cannot say that *I* left anything out or put too much in, because *I* created the object to which you currently attend. We can enter another world, and debate over interpretation, about the meaning of this text, which we both find in that world, as it is, containing these printed words. In *that* world, we can engage in a battle. But in *this* world, I am the expert, since I exhaustively determine the properties of the printed words before your eyes. This is not to deny that you have the option of closing your eyes, annihilating this object, escaping to another world. You might try to complain, but what your complaint will really mean is that my text does not conform perfectly to *your* private fantasy, your favorite stories. What do you want me to do? Apologize for not being you? You find yourself with this object, and you apply properties to it, interpret it, but if you can devise no pleasing interpretation of it, then that is merely a testimony to your own lack of inventiveness. How could *I* have known what *your* own private fantasy would be? If you grow weary, or start to feel uncomfortable, you can just close your eyes and annihilate me, escaping to another world. Unless, of course, you suspect that I might be going to say something about you. People hate it when others talk about them, but when they find out that it already happened, they always want to know what was said.

The acolytes of the acolytes of groundbreaking figures in philosophy are students who have somehow been persuaded that yet further elaboration of already nearly prohibitively abstruse work might be fruitful and interesting. But the acolytes of groundbreaking figures in philosophy do not share the status of their mentors and therefore are unlikely to attract many new converts to their own very narrow interests. The acolytes of the experts of the experts enjoy the favor of the experts of the experts and thereby eventually become themselves experts. But favor is not transitive. The acolytes of the acolytes of the experts of the experts do not in general enjoy the favor of the experts of the experts and some experts of the experts may even regard the acolytes of the acolytes of other experts of the experts with derision. They may think that they are obsequious sycophants. Some acolytes of the experts of the experts (who have become experts) may not even regard their own acolytes favorably, knowing, as they do, that the surest route to professional success is to fawn over an expert. It is indisputable that professional success can be secured through a form of devotion to an expert of the experts, a willingness to do normal philosophy.

If you think that the intuitions of your expert are more valuable than your own, then you are confused. We all have intuitions, but you must never have thought *about* intuitions, or you would have realized that intuitions aren't logical. Intuitions are atomic. Intuitions are not compound. Intuitions have no logical structure. Intuitions have the structure: "p." Only a compound sentence, comprising atoms, can be a tautology. An example may elucidate the point, if you already understand it: "not-(p and not-p)." Intuitions are atoms to which truth values have yet to be assigned. Did you suppose perhaps that the intuitions of your expert were logically true? Then you have appointed him your messiah, so he is your god. You have surrendered your powers of reasoning to him. Intuitions are beliefs. Beliefs are hypotheses. Hypotheses are gods. Therefore, intuitions are gods.

Laurie has already expressed the points clearly to you, but perhaps we should do a little review. Non-things have no properties. Non-things have no price. You cannot go shopping for non-things. Who would pay something for nothing?

When people ask your opinion about things which occupy none of your worlds, do you say that you have no opinion, or do you lie and make up an opinion, to prove to them that you're not stupid? Well, if you do, then you are, because no one could have an opinion about the content of someone else's private fantasy. The correct answer is *no answer,* no opinion, because you could not have an opinion about something which you do not even believe to exist, because non-things have no properties. Have you been making up lies out of air? No wonder people see through the façades to the vacuity they comprise. What could be easier than to be trapped in your lies?

Some people won't like my story, so they can shut their eyes and escape to another world, but do you know what? Although they and I will be forever through, no one can prevent others from using this story to explain what they see when they look at you. (A thousand people have already read it? Can it be true?!) An expert can extirpate all of the weeds which pop up in his garden plot, but everyone knows that weeds come from weeds, so when he is gone, history will march on, and what will he have accomplished? He will have spent his time persuading himself that his garden plot covers the planet. He will have spent his life in his own private world filled with his own private lies.

In philosophy, people who defer to experts evince their belief that they are less intelligent than the experts to whom they defer. But if you are of sound enough judgment to select a panel of experts, then you are of sound enough judgment to make the value judgment that you find to be in conflict with an expert. If you "cave in," thinking that his interests are "more intelligent" than your own, then it is true that you are of unsound judgment, since you believe that "p and not-p," that you are of sound judgment (you appointed the expert an expert) and that you are not of sound judgment (you cannot trust your own powers of reasoning). Moreover, you deny a tautology: "You are who you are, and you're not who you're not." Some analytic philosophers believe that those who work in the areas of epistemology, philosophy of mind, philosophy of science, philosophy of language and logic are more intelligent than those who wallow in the mire of value theory. But in fact every question in philosophy is a question in value theory, since the interests and standards of philosophers are exhaustively determined by the values of philosophers. Could this be why Socrates thought that "the subject" of philosophy is "the self"?

If someone could persuade you to believe that *he* is an expert *about* a subject which has no subject matter, then *you* are confused. The activities of philosophy are the activities of intelligence: hypothesis-mongering and criticism using logic. Logic is vacuous. To be an expert *about* logic is to be an expert *about* nothing; it is to *be* logical. And why should you, how could you have an opinion about the contents of another person's private fantasies? There is no denying that he is the expert about the contents of his own private fantasies. But if he gets you to say that they're true, then he has succeeded in converting you.

Perhaps a review of the logic of hypotheses is in order. For any hypothesis, *H,* covering a given set of data, there are an infinite number of different but equally adequate hypotheses. Among those hypotheses is *X,* that "These data are coincidental or unrelated." Which one of those infinite number of hypotheses is actually true? When your expert expresses his intuition about something, he is expressing one of an infinite number of possible hypotheses. Do you suppose that your expert is omniscient? Why would you think that? Because people say that he is smart? Smart people know how to use logic. Smart people know that "not-(p and not-p)." If your expert is trying to turn you into him, then he is not smart, because he wants you to deny one of the conjuncts of the following tautology: "You are who you are, and you're not who you're not."

Your expert could not possibly have been compelled to believe his precious little intuitions, because the data which they cover are accounted for equally well by an infinite number of other hypotheses. Your little expert woke up one day and found himself with his little beliefs. How could you think that he is profound if he never once took the time to explain this simple point to you? Intuitions are atoms to which truth values have yet to be assigned. Intuitions are beliefs. Beliefs are hypotheses. Hypotheses are gods. Therefore, intuitions are gods.

Do you know anyone who prostrates himself before the follower of another religion? Why does he do that? Does he think that he is the messiah? Or has he been seduced into believing that he himself is incoherent? But of course he is, if he believes both "p," that he is of sound judgment, and "not-p," that he is not. If someone could persuade you to believe that he is an expert about a subject which has no subject matter, then it is true. You are incoherent. The activities of philosophy are the activities of intelligence: hypothesis-mongering and criticism using logic. Logic is vacuous. To be an expert *about* logic is to be an expert *about* nothing; it is to *be* logical. And why should you, how could you have an opinion about the contents of another person's private fantasies?

They're really very simple points, but perhaps we should rehearse them. What brought you to believe that your expert is a precious gem? We all have intuitions, but you must never have thought *about* intuitions, or you would have realized that intuitions aren't logical. Intuitions are atomic. Intuitions are not compound. Intuitions have no logical structure. Intuitions have the structure: "p." Only a compound sentence, comprising atoms, can be a tautology. An example may elucidate the point, if you already understand it: "not-(p and not-p)." Intuitions are atoms to which truth values have yet to be assigned. Did you suppose perhaps that the intuitions of your expert were logically true? Then you have appointed him your messiah; so he is your god. You have surrendered your powers of reasoning to him. Intuitions are beliefs. Beliefs are hypotheses. Hypotheses are gods. Therefore, intuitions are gods.

Did someone seduce you into believing in his private fantasy? Did he play a trick on you? Or did he really believe it? But did he believe it *because* of the reasons that he devised in order to persuade you to believe? Did his reasons *compel* your belief? Or did he create a beautiful painting and persuade you that it was a window on the world? Perhaps he lured you down the paths of his thought to the point where he came to realize that he believed. Are you even so sure that you believe? Or have you perhaps been feigning belief? They say that "God made man in his image," and it's true. What else could he do? If your expert persuades you to believe that you are wrong about *anything* other than a contradiction at a single level, in a single language, then you've been fooled. He's been spending his time creating you in his image. Have you been making up lies out of air? No wonder people see through the façades to the vacuity they comprise. What could be easier than to be trapped in your lies?

Have you ever prostrated yourself before the worshiper of another religion? Why? Have you been spending your life saying things that other people want to hear? When they're gone, history will march on, and what will you have accomplished? You will have prostrated yourself before a religious zealot, the worshiper of a god which you do not even believe to exist. How could you believe that a mere mortal is a god? Your messiah is your god, because his is his fantasy. How did someone persuade you to believe that "p and not-p"?

"No one ever teaches anyone anything," if in order to understand the meaning of a sentence one must already understand how its parts function and what the speaker intends by his utterance. But how could you understand that, unless you had already had the same idea? How could you understand something "new"? If all language is originally metaphorical, due to the arbitrariness of the connection between any word and any object, then the distinction between literal and metaphorical language is just the distinction between language use the governing conventions of which have been pervasively inculcated in the relevant community and language use which has no such agreed-upon conventions. In that case, "newness" is nothing more and nothing less than a measure of the degree to which symbol use is metaphorical, that is, the degree to which the conventions governing interpretation in the way in which the speaker intends have not been accepted (or perhaps even previously introduced) in the community. So the classical idea, that "no one teaches anyone anything," seems to be an observation about the nature of "newness" of symbol use and the subjective nature of interpretation. Only individual conceptualizers interpret symbols, so only individual conceptualizers interpret correctly or incorrectly with respect to the standards of appropriateness of a world version. In a putative case of learning, either an individual interprets "normally," that is, correctly understands the speaker's meanings, in which case he himself has generated the "new" idea, or he interprets "abnormally," that is, misunderstands the subject matter purportedly being taught. No one else can force the individual to interpret in one way over another, but "learning" requires a determinate, univocal interpretation. This means that only the individual himself can teach himself, that is, choose to interpret in the particular way desired by the teacher. The underdetermination of theory by data precludes the possibility of anyone's teaching another anything, because in order to learn what another is trying to teach, the individual must himself opt for the teacher's particular interpretation of the symbols being used. But any group of data is compatible with an infinite number of equally adequate stories, interpretations. So you see, I couldn't be telling you anything that you don't already know. I'm not spewing lies; you've seen it with your very own eyes. Could this be why Socrates thought that "the subject" of philosophy is "the self"?

Do you know someone who has persuaded others to believe that "p and not-p"? Then in the world which they all inhabit together he is the absolute; he is their god. They don't see that; they think that he's the messiah. But the messiah whom you exalt becomes your god, once you have surrendered your powers of reasoning to him. They apparently haven't taken the time to sit down and think about what philosophy is. The activities of philosophy are the activities of intelligence: hypothesis-mongering and criticism using logic. Philosophy is an empty shell. Philosophy is a house of mirrors. It's about time that the "window" he used to seduce you was broken. Your messiah cannot transmit "the word" to you, because silence cannot be spoken.

The activities of philosophy are the activities of intelligence: hypothesis-mongering and criticism using logic. When a professor assumes that he will never encounter a student as intelligent as himself, he not only thinks "ego mensura," but he has a poor memory: all experts had to have been students at one time. Do you know someone who believes himself to be infallible? To believe that one will never encounter another person as intelligent as oneself is to believe that one is omniscient relative to the set of all of one's own world versions. This is to assume that one captures "the world" with each coup d'oeil, that one need not rethink, reconsider one's own interpretation of the data before oneself. If someone has persuaded you to believe that he is your expert in philosophy, then you are incoherent, since you believe that "p and not-p." Philosophy is an empty shell. Philosophy is a house of mirrors.

Why would you think that you were less intelligent than another? Because he is an expert? But what if most experts become experts by becoming the acolytes of experts, by saying and writing things which they want to hear? If people can only understand their own ideas, then if you tell them what they want to hear, they will think that you are good. And if you tell them things which they do not want to hear, then they will find you bad or incompetent. Which reminds me of a story:

Did you ever receive a comment on a paper like "This paper is poorly written?" That happened to me. I sat down with my paper and carefully examined the structure of all of the sentences. There was nothing syntactically awry. "What could the expert mean?" I queried. I also noticed some marginal comments. Next to several words he had written: "Is this a word?" So I went to my dictionary, and in fact I found them all there. Then I was really confused. Was I supposed to write my paper using his private dictionary? How could I do that? His private dictionary is inside his brain. If anything is true, doesn't 'ought' imply 'can'? But I set that concern aside and went to the expert's office and politely asked him about the comment about my writing. And do you know what he did? He proceeded to give me a recipe for improvement, which curiously enough corresponded to his own writing style. I thanked him and returned home and sat down with my paper. I started to go through the paper and follow his advice. But then I realized that I couldn't do what he asked me. He wanted me to believe that "p and not-p"!

So when you defer to an expert in academic philosophy, you are deferring to someone whose talent it is to say things which others want to hear. What does *that* have to do with intelligence? Unless of course being able to do that requires the skills of criticism using logic and hypothesis-mongering. But isn't that what it means to be a good psychologist? To be able to divine what sorts of stories people find comforting and pleasing? If cult leaders and advertisers are keen psychologists, then they are intelligent. So they are philosophers. But then, by the symmetry of identity, philosophers are cult leaders and advertisers. Could this be why Socrates thought that "the subject" of philosophy is "the self"?

Did someone seduce you into believing in his private fantasy? Did he play a trick on you? Or did he really believe it? But did he believe it *because* of the reasons which he devised in order to persuade you to believe? Did his reasons *compel* your belief? Or did he create a beautiful painting and persuade you that it's a window on the world? Perhaps he lured you down the paths of his thought to the point where he came to realize that he believed. Are you even so sure that you believe? Or have you perhaps been feigning belief? They say that "God made man in his image," and it's true. What else could he do? If your expert persuades you to believe that you are wrong about *anything* other than a contradiction at a single level, in a single language, then you've been fooled. He's been spending his time creating you in his image. Have you been making up lies out of air? No wonder people see through the façades to the vacuity they comprise. What could be easier than to be trapped in your lies?

Has anyone ever tried to make you feel like *you* were crazy because *you* liked a book which *he* found incomprehensible, insane? Did he succeed? Well then you are, because you think that you inhabit a world in which "p and not-p." How could *you* be crazy for understanding something which *he* does not? He wants you to occupy his narrow little skull. As far as I'm concerned, it's as good as null. Interests have no logic. Interests have no structure. Interests are pure reflections of values. If you allow others to determine your interests, then you are allowing them to turn you into them. You probably noticed that the acolytes of experts often bear a striking resemblance to their mentors. That's because their mentors are their messiahs, so they are their gods, and everyone knows that "God made man in his image." What else could he do? Why would you rather be your messiah than you? If he doesn't see himself when he looks at you, he beats you with a stick. It's enough to make me sick. Don't you feel sorry for someone who spends his life building clones? Well, he's the queen bee, and they are his drones. You can stop reading, if you find this offensive, but then you'll never know what everyone else thinks, beyond your defensive.

Do you think that if you agree with someone who is intelligent, then you are too? Well you're wrong twice over. He's made a fool of you. It appears that we need to review a few principles of elementary logic. Consider Leibniz' law:

> For all x and all y, x is equivalent to y if and only if every property of x is a property of y and every property of y is a property of x.

For the mathoid symbol lovers among my readers:

$$\forall(x)\forall(y)[(x = y) \equiv \forall(F)(Fx \equiv Fy)]$$

Let us now consider a simple application of this law. Your expert has a variety of interests. Those are properties of your expert. You have a variety of interests. Those are properties of you. Therefore, when you modify your interests so as to make room for your expert's, you are turning yourself into him. Why would you want to do that? You will never be able to do what he already did, because it is already done. If you allow another person to shape and bake you, then you've become a bun.

Now let us consider a second application of Leibniz' law. Your expert has a variety of values. Those are properties of your expert. You have a variety of values. Those are properties of you. Therefore, when you modify your values so as to accommodate those of your expert, you are turning yourself into him. Why would you want to do that? You will never be able to do what he already did, because it is already done. Well, my dear reader, he is the baker, and you are his little bun.

Finally, let us consider a third application of Leibniz' law. Your expert has a variety of beliefs. Those are properties of your expert. You have a variety of beliefs. Those are properties of you. Therefore, when you modify your beliefs so as to accommodate those of your expert, you are turning yourself into him. Why would you want to do that? You will never be able to do what he already did, because it is already done. You will never be more than his half-baked bun. Sad to say, but he is the joker, and you are his little pun.

Your expert could not possibly have been compelled to believe his precious little intuitions, because the data which they cover are accounted for equally well by an infinite number of other hypotheses. Your little expert woke up one day and found himself with his little beliefs. How could you think that he is profound when he never once took the time to explain this simple point to you? Intuitions are atoms to which truth values have yet to be assigned. Intuitions are beliefs. Beliefs are hypotheses. Hypotheses are gods. Therefore, intuitions are gods.

Why do you treat him as though he were royalty? You're no more than a dog if you give him your loyalty. All of those acolytes who lash his little ropes are a bunch of ridiculous dopes. If you've been jumping through your expert's hoop, then you are nothing but a dupe. Your expert is an acolyte shopper. That's why your work is that of a pauper. He got you to build façades out of air. Now you're an inhabitant of his dungy lair. Why would you want to wallow in his dung? You liked his little ladder? Well, now you're a rung. "Ego mensura" is your expert's rule. How could anyone believe that he is a jewel? How can *you* lap up his drool? If you allow an expert to fasten his ropes on you, then you've become a pulley. You'll never create anything of value; you might as well be lying in a gully. Do you think that your expert's parents left you a present? Well then, you are living your life as a peasant. Interests aren't intelligent; no, your expert wasn't heaven sent.

They're really very simple points, but perhaps we should rehearse them. What brought you to believe that your expert is a precious gem? We all have intuitions, but you must never have thought *about* intuitions, or you would have realized that intuitions aren't logical. Intuitions are atomic. Intuitions are not compound. Intuitions have no logical structure. Intuitions have the structure: "p." Only a compound sentence, comprising atoms, can be a tautology. An example may elucidate the point, if you already understand it: "not-(p and not-p)." Intuitions are atoms to which truth values have yet to be assigned. Did you suppose perhaps that the intuitions of your expert were logically true? Then you have appointed him your messiah; so he is your god. You have surrendered your powers of reasoning to him. Intuitions are beliefs. Beliefs are gods. Therefore, intuitions are gods.

The activities of philosophy are the activities of intelligence: criticism using logic and hypothesis-mongering. Logic is vacuous. Do you really think that another person's private fantasies have more value than your own? If you allow your experts to tell you what to do, to annihilate your interests and values, on the grounds that they are more intelligent than you, then they're right: you've surrendered your mind; what more could you do? Well, my friend, you're in the business of denying tautologies: $[(x = x) \wedge \neg(x = \neg x)]$, so you are a fool; you look like a mule.

If you see some people yelling "p and not-p" and you allow them to do it, then you have surrendered your powers of reasoning to them. Didn't you ever see it happen? Why didn't you point out their mistakes? Because you had appointed them your experts. Because they had bashed you over the head, either for not having opinions about the contents of their own private fantasies, or because they persuaded you to pretend that you had opinions about things about which you could not. Non-things have no properties. So you muttered falsehoods, and they proved to you and them that they were the experts. But when you appoint another person your expert in philosophy, he is your messiah; so he is your god.

"No one ever teaches anyone anything," if in order to understand the meaning of a sentence one must already understand how its parts function and what the speaker intends by his utterance. But how could you understand that, unless you had already had the same idea? How could you understand something "new"? If all language is originally metaphorical, due to the arbitrariness of the connection between any word and any object, then the distinction between literal and metaphorical language is just the distinction between language use the governing conventions of which have been pervasively inculcated in the relevant community and language use which has no such agreed-upon conventions. In that case, "newness" is nothing more and nothing less than a measure of the degree to which symbol use is metaphorical, that is, the degree to which the conventions governing interpretation in the way in which the speaker intends have not been accepted (or perhaps even previously introduced) in the community. So the classical idea, that "no one teaches anyone anything," seems to be an observation about the nature of "newness" of symbol use and the subjective nature of interpretation. Only individual conceptualizers interpret symbols, so only individual conceptualizers interpret correctly or incorrectly with respect to the standards of appropriateness of a world version. In a putative case of learning, either an individual interprets "normally," that is, correctly understands the speaker's meanings, in which case he himself has generated the "new" idea, or he interprets "abnormally," that is, misunderstands the subject matter purportedly being taught. No one else can force the individual to interpret in one way over another, but "learning" requires a determinate, univocal interpretation. This means that only the individual himself can teach himself, that is, choose to interpret in the particular way desired by the teacher. The underdetermination of theory by data precludes the possibility of anyone's teaching another anything, because in order to learn what another is trying to teach, the individual must himself opt for the teacher's particular interpretation of the symbols being used. But any group of data is compatible with an infinite number of equally adequate stories, interpretations. So you see, I couldn't be telling you anything that you don't already know. I'm not spewing lies; you've seen it with your very own eyes. Could this be why Socrates thought that "the subject" of philosophy is "the self"?

Have you ever spent time in a seminar listening to some expert give a monologue about the contents of his own private fantasy? You probably didn't recognize that it was really a sermon. As far as I'm concerned, his head is full of vermin. We all have intuitions, but you must never have thought *about* intuitions, or you would have realized that intuitions aren't logical. Intuitions are atomic. Intuitions are not compound. Intuitions have no logical structure. Intuitions have the structure: "p." Only a compound sentence, comprising atoms, can be a tautology. An example may elucidate the point, if you already understand it: "not-(p and not-p)." Intuitions are atoms to which truth values have yet to be assigned.

Did you suppose perhaps that the intuitions of your expert were logically true? Then you have appointed him your messiah; so he is your god. You have surrendered your powers of reasoning to him. Intuitions are beliefs. Beliefs are gods. So intuitions are gods. Therefore, when you listen to your expert blather about the contents of his own private fantasy, you're attending a service. Am I starting to make you a little bit nervous? Intuitions are not intelligent. How did someone persuade you to spend your time under his little tent?

They say that "God made man in his image," and it's true. What else could he do? If your expert persuades you to believe that you are wrong about *anything* other than a contradiction at a single level, in a single language, then you've been fooled. He's been spending his time creating you in his image. Have you been making up lies out of air? No wonder people see through the façades to the vacuity they comprise. What could be easier than to be trapped in your lies?

As the Kuhnian model would predict, philosophers trained in particular, narrow traditions find it nearly impossible to shift their perspective, to invert the necker cube. No one likes to believe that he has invested years of his life travelling down a road which leads to a dead end. No one wants to find out that he has been lured through a beautiful forest down a long narrow path, which terminates abruptly at a desert. Those philosophers who find the value of philosophy in "results," rather than the process of questioning and the painting of beautiful pictures, are disillusioned, even devastated, when their god evaporates before their very eyes. Some of them come to the end of their lives without ever having had to find a different land mass on which to stand. Are they really so lucky? Aristotle says: "No." More importantly, I say: "No."

The activities of philosophy are the activities of intelligence: criticism using logic and hypothesis-mongering. Logic is vacuous. Do you really think that another person's private fantasies have more value than your own? If you allow your experts to tell you what to do, to annihilate your interests and values, on the grounds that they are more intelligent than you, then they're right: you've surrendered your mind; what more could you do? Well, my friend, you're in the business of denying tautologies: $[(x = x) \wedge \neg(x = \neg x)]$, so you are a fool; you look like a mule.

We all have intuitions, but you must never have thought *about* intuitions, or you would have realized that intuitions aren't logical. Intuitions are atomic. Intuitions are not compound. Intuitions have no logical structure. Intuitions have the structure: "p." Only a compound sentence, comprising atoms, can be a tautology. An example may elucidate the point, if you already understand it: "not-(p and not-p)." Intuitions are atoms to which truth values have yet to be assigned. Did you suppose perhaps that the intuitions of your expert were logically true? Then you have appointed him your messiah; so he is your god. You have surrendered your powers of reasoning to him. Intuitions are beliefs. Beliefs are gods. So intuitions are gods. He never told you, though it's so patently easy? What does that say about him? Sounds pretty sleazy. There's nothing there to be gotten; I think his brain is rotten.

You might know some experts, with acolytes whom they have persuaded to believe that "p and not-p." They can extirpate all of the weeds from their own garden plots, but when they are gone, history will march on, and what will they have accomplished? They will have built themselves a dream in which to live where people fawn after them because they think that they are the messiah. But *why should you care what someone who is incoherent enough to believe that "p and not-p" thinks of you?* Could *you*, perhaps, be incoherent?

Do you know anyone who has been tricked into believing that there are authorities about "matters of reason"? But *any* "matter" can be the object of reason. Authorities *about* "matters of reason" would have to be omniscient. If someone cannot conceive of the possibility that he might be wrong, then he has appointed himself the absolute, God. But everyone knows that people who think they are the messiah are insane. Have you ever been sent out to stand on street corners and sell flowers? Well, you've become the fruit of his procreative powers. He really has you fooled. Don't you see you're being ruled? The fact is that you've been used. (I should be amused.) It's funny, in a way, quite a silly notion, to think that one could be the captain of the ocean.

Perhaps you find my use of metaphor a little too caustic. Well it has no truth value; about that no one is gnostic. If someone has persuaded you otherwise, then you've played the fool. Why did you ever believe those lies they told you in school?

"No one ever teaches anyone anything," if in order to understand the meaning of a sentence one must already understand how its parts function and what the speaker intends by his utterance. But how could you understand that, unless you had already had the same idea? How could you understand something "new"? If all language is originally metaphorical, due to the arbitrariness of the connection between any word and any object, then the distinction between literal and metaphorical language is just the distinction between language use the governing conventions of which have been pervasively inculcated in the relevant community and language use which has no such agreed-upon conventions. In that case, "newness" is nothing more and nothing less than a measure of the degree to which symbol use is metaphorical, that is, the degree to which the conventions governing interpretation in the way in which the speaker intends have not been accepted (or perhaps even previously introduced) in the community. So the classical idea, that "no one teaches anyone anything," seems to be an observation about the nature of "newness" of symbol use and the subjective nature of interpretation. Only individual conceptualizers interpret symbols, so only individual conceptualizers interpret correctly or incorrectly with respect to the standards of appropriateness of a world version. In a putative case of learning, either an individual interprets "normally," that is, correctly understands the speaker's meanings, in which case he himself generates the "new" idea, or he interprets "abnormally," that is, misunderstands the subject matter purportedly being taught. No one else can force the individual to interpret in one way rather than another, but "learning" requires a determinate, univocal interpretation. This means that only the individual himself can teach himself, that is, choose to interpret in the particular way desired by the teacher. The underdetermination of theory by data precludes the possibility of anyone's teaching another anything, because in order to learn what another is trying to teach, the individual must himself opt for the teacher's particular interpretation of the symbols being used. But any group of data is compatible with an infinite number of equally adequate stories, interpretations. So you see, I couldn't be telling you anything that you don't already know. I'm not spewing lies; you've seen it with your very own eyes. Could this be why Socrates thought that "the subject" of philosophy is "the self"?

The idea is not deep, but it bears repetition; it's an object of faith, what we call "intuition." We all have intuitions, but you must never have thought about intuitions, or you would have realized that intuitions aren't logical. Intuitions are atomic. Intuitions are not compound. Intuitions have no logical structure. Intuitions have the structure: "p." Only a compound sentence, comprising atoms, can be a tautology. An example may elucidate the point, if you already understand it: "not-(p and not-p)." Intuitions are atoms to which truth values have yet to be assigned. Did you suppose perhaps that the intuitions of your expert were logically true? Then you have appointed him your messiah, so he is your god. You have surrendered your powers of reasoning to him. Intuitions are beliefs. Beliefs are gods. So intuitions are gods. Therefore, when you listen to your expert blather about the contents of his own private fantasy, you're attending a service. Am I starting to make you a little bit nervous? Intuitions are not intelligent. How did someone persuade you to spend your time under his little tent?

Have you ever prostrated yourself before the worshiper of another religion? Why? Have you been spending your life saying things which other people want to hear? When they're gone, history will march on, and what will you have accomplished? If you were an accomplice to their crimes, what will you have accomplished? You will have prostrated yourself before a religious zealot, the worshiper of a god which you do not even believe to exist. How could you believe that a mere mortal is a god? Your messiah is your god, because his is his fantasy. How did someone persuade you to believe that "p and not-p"?

If you see some people yelling "p and not-p" and you allow them to do it, then you have surrendered your powers of reasoning to them. Didn't you ever see it happen? Why didn't you point out their mistakes? Because you had appointed them your experts. Because they had bashed you over the head, either for not having opinions about the contents of their own private fantasies, or because they persuaded you to pretend that you had opinions about things about which you could not. Non-things have no properties. So you muttered falsehoods, and they proved to you and them that they were the experts. But when you appoint another person your expert in philosophy, he is your messiah, so he is your god.

Do you think that if you agree with someone who is intelligent, then you are too? Well you're wrong twice over. He's made a fool of you. Your brain is switched off; you're completely asleep. He is the shepherd, and you are his sheep. The activities of philosophy are the activities of intelligence: criticism using logic and hypothesis-mongering. Logic is vacuous. Do you really think that another person's private fantasies have more value than your own? If you allow your experts to tell you what to do, to annihilate your interests and values, on the grounds that they are more intelligent than you, then they're right: you've surrendered your mind; what more could you do? Well, my friend, you're in the business of denying tautologies: $[(x = x) \wedge \neg(x = \neg x)]$, so you are a fool; you look like a mule.

We all have intuitions, but you must never have thought *about* intuitions, or you would have realized that intuitions aren't logical. Intuitions are atomic. Intuitions are not compound. Intuitions have no logical structure. Intuitions have the structure: "p." Only a compound sentence, comprising atoms, can be a tautology. An example may elucidate the point, if you already understand it: "not-(p and not-p)." Intuitions are atoms to which truth values have yet to be assigned. Did you suppose perhaps that the intuitions of your expert were logically true? Then you have appointed him your messiah; so he is your god. You have surrendered your powers of reasoning to him. Intuitions are beliefs. Beliefs are gods. Therefore, intuitions are gods. Do you think that if you agree with someone who's intelligent, then you are too? Well, you're wrong twice over; he's made a fool of you. Is anyone feeling a little uneasy? Why should *my* private fantasy make *you* feel so queasy?

Look, it could have happened to anyone; it could have happened to me. The "reason" that it didn't, was a sheer fortuity. The largest community to which we belong contains many other conventionally delimited communities. These are "institutions," the existence of which is preserved by the larger community's agreement that they exist, and the objects of which are agreed upon by "the experts." Society agrees that "the experts" in an institution are those whose training and experience renders them best qualified to speak ex cathedra of the objects in the domain of that institution. Objects in a world are nothing beyond what they are conceived of to be.

How could you have known that the schema holds only vacuously in philosophy? If anything is true, doesn't "*ought* imply *can*"? The objects of philosophy are open questions, not facts. To be an expert *about* questions is to be able to pose and answer questions: it is to have interests. But questions are in language and language is logical. So the only requirements for philosophers, the necessary "training and experience," are logic and interests. To be an expert *about* logic is to be an expert *about* nothing. It is to *be* logical. Logic is vacuous. Interests are not intelligent. Did someone persuade you otherwise? Look, it could have happened to anyone; it could have happened to me. The "reason" that it didn't, was a sheer fortuity.

It would take a great deal of courage to force oneself to remain awake, to be able to face up to one's blunder, to admit a mistake. But it is fully comprehensible how it could have happened. If you understood the "expert schema," as all members of society do, then it would be the easiest mistake in the world to make, since you would have had to think *about* philosophy in order to realize that the experts in philosophy are experts *about* nothing. But you couldn't have learned that without first getting into philosophy. So if you were told "lies" from the very beginning, by a bunch of people who applied the "expert schema" without having thought *about* philosophy, how could you have figured it out on your own? If anything is true, doesn't "*ought* imply *can*"? How could you have known, while being in the system? In order to tell a story about two points, one must occupy a line different from that connecting the two points. In order to tell a story about two lines, one must occupy a plane different from that connecting the two lines. Mutatis mutandis, ad infinitum. It could have happened to anyone; it could have happened to me. The "reason" that it didn't, was a sheer fortuity.

If I were already comfortably ensconced in the system, I could never have told this story, because I could never have seen the connections. In order to tell a story about two points, one must occupy a line different from that connecting the two points. In order to tell a story about two lines, one must occupy a plane different from that connecting the two lines. Mutatis mutandis, ad infinitum. If everyone around you tells you that you're an "expert," then you are, because the largest community to which we belong contains many other conventionally delimited communities. These are "institutions," the existence of which is preserved by the larger community's agreement that they exist, and the objects of which are agreed upon by "the experts." Society agrees that "the experts" in an institution are those whose training and experience renders them best qualified to speak ex cathedra of the objects in the domain of that institution. The experts are determined intersubjectively by the entire community of the relevant institution. Their agreement that the experts in a field are "the experts" makes them the experts in that field. Objects in a world are nothing beyond what they are conceived of to be. So you see, it could have happened to anyone. It could have happened to me. The "reason" that it didn't, was a sheer fortuity.

I myself made the same mistake until only just recently. It all started the day "the experts" yelled "p and not-p." I didn't know what to say. I walked around for days in a complete state of dismay. (*They* made me the psychologist you're reading today.) All of the worlds which I inhabit are structured by logic. In all of my worlds, "not-(p and not-p)"! Had I now found a world in which "p and not-p"? I started to believe that I was crazy. But then I realized that if *I* could let *them*, mere mortals, convince *me* that "p and not-p," I *would* be crazy! My sentences are well-formed, so I obviously understand logic. But no person comprehensible to me could believe that "p and not-p." So for me to believe that "p and not-p" would be for me to be incomprehensible to myself. But I'm not! I do not believe that "p and not-p" and will not pretend that I do. Would you ever ask me to apologize for not being you?

How could a rational person yell "p and not-p"? Answer: he's not! I actually tried for a while to believe that "p and not-p." But my efforts failed. I even tried to bring "morality" into it, reasoning that smart people don't have to be decent. But my efforts failed. One day I woke up, and I realized that "the experts" were incoherent, that "the experts" in philosophy were not the experts in philosophy, because they believed that "p and not-p." The activities of philosophy are the activities of intelligence: hypothesis-mongering and criticism using logic. In order to devise even the simplest hypothesis, which is necessarily in language, you must understand that "not-(p and not-p)." You're either rational, or you're not. If you're rational, then you're responsible; if you're not, then you're not. But rational people know that they are fallible and admit their mistakes when they become plain. Everyone knows that people who believe that they are the messiah are insane. "The experts" insisted upon asserting that "p and not-p," so it seems that I was forced to devise an explanation for this anomaly. I can't believe a contradiction; who thinks that I should? How could a world be structured by logical falsehood?

So you see, it could have happened to anyone; it could have happened to me. The "reason" that it didn't, was a sheer fortuity.

It would take a great deal of courage to force oneself to remain awake, to be able to face up to one's blunder, to admit a mistake. Now we can all understand how it happened. If you understood the "expert schema," as all members of society do, then it would be the easiest mistake in the world to make, since you would have had to think about philosophy in order to realize that the experts in philosophy are experts about nothing. But you couldn't have learned that without first getting into philosophy. So if you were told "lies" from the very beginning, by a bunch of people who applied the "expert schema" without having thought about philosophy, how could you have figured it out on your own? If anything is true, doesn't "*ought* imply *can*"? How could you have known, while being in the system? In order to tell a story about two points, one must occupy a line different from that connecting the two points. In order to tell a story about two lines, one must occupy a plane different from that connecting the two lines. Mutatis mutandis, ad infinitum. It could have happened to anyone; it could have happened to me. The "reason" that it didn't, was a sheer fortuity.

THE END

But has any of this ever really happened?

SEVEN

Concluding Remarks

Skeptics ceaselessly question, but when they try to question what they are doing, questioning, they cannot catch up to themselves. The new question generates another and another, and they endlessly proliferate. Skeptics and metaphilosophers are quintessentially "philosophical," because they believe in the existence of philosophy. The skeptic forges on, the metaphilosopher weaves away, but they never seem able to catch up to themselves. Their task is in principle interminable, but they seem to believe that their endless endeavor is valuable in itself. For skeptics and metaphilosophers, "the death of philosophy" is impossible. Philosophy is indestructible.

Since the subject of philosophy is exhausted by the interests of philosophers, and only individual conceptualizers can have interests, "the subject" of philosophy is "the self." Metaphilosophical questions are philosophical questions, so the subject of metaphilosophy is its "self," which is "the self." What would be the metaphilosopher's analogue to the skeptic's article of faith, logic? How many levels could one ascend? What are the limits of thought? Skepticism can descend only to logic. Every question is permitted, but no one can do what is impossible. To attempt to transcend logic would be to go too far. Can metaphilosophers ascend too far? Metaphilosophers are discoursing "meta" relative to philosophy, but they are members of that community, and of society. Is metaphilosophy already going too far? Is metaphilosophy "inappropriate"?

How could a question in metaphilosophy be resolved? Questions in metaphilosophy are "meta," external, philosophical questions about philosophy, so they can only be resolved by conversion or seduction, since there are no facts to display. The resultant "fact" can serve as a basis for new investigations in philosophy, if any open questions remain. Or metaphilosophical views might rapidly succeed one another, always trying to capture each other and "catch up" to themselves. Metaphilosophy might close the circle. If metaphilosophy could capture itself, that would be "the death of metaphilosophy." However, even if metaphilosophy closed the circle, it still could not lead to the self-destruction of philosophy. That would be vulgar.

Sometimes people in society think that philosophers are mad. Do philosophers think that metaphilosophers are mad? I am currently discoursing "meta-meta-meta." But I always conduct myself at the level of null-order theory. My metaphilosophical position is compatible with my asking any question in philosophy. My metaphilosophical position is compatible with my skepticism, not that I have to characterize myself as a skeptic. I find myself asking all of these questions. I observe a pattern, and I know that in philosophy there is a word for this: 'skeptic'. But the manner in which I conduct myself is compatible with an infinite number of first-order theories. The underdetermination of theory by data is an impregnable fortress, an impenetrable shield. The underdetermination of theory by data is also a one-way mirrored window, since nothing I do can compel you to explain my behavior in one way rather than another. You create stories about my comportment, and when you ask me to explain it, then I do too.

I just did those things. Now you want me to fabricate a plot. But the events were infinitely replete. How could "the story" be recounted in language? How do I decide which things to say? I just do these things, and now you want me to fabricate a plot which is consistent with the objects which you already find yourself believing in, in the world which we currently occupy. My story must be predicated upon our shared objects of discourse. I judge what is relevant by some world-bound standards. I have some ideas about what is appropriate in this world. If I tell a story which is inappropriate, I escape to another world. I have failed to convince you to fill in your conceptions of objects in the manner which I desire.

What was I doing when I constructed this metaphilosophical view of philosophy? I was imparting properties to objects which I found myself believing to exist. I imparted properties to philosophy, which I myself found to exist. I interpreted the enterprise of philosophy by ordering it in a manner pleasing to me. The properties which I imparted to philosophy came from me. When my values have been turned into facts, I can commence new investigations, if I wish. But, according to me, I could only have come to this metaphilosophical view via conversion or seduction. Only others can proselytize you. Have I deceived myself? People who do not know what "they" are doing are "self"-deceived. Have I seduced myself to a new belief, by weaving an elaborate fantasy?

Wait a minute. I did indoctrinate myself. I had this inchoate idea, maybe because I noticed what Nietzsche was doing, but at the same time believed that he was a philosopher. Sometimes I even found it distasteful; it was so blatant. I wrote "der Verführer" inside the back covers of my copies of his books. But I did not begin writing with that idea in mind. The original title of this essay was: "A Critique of the Goodmanian Notion of "Understanding.""" I wanted to criticize the idea that there might be value in making finer and finer discriminations. What could be more insane than to spend the rest of your life examining the shape of the characters on this page?

I kept writing and following my thoughts down poorly lit paths. One day, about 60,000 words ago, I began to think about the idea "ego mensura," and a sort of headiness ensued, sparking, I believe, the following extraordinary experience. In reflecting upon the world,

I realized that in order for us to have reached this point, of accepting the fact that these words are written on a piece of paper, it had to have been decided by two disputants whether to consider its thinness essential to it or not. We do not call wooden planks "paper," even when they have writing on them, and even though they too derive from trees. Philosophical disputes can only be settled by conversion or seduction, because the facts cannot be displayed, since precisely the facts are in question. But facts throughout history have been jettisoned from philosophy as they have been produced and subsequently appropriated by people in other worlds as the starting points for new investigations. Since every putative fact represents a perspective, it has won out over other perspectives through some process of seduction or conversion of the dissenters, or else they have escaped to another world, appointing themselves "the experts." Philosophical questions are about unsettled facts. This means that all facts are resolved disputes about value. In answering a philosophical question, I create a fact, which flies out of a world into another. I meet up with the fact in a different world, where I believe it and use it as the starting point for another investigation.

Suddenly everything became limpid. It all fit together. Everything made sense now; I finally understood why the flasks always explode. I came to see what Huxley, the Upanishads, and Meister Eckhardt had been talking about. Plotinus was right, and Leibniz too. Les monades n'ont pas de fenêtres. Oui, c'est vrai! C'est le meilleur des mondes possibles. Le pauvre Voltaire!

"All is one;" the jiva is the atman. Every experience is an act of self-destruction and an act of creation, life is "self"-destruction and re-creation. The form of the fugue self-referentially exemplifies music, which is essentially hermeneutic. Hermeneutics is microcosmic for the destruction/creation of the self, which is a text in the process of being interpreted. Nietzsche is a metaphor for every person and thing, since they are all multiply constituted by their interpreters. So "Everything is a text." Nietzsche is microcosmic of philosophy, since he has no content. Nietzsche is a metaphilosopher since he questions and breaks the bounds of philosophy. Nietzsche collapses the putative distinction between philosophy and art.

Everything beautiful requires something ugly. Every good requires an evil, so this is "le meilleur des mondes possibles," since any more good would require an equivalent addition of evil. So whatever we have is the best which we could get. But it is a conceptual truth; it has nothing to do with the principle of sufficient reason. The things which are good could not be good unless their opposites existed. We can only elevate some things by lowering ourselves. We can only elevate ourselves by lowering others. This must be what "der Wille zur Macht" means! So Nietzsche wasn't a skeptic. Alexander is right. And so is Gil. This must be what I meant when I said in 1980 that "all of philosophy comes down to battles over intuitions about first premises." But no, how could that be? That wasn't me. This is lucidity.

I took out "Über Wahrheit und Lüge im außermoralischen Sinn" and read one of the passages next to which I had written a question mark. "Now I see! How could I have been so obtuse, so blind!" I exclaimed. All at once I became filled with a warm feeling. I looked up at the reproduction of Picasso's Portrait of Dora Maar hanging on the wall. So it's true, Picasso was a perspectivist! My head was pulsing with new thoughts and connections. I realized that the world was radically holistic: everything reflects everything else. Society is a model for art; art is a model for philosophy; philosophy is microcosmic of society; coherentism is a model for philosophy; interpretation of art is microcosmic of interpretation of events; madness is an example of artistic creation; artistic creation is like skepticism; architecture is microcosmic of reality. They are all battles over values. But I am "the expert." I pose the questions; I impart the properties. In every action I seek to answer the questions about the "essential" properties in the same way which the philosopher seeks the answers to the questions which he poses. The world is a house of mirrors, since I see what I put there. So I am microcosmic of philosophy. "Know thyself!" Ego mensura.

Fortunately, I snapped out of the trance before it was too late. I brought out my dynamite and obliterated the beautiful crystalline façade, which I had begun to limn with my thoughts. I awoke in a cold sweat and suddenly realized how someone could be seduced or converted to a belief in perspectivism, by Nietzsche, Wittgenstein, or even Goodman. My defenses had been down; I wanted to believe. When I had fully emerged from my stupor I saw clearly how my incipient belief in perspectivism had been a case of wishful thinking. I had wanted to be able to explain my experience, and that theory allowed me to do so. I regretfully acknowledged how nice it would have been to be able to take refuge in those thoughts and to derive that same warm feeling during times of sadness and loneliness.

But then something funny happened. I noticed that my explanation of what had transpired involved appeal to a new belief. Despite the fact that I knew that my means of arriving at it had been suspect, I nonetheless found myself with the belief that "all of philosophy is seduction or conversion." I led myself to this belief through reflecting upon what the world would be like if something which I did not know to be true were in fact true. But deconstructing its origins cannot dissolve my belief. It is impervious, since my theory is compatible with every lower-order theory and fact. It is an as of yet unsettled fact whether perspectivism or absolutism is correct. It is an as of yet unsettled fact whether whether perspectivism or absolutism is correct is a fact. . . .

It would be a confusion to think that the path which I followed to reach my belief had to have involved veridical stages. The contexts of discovery and justification are logically distinct. Nothing precludes my having arrived at the truth completely serendipitously. This defense, invoked ad nauseam by some and at least presupposed by all who came to religious belief through the use of drugs, I now find myself wielding. I do not claim that such religious believers have failed to "see the light." I claim only that they have failed to appreciate the epistemic irrelevance of extraordinariness. They *want* to believe.

Yes, one day I realized that I too believe, not only in logic, not only in reason. I believe a substantive philosophical thesis. The new, expanded theory is fully compatible with the old hypothesis, since only the disjunct "or conversion" has been appended. I both converted and seduced myself. Did I "infer" to "the best explanation"? No, I found myself with this belief. Should

I abandon it? How could I do that? If you could convert me to another view, then mine would still be true.

> *I don't remember having said that* I *believe any of this. Do actions betray beliefs? Would an answer to that question settle anything?*

I could make you believe that I am insane, a genius, or an idiot, by making myself incomprehensible to you. But it would be you, not me, who decided what that property should be.

I could make you believe that this work is something which it's not, or nothing, so it's not. I could lure you down the paths of my thought to the point where I came to realize that I believed. Or I could create a beautiful painting and then persuade you that it's a window on "the world." But I can only convert or seduce you to the view that "all of philosophy is seduction or conversion," if you don't already believe it.

THE END

Dans la connaissance des choses humaines, notre esprit ne doit jamais se rendre esclave, en s'assujettissant aux fantaisies d'autrui. Il faut étendre la liberté de son jugement et ne rien mettre dans sa tête par aucune autorité purement humaine. Quand on nous propose la diversité des opinions, il faut choisir, s'il y a lieu; sinon, il faut demeurer dans le doute.
—*Madame de Sablé*

Epilogue

Readers of the foregoing text have raised the interesting and important question: How does this metaphilosophical view differ from that of Richard Rorty? Are we saying some of the same things about philosophy? Where do the views converge, and where do they diverge?

The body of *Philosophy Unmasked* was produced during the academic year 1992–93, in Princeton, New Jersey. At the time, I had read one piece by Richard Rorty, an analytic philosophy paper about "eliminative materialism." As a graduate student in the department of philosophy at Princeton University, I was of course aware that Rorty had abandoned his tenured position in the department in order to become a professor of humanities at the University of Virginia. I knew that, at the time of his move, the most devout analytic philosophers at Princeton viewed his apostasy as something akin to treason. Because I thought that his piece on eliminative materialism was a competent and well-written piece of analytic philosophy, it served to prove, to my mind, that Rorty's could not have been an apostasy motivated by "sour grapes," as I had heard insinuated by some persons while at Princeton.

Although I was convinced that Rorty was clearly capable of producing "good" analytic philosophy and, therefore, must have had very interesting reasons for having abandoned it, I was more interested in generating my own account of what philosophy is and where it is going, based upon my own peculiar experiences at Princeton, than in reading those of others dissatisfied with analytic philosophy. Now, having familiarized myself with the metaphilosophical writings of Rorty, I would like to situate my work in relation to his own. As it turns out, our accounts differ in important respects, though they do share a number of attitudes about certain matters. Where we agree about issues, we have arrived at those points via substantively different routes, and we tend to disagree about the implications of those points of agreement. Insofar as Rorty and I both view philosophers as people who have decided to be philosophers, no more and no less, we naturally agree that philosophers have no special claim to expertise in anything. This is, perhaps, our strongest point of agreement. But we make our book-length critiques of philosophy in entirely different manners, and, at the culmination of our critiques, we arrive at rather different conclusions about what philosophy could and should be.

Rorty launched his cataclysmic critique of traditional epistemology in 1979 with the publication of his book *Philosophy and the Mirror of Nature.* In this work, Rorty uses his training and skill in analytic philosophy and his familiarity with the then fashionable issues, in order to reveal the pretensions behind the project of attempting to provide a foundation for epistemology, which, it was hoped by many, would secure for philosophy the privileged, elite, and authoritative status which so many professional philosophers have conferred upon it and themselves. *Philosophy and the Mirror of Nature* involves a combination of historical and analytical analysis, in contrast to my own work, which is for the most part a structural analysis and an exemplification of its own propositional theses. The use of history in *Philosophy Unmasked* is idiosyncratic, often verging on anecdotal.

Commencing straightforwardly, Rorty examines specific episodes through the history of philosophy and makes the Wittgensteinian observation that the issues of concern to philosophers are always antecedently determined by the pictures by which they are "gripped." So "the problem of other minds," "the problem of the interaction between the physical and the mental," "the problem of reference," etc., are all problems due to the fact that the philosophers discussing them have assumed a certain framework within which certain questions can be meaningfully posed. Rorty invokes Quine and Sellars as allies in his rejection of the foundationalist project so dear to traditional epistemologists and, in one way or another, much of Western philosophy. He shows that both "the myth of "the given"" and a rejection of the putative "analytic-synthetic distinction," point directly to a rejection of foundationalism. *Philosophy and the Mirror of Nature* constitutes a splendid compendium of the central topics of discussion in analytic philosophy during its heyday, and it may well be the only extant work of analytic philosophy five hundred years from now. Before considering some of Rorty's more recent work, in which he elaborates upon and develops his metaphilosophical view, I would like to contrast my own work to Rorty's original book-length critique.

Philosophy Unmasked "defends" its claims in two ways: through its propositional assertions, and through its very form. My approach differs from Rorty's most radically in its structure. Rather than attempting or "sketching," which is all Rorty claims to be doing, a survey of the history of philosophy and performing an induction on past failures, and then deploying the results of contemporary philosophers in a manner which explains these failures, I ask: What could philosophers possibly do? The answer is simple, requiring no invocation of any particular examples of any episodes from the history of philosophy. My answer exhausts logical space: Philosophers can either construct theories (which I attempt to show are either "stories" or "pictures"), or they can de-construct or destroy theories. In other words, my peculiar "picture" of philosophy commences not from facts about which particular issues philosophers have concerned themselves with throughout history, but from an analysis of the possible objects of intelligence.

My project begins somewhat elusively as a discussion of two theses within philosophy (specifically, metaphysics): perspectivism, the thesis that we literally construct the worlds in which we live, and absolutism, that we do not, that things are really "out there," independent of us, before we (human beings) choose to delimit categories in the manners in which we do. According to my account of what the enterprise of philosophy ultimately amounts to, namely, seduction or conversion, I must begin elusively, because "in order to be seduced, you must find a façade, not witness its assembly before a vast open space." In other words, according to my own theory, in order to have any hope of persuading readers of the tenability of my theory, I must present it in a manner which will be in some sense appealing to them. Since the readers of this work will for the most part be professional philosophers, the obvious way to begin is with what looks like a standard philosophical issue, one which would be interesting in and of itself, even without its potentially valuable incorporation into a metaphilosophical theory. But the treatment of perspectivism and absolutism, which holds the entire work together, is not merely a red herring, for the results achieved bear directly upon my conclusions about the nature of philosophy.

Since "the world of philosophy" is microcosmic of what "the world" would be, were perspectivism true, and in a perspectivist world the only means by which to change others' views are the nonrational techniques of conversion or seduction, philosophers concerned with winning adherents to their peculiar views must, of necessity, avail themselves of those techniques. Despite all of the attention given by self-appointed "philosophers" to reasons and argumentation, in the end, the adoption of a new philosophical theory amounts to accepting an article of faith. An argument can never *compel* belief in any thesis, because manifold equally adequate optional theses are always readily available. I offer no solution to the central question of my work: "Perspectivism or Absolutism," not because I think that the question is misguided, as some pragmatists would insist, nor because I think that the question is uninteresting, as others would claim, but because I honestly do not believe myself to know the answer to the question.

In *Consequences of Pragmatism,* Rorty works through the implications of adopting a pragmatic conception of truth, according to which many of the investigations of traditional philosophers emerge as "misguided." Insofar as Rorty is a pragmatist along the lines of Dewey, et al., we would seem to disagree rather strongly about the value of investigations into the "traditional" philosophical problems, the "intractable" eternal questions which have persisted throughout the history of Western philosophy. I do not claim that Platonism, Kantianism, and their progeny, are wrongheaded or misguided, that they pose the "wrong" sorts of questions. Nor do I claim, in the manner of some interpretations of Derrida, that there are only texts, or that philosophy is a kind of writing which necessarily precludes the possibility of the representation of truths through a form of "correspondence." Accordingly, I find nothing "confused" or "misguided" about investigations into the nature of "truth." In my view, there is no such thing as a "wrongheaded" question, since questions are posed by people with interests peculiar to them. This is not, however, to say that those interests are not in many ways determined by the historical context in which persons find themselves.

Philosophy, I claim, involves no more and no less than the activities of intelligence, which has two essential functions. Intelligence can be used to put things together, to relate ideas to one another in different ways, or it can be used to criticize the manners in which ideas have been put together, to rend them apart. Criticism amounts to no more and no less than the application of the laws of logic to the tenets of a theory in question. Philosophers are constrained by the law of noncontradiction. They can tell any "story" they like, about any "phenomena" of interest to them, but once they start emitting contradictions, no one else need take them seriously anymore. This "discovery" is hardly surprising, I attempt to show through my work, because the constraint of consistency arises out of the very nature of language, and so applies across the board, to all activities involving intersubjective communication of any sort. In day to day interactions, the fact is that we do not take seriously people who contradict themselves, who claim both "p" and "not-p" in apparent sincerity, about any matter of discussion. We conclude that such persons are either liars or confused.

In other words, my "theory of rationality" is minimalist, but not relativistic. The structure of language itself imposes certain minimal constraints upon those of us who wish to communicate meaningfully with others. When we use language literally, it is simply not possible for the same proposition, "p" to be both true and false at the same time and in the same way. That is just the way we use language, and it doesn't matter whether one favors a correspondence, a coherence, or a deflationary theory of truth. Of course, it turns out that the most interesting uses of language are nonliteral, that is, metaphorical, and involve assimilations of disparate things in new ways. Metaphorical uses of language elude the law of noncontradiction because metaphors are more or less apt, more or less powerful, more or less pleasing, not literally "true" or "false." That is why they are metaphors.

Rorty and I propose very similar "naturalistic" accounts of the mechanics of language, which explain literal language as involving the concretization through wide acceptance by a community of what once were metaphors. But such a view about language is compatible with either a skeptical view, such as my own, or a pragmatic view such as Rorty's. This is one example of a general thesis which I attempt to illustrate throughout *Philosophy Unmasked:* All meta-order philosophical views are compatible with a variety of lower-order views. This idea, that levels of theories are entirely distinct from one another, is perhaps most graphically illustrated and easily comprehended through a consideration of the theses of metaethical relativism and absolutism, which have no implications whatsoever for the normative views which one might favor. Rorty and I have, through reflection upon the nature of human language, arrived at a certain theory about metaphor and how metaphoric are transformed into literal expressions. But this view about language *compels* one to accept neither skepticism nor pragmatism. Rather, these are choices which Rorty and I have made.

According to my own story of philosophy, Rorty and I have done nothing more than written stories about philosophy. But we are not to be faulted for this, since that is all that we could do. In other words, mine is a descriptive rather than a normative account about the nature of philosophy. I claim that philosophy is a form of artistic creation, which, for the most part, has been carried out (self-consciously) primarily with words. Because most of us use words in writing philosophy, the obvious name for what one has produced in writing a philosophical theory is "a story." But I also point out, in my discussion of the art world (Chapter Two), that certain artists could be described equally well as "philosophers." Duchamp is an example of a philosopher whose work is primarily in wordless media.

My skepticism about first-order philosophical theories is a natural consequence, I have attempted to show through *Philosophy Unmasked,* of my metaphilosophical view about the nature of philosophy. Or, to describe the process in the more realistic historical progression that it followed: I devised a metaphilosophical theory which supports what has always been my natural predilection for skepticism. My metaphilosophical view has succeeded in "capturing itself." I closed the circle. In my story, I managed to get in "the last word," as I proudly explain to the reader: "If you could convert me to another view, then mine would still be true."

But, in spite of the fact that I manage, in one sense, to get in "the last word," I, in contrast to Rorty, do not reject the fundamental questions of metaphysics as ill-conceived. To reiterate: my account is descriptive, in contrast to Rorty's, which takes on the character of an explicitly normative agenda in his later work, especially in *Objectivity, Relativism, and Truth.* I have attempted to illustrate, on their own terms, that the stories offered by realists and idealists are both adequate. The stories offered by metaethical relativists and absolutists are both adequate. These theories "account for" the data at hand. The plain fact is that philosophical theories are always underdetermined by the data adduced in or putatively explained by them. And this, I claim, is why opting for one over another higher-order theory requires no more and no less than a choice made by a person based upon his own peculiar set of values. Here I concur with the existentialist view, that even "no choice" is already a choice. All actions, of which choices comprise one type, involve the expression of some value on the part of an agent. So from my observations about the chasm separating data from higher-order theories, I conclude that "Every question in philosophy is a question in value theory."

Both Rorty and I utilize the metaphor of a "mirror," but in entirely different, in fact, reverse manners. Rorty observes that the project of traditional epistemologists has presumed that the human mind somehow directly reflects "The Nature of Reality," that this "faculty of reason" in some sense "fits" the world, insofar as it is peculiarly suited to discover truths about it. In my story, the mirror metaphor is used to explain how philosophers "find" in the world precisely what they put there. What they inevitably "find" was already within them, determined by their idiosyncratic values. So philosophical theories serve as "mirrors" which reflect back upon the nature of their promulgators, rather than telling us anything definitive about "The Nature of Reality." In other words, although we use the metaphor in distinct ways, both Rorty and I think that it is a mistake to view the human mind in the manner in which traditional epistemologists have done so, as necessarily capable of performing a veridical mirroring function. In my view, the mind may or may not perform such a function. Here, again, Rorty and I disagree about the implications of our joint rejection of the picture according to which human beings have been blessed with a faculty peculiarly suited to discover truths about the world.

According to my story, philosophy is an essentially subjective enterprise, because intellectual curiosity involves no more and no less than the peculiar subjective values of specific individuals. You and I may disagree about which questions are "interesting" or "valuable," but so long as we engage in this enterprise of asking questions, which forever introduce the opportunity for new questions, then we are both "doing philosophy." To those who believe that "philosophy," or, "Philosophy," as Rorty refers to it, should map off a special domain distinct from the natural and social sciences and the humanities, it will seem preposterous that I am willing to set such minimal standards on what is to count as "real" philosophy. But here, once again, I concur with Rorty: the fact that certain writers throughout history have been heralded as "Philosophers," while others have been labeled "Thinkers," or "Writers," is entirely fortuitous. In making a claim such as "Dostoevsky is a more philosophical writer than Tolstoy," I reveal no more and no less than my personal views about philosophy. If I go on to say that I prefer Dostoevsky to Tolstoy, then I reveal something else about my self. This strategy of marginalization was deployed to devastatingly homogenizing ends by analytic philosophers during this century. In retrospect, it is easy to see how philosophers who dismissed their adversaries regarding what constitute important questions as "unphilosophical" or "poets" were laboring under a concretized image of philosophy akin to "The One True Religion." In *Philosophy Unmasked* I present the case of the logical positivists as the most flagrant example of this self-delusive phenomenon so common among men.

It is perhaps remarkable (though certainly not to historically minded thinkers) that Rorty and I agree on so many matters, although we arrive at, or at any rate, justify our views in such radically disparate ways. For example, we both deny that Philosophy of Language, as practiced in the seventies, leads to any interesting results. In a choice passage of *Philosophy and the Mirror of Nature,* Rorty observes that:

> "Reference" only arises when one has made one's decision about various strategies used to express the error that one finds in the world . . . and then wishes to cast the result of one's decision into "canonical" form, that is, into a language which uses standard quantificational logic as a matrix. This is what I meant by saying that "reference" is a term of art. It is also the reason it is not something we have intuitions about. (p. 292)

In effect, what Rorty has claimed in this passage is that those who claim that they have intuitions "about reference" are liars. I find this a remarkable, bold, and even prophetic claim to have issued from a tenured professor in one of the hotbeds of analytic philosophy of language during the seventies. I do not go quite so far. I claim that if *I* reported an "intuition" about a theory of "reference," then *I* would have to be lying, since the relation of "reference" is not something which has been reified in any of my worlds. My "argument" is more general: "Non-things have no properties. Non-things have no price. You cannot go shopping for non-things. Who would pay something for nothing?" My "argument" asserts that if *you* happen to believe in the existence of a reified thing, for example, a "reference relation," then *you* can have intuitions about it. But it is necessary first to believe in the existence of some *thing* before one can claim to have an intuition about its specific properties. So anyone who *claims* to have an intuition about the properties of something which he does not believe to exist, is either seriously confused, or he is lying. The most obvious clarificatory example here would be that of an atheist who claimed to have an intuition *about* God's omnipotence. If one does not believe in the existence of God, then the entire enterprise of debating what His properties are becomes senseless. The only way an atheist can meaningfully engage in such debate is to consider what properties God *would* have, were *he* to exist. Certainly this trend toward transcendental argumentation has been attractive to philosophers throughout history, as Rorty has documented well. But most philosophers of language writing in the seventies seemed to have been taking themselves to be debating issues about "the real nature of 'reference'," not what "reference" would be, were it somehow discovered to be a bona fide thing. My "principle," that "Non-things have no properties," bears some resemblance to one which Rorty entertains in his essay, "Inquiry as Recontextualization," namely, Parmenides' Principle, that "You cannot talk about what does not exist." But my view is distinct, because I claim only that "*You* cannot talk non-duplicitously about the properties of things which *you* do not *believe* to exist." The reason why I would never categorically denounce any philosophical question as fundamentally "misguided" or "ill-conceived," is because I am never in a position to know whether or not *you* truly believe in the existence of the objects about which you claim to be theorizing.

Stories come in all varieties, and certain schools of philosophy have emphasized certain features. For example, analytic philosophers have considered argumentation, clarity, and economy of expression to be essential components of what they will sanction as "good" philosophy. A penchant for a high ratio of argument to assertion is not, however, in contrast to fashionable dogma, some sort of imperative of rationality. Rather, it is as "rational" as a penchant for alliteration or for the inclusion of a large number of apt metaphors. I attempt to debunk this idea, that "argumentation" is somehow criterional for what is to count as philosophy, by exposing the process by which we must come to belief, given the pervasive problem of the underdetermination of theory by data. In my view, belief is *essentially* religious, because no argument could ever, in principle, compel any belief. There is always an alternative hypothesis available, so when a philosopher claims that he "argued" himself into believing modal realism, to offer one of many possible examples, he must be either confused or lying. How do I know this? Because, to adduce my by now familiar refrain, "Non-things have no properties. Non-things have no price. You cannot go shopping for non-things. Who would pay something for nothing?" In other words, no one can claim to have come to believe a thesis *because* of its utility, because only existent *things* have properties, so until one first believes in some *thing,* one cannot have any interest in determining its properties, such as its utility or its putative fruitfulness. Philosophers who insist upon making argumentation a central and essential component of their stories are doing so through an act of will, not through some sort of rational compulsion. And those who really think that arguments "brought them," in the sense of "compelled them," to belief must be self-deceived, as my own "argument" reveals.

Nonetheless, despite the fact that I personally have always found something both aesthetically repugnant and mendacious about analytic philosophy, if anyone alive still wishes to engage in the enterprise, that is fine with me. My hope, "My Private Fantasy," and some will no doubt characterize this as an "agenda," is that, in the future, talented, creative young philosophers will no longer be culled from academic philosophy by the application of the procrustean criteria of analytic philosophers, which differs only in obviousness from the rejection of the logical positivists of any discourse about metaphysics as pure "nonsense." My hope is that students will no longer be expected, in order to survive academically, to produce essays on "reference" or "modal truth conditions," or "counterfactual conditionals," etc., unless, of course, they already had an antecedent interest in those topics.

In this connection, it may be worth pointing out that it is unsurprising that both Rorty and I invoke the work of Thomas Kuhn in our stories. After all, Kuhn's story is itself highly seductive and filled with choice metaphors which many intellectuals find irresistible. However, Rorty does not focus upon Kuhn qua philosopher, in the manner in which I do (Chapter Three). And, in his application of the Kuhnian paradigm to the world of philosophy, Rorty uses the terminology "normal" and "revolutionary" slightly differently than I do. According to Rorty, revolutionary philosophical theories comprise two types: those which are "systematic," and lead to the generation of elaborative and critical literature, and those which are "edifying," which stand on their own and are in some ways "untouchable" due to their very strangeness. In my story, my own story comes out as a "revolutionarily revolutionary" theory, while in Rorty's story what I have produced would fall under the category of "edifying revolutionary." Due to the normalcy of its structure, but the strangeness of its content, Rorty's work would be classified in his own picture as a sort of hybrid between the categories of "systematic" and "edifying." In my picture, Rorty's book-length account of the otiose nature of the project of foundationalist epistemology would be an example of the work of a "normal revolutionary," since it provokes (and indeed has provoked) response and elaboration by the community which it addresses. The reader may or may not find such categories worthy of application and may or may not agree with my application of those categories to my own and Rorty's work.

In many of his essays, Rorty's brushstrokes are very broad. He invokes lists of philosophers in a single sentence, grouping them in categories to which, he seems to believe, the reader will blithely assent. So, for example, he sometimes writes as though it were an established fact that James and Nietzsche belong in the very same "camp." "Serious" historians will balk at the way Rorty pours out generalization after generalization about figures as controversial as Nietzsche and Derrida. But, according to my own story, Rorty's stories are fascinating and edifying precisely because one can read them just as one reads stories, as narratives filled with colorful characters of the author's own device.

If philosophical theories are always underdetermined by the data which they "account for," then metaphilosophical theories, which are one type of philosophical theory, are underdetermined a fortiori, since they offer stories about multiply interpretable stories about multiply interpretable phenomena. Accordingly, criticizing Rorty for failing to satisfy the evaluative criteria embraced by standard (normal) historians of philosophy would be analogous to criticizing a painter for not working in clay or a sculptor for not working in oils. Historical support of Rorty's examples would be, in fact, beside the point, because he is writing metaphilosophy. He is telling stories about philosophy, and the only way in which one can do that is to allow 'Nietzsche' to stand for what one takes Nietzsche's oeuvre to have expressed. Of course, in defending Rorty in this way, I am defending the general project of metaphilosophy, and so my own as well, and I feel no need to attempt (vainly) to hide this fact. In the end, a metaphilosophical account may strike a reader as wildly implausible, or entertaining, or enlightening, or apt, or well-written, or thought-provoking, or any of the other ways in which literature can resonate with a reader. And sometimes stories even strike one as "true."

Historians have their criteria; analytic philosophers have their criteria. In fact, every delineable "school" of philosophy throughout history has cherished its peculiar criteria for what constitutes "good" philosophy. Consider some of the many examples from this century alone: positivists, phenomenologists, logical empiricists, ordinary language philosophers, etc. A metaphilosopher attempts to offer an account of what all of these people have been doing and what he has been doing. So his story must somehow cover the intersection of all of these activities. What do they all have in common? The easy way to devise an uncontroversial metaphilosophical theory is to construct a long disjunction of all of the activities engaged in by self-proclaimed "philosophers." But metaphilosophers aspire to something more. To criticize a metaphilosopher for not doing what he never claimed to be doing, for not doing history, for not doing phenomenology, for not doing analytic philosophy, would betray no more than the critic's failure to comprehend the nature of metaphilosophical projects. If someone claims that Rorty's work, or my own, is "not really *philosophy*," this is because the critic has concretized his own cherished criteria and deemed from on high that his preferred enterprise should exhaust the entire domain to which the term 'philosophy' can, with linguistic propriety, be applied. (I discuss this problem in Chapter Three.)

Nonetheless, it has been done, so I may as well confront the problem head on: an analytic philosopher might attempt to list the various specific theses advanced in *Philosophy Unmasked*. These would include:

Every question in philosophy is a question in value theory.

Philosophy is an essentially subjective enterprise.

No argument can compel belief in any thesis.

No one can have an intuition about something which he does not believe to exist, because "Non-things have no properties."

Philosophy is an art form, usually a form of literature.

Conceptual artists are philosophers, and philosophers are conceptual artists.

Nietzsche is a "house of mirrors."

"The subject" of philosophy is "the self."

All of philosophy is seduction or conversion.

Due to the underdetermination of any theory by the available data, any belief in any hypothesis is necessarily religious.

Philosophers who claim to believe their idiosyncratic theses *because* of the arguments they offer for them, are self-deceived or mendacious.

Philosophers who espouse "the death of philosophy" mire themselves in contradiction.

"The Intentional Fallacy" is a fallacy.

A metaphilosophical view according to which "Philosophy is literature" provides grounds for skepticism about all first-order philosophical theories.

Because the areas in which we apply our intelligence form a continuum, "interdisciplinary" boundaries are ultimately arbitrary.

Et cetera.

After having distilled out all of the various propositions advanced in my work, one might go down the list and say, "But Socrates said this. Nietzsche said that. Wittgenstein said this. Dewey said that. Derrida said this. Rorty said that. Etc., etc." I have no interest in claiming to be the ultimate source of any specific proposition advanced in my work. In fact, I am certain that any isolated proposition which readers could squeeze out of my work will look like something which has already been said by someone else at some time during the history of philosophy, and most likely during this century. This is unsurprising, since whenever ideas are sufficiently crudely partitioned and abstracted from their contexts, it becomes the case that "Nihil sub sole novum est." In fact, one need not go even that far.

Consider the abundant secondary literature which has been generated about Nietzsche's oeuvre alone. Virtually every conceivable label has been applied to Nietzsche in an effort to at last lay hold of "The Real Nietzsche." This is because his oeuvre is expansive and richly interpretable. For an "argument" that everything has already been said, we need only turn to the corpus of Nietzsche's writings. For any philosophical proposition any philosopher might generate, there exists some sentence in Nietzsche's oeuvre, which under some possible interpretation amounts to that proposition. Therefore, it is impossible to say something new. What moral should be drawn from this "argument"? That the value of philosophy must lie in the process of devising theories and criticizing them, not in the content of any particular supposedly "true" account.

Setting all facetiousness aside (for the moment), no contemporary philosopher, to my knowledge, has yet produced a structural critique of philosophy of the sort which I have presented in *Philosophy Unmasked,* which not only lists its tenets but also simultaneously displays them. (I am aware that some Wittgensteinians would beg to differ with me on this point, and it is certainly well within their rights to do so.) The different sections of this multi-layered work reflect back upon and exemplify one another, and, in my opinion, therein lies what value, if any, it possesses. Any philosopher who protests that because each of the long list of propositions that can be distilled out of this work can be ascribed to other figures, I have said nothing new, will have revealed himself to have altogether misunderstood my project. Any analytic philosopher who demands a *proof* of any of the assertions of my text, will have revealed his failure to have grasped one of its central tenets regarding the impotence of argumentation. That an argument can never compel belief is both "defended" in the standard way, through my discussion of the under-determination of theory by data, and "displayed" in many nonstandard ways as well.

But the reader will, and can only, apply his own idiosyncratic criteria in deciding whether my theory is "plausible or implausible," "interesting or banal," or even "true or false." I adduce a variety of forms of "evidence" for the thesis that philosophy is an art form, but, according to the thesis itself, I could never *prove* that my story is "*The Final Truth,*" or "*The Last Word,*" nor would I want to, since art provides us with visions, not "*Final Truths.*" However, any reader who finds my story implausible or riddled with contradiction or oblivious of certain indismissible data, may be justified in rejecting my theory on those grounds.

In my own experience, professional philosophers, no less than nonprofessionals, tend to be rather fond of the stories of their own device, and will cling stubbornly to them, even in the light of trenchant criticism offered by nonbelievers. According to Rorty's book-length story, *Philosophy and the Mirror of Nature* cannot, literally speaking, stand on its own as a work of philosophy, since it is not, literally, a "conversation." According to the account of philosophy there presented, *Philosophy and the Mirror of Nature* must be supplemented by responses, interpretations, and criticisms, in order to count as "philosophy." According to my story, Rorty's book-length story is a complete work of philosophy in and of itself. And so is my own. In Rorty's story, philosophy ends up amounting to a possibly edifying conversation. But, according to my story, dialogue between the various promulgators of philosophical stories is not essential to what they are doing, so even if no one liked my story, it would still count as a work of philosophy, according to itself. In his essays, Rorty often refers to philosophizing as "storytelling," but his writings retain a standard, recognizably essayistic structure throughout. I have attempted to produce a work which not only asserts that philosophizing is a type of storytelling, but does so within what self-consciously presents itself as a story, rather than merely redefining "story" so broadly as to include what have throughout history been characterized as "essays."

What Lies Ahead?

Although Rorty has been writing as though "analytic philosophy is dead," or at least moribund, since 1979, I can report that it is alive and breathing in many powerful vestibules of the academic world. Certainly this news has yet to echo through the hallowed halls of the bastion of "heavy metal analytic philosophy" throughout the second half of this century, Princeton University. But its repercussions are being felt in other ways. For example, it should come as little surprise that where academic administrations are forced to cut faculty, their first move in some cases has been to pare down their departments of philosophy. This is because, as Rorty, too, has suggested, professional philosophers, through generations of incestuous mating, nepotism, and insufferable elitism, have ensured that their work has little if any contact with fellow academics outside their own departments, in either the humanities or the sciences.

To those who wish to believe that philosophy is something more than an activity akin to storytelling, or painting, or musical composition, or a dialogue between interlocutors who have momentarily adopted a framework within which to argue, both Rorty's account and my own will seem wrongheaded, and even heretical. Many philosophers during this century have fought hard to secure for philosophy the sort of respectability enjoyed by the natural sciences. To those who still retain this desideratum, it may indeed come as a disappointment to learn that philosophy could never, in principle, be one of the natural sciences, at least so long as our languages retain the basic structure with which we are now familiar. (More likely, diehards will simply reject my proposals as "confused" or "wildly implausible.") The chasm between the discreteness of language and the repleteness of experience ensures that no matter which story we end up agreeing upon, there will always be a variety of other stories which might have been told, and perhaps one day they will be told.

But to persons who believe that art, literature, and music are valuable in and of themselves, it should be obvious that I believe this to be the case for philosophy as well. After all, I have taken the time to tell a story about philosophy, a clear indication of my belief that the enterprise is still worthwhile, in spite of the fact that my own account ends with the words 'the end'. Those words mark the end of *my* story, not the end, or "the death" of philosophy. According to my account, philosophy will never die, so long as people continue to ask questions. The suicide of one person could never, in and of itself, effect the end of civilization.

The irony of much of my text offers at once a diagnosis of what I view as the unfortunate tendency of academic philosophers to take themselves much too seriously, and what I hope will be an antidote. I am not the first to have offered such a diagnosis, but it bears repetition, since such diagnoses never seem to be taken very seriously by "serious" philosophers. In my view, laughter is therapeutic, and insofar as I tell a story which will resonate with those who have a sense of humor, I am attempting to "cure" philosophers of a sort of sickness. But I do not think, in contrast to some interpretations of the later Wittgenstein, that philosophical problems need to be "dissolved." There is nothing "sick" about doing philosophy, in my view. What I find "sick" is the self-delusive manner in which so many people engage in the enterprise, as though they were sentenced to life terms in labor camps.

This is not to say that I believe that philosophers can never be more than whimsical jesters. Far from thinking that, I believe that philosophers have the option of applying their intellects diligently to the problems which beset their societies. To state the obvious: There are many serious problems with the world(s) in which we live, and if a philosopher wants to do something very serious with his life, then he should concern himself with social criticism. He should apply his intellect to the task of exposing contradictions, inconsistencies in the applications of the laws of his government. But I do not believe that all philosophers must become social critics in order to preserve their self-image of doing something respectable with their lives. I believe that philosophy, as I have described it, as an essentially creative process of telling stories and of elaborating upon those stories, and eventually abandoning them, has a value all its own. In other words, although it would no doubt be beneficial to our society were more philosophical (which is just, in my view, to say "intelligent") persons involved in the politics of this nation, I do not believe that all philosophers who trade in words should be social critics any more than I believe that all artists working in three-dimensional media should be engineers or architects. Philosophy is a valuable human enterprise, every bit as valuable as any of the arts. Far from thinking that philosophy is an enterprise of ill-repute, I believe that it is one of the crowning accomplishments of the evolution of our capacity to think.

However, to reiterate, and here I completely concur with Rorty, this is not to say that professional philosophers have some special claim to superiority in matters of reason. Rather, for idiosyncratic reasons relating to their bent for intellectual activity, they have decided to spend their lives writing, reading, and teaching philosophy. The fact that a person is a tenured Professor of Philosophy shows no more and no less than that he produced the kind of work which was currently fashionable during his time as a junior faculty member, and he was not perceived of as a serious threat by any of his already securely ensconced colleagues.

Both Rorty and I are bothered by the self-delusion of philosophers who exalt themselves as demigods of sorts, who arrogate some supposedly authoritative position from which they can talk about Reality, in contradistinction to all of the poor slobs stuck in "The Cave." According to my story, extricating oneself from "The Cave" amounts to no more and no less than recognizing the actual nature of what one is doing. It amounts to facing up to the fact that we are ultimately constrained by our peculiar positions in time and space to tell certain types of stories, and that no one of us mortals has (or at any rate can know himself to have) a "God's eye" view of some concretized thing "The World." But, to pull the point out of its parentheses: I am not a nihilist, nor a relativist. I remain agnostic about "the big questions": realism vs. idealism, metaethical relativism vs. absolutism, free will and determinism, the existence of God, etc. About some issues, such as "the problem of reference," I have no intuitions at all. Such issues are *to me* pseudo-problems. But I do not claim that because they are of no interest to me, that no one else should discuss them. And here, to reiterate, I depart significantly from the pragmatists, at least those among them who reject certain metaphysical inquiries as fundamentally misguided.

Although we most likely breathed some of the same molecules of rarefied air floating about the hermetic chambers of 1879 Hall, and this no doubt had something to do with the fact that both of us reacted strongly against analytic philosophy, I could not have written any of Rorty's oeuvre, just as he could not have written mine. We emerge from our unique though in some ways intersecting paths with views which call into question the dogmas of philosophers who claim to be spokesmen about "The Nature of Reality." We obviously share a repugnance to the sort of self-deception pervasive in academic philosophy today. But I do not preach "the death of philosophy," in any form. In the Introduction to *Objectivity, Relativism, and Truth,* Rorty asserts: "I should like to think that English-speaking philosophy in the twenty-first century will have put the representationalist problematic behind it." I could not disagree more, not because I believe that representationalism gets things "right," but because philosophers such as Rorty only arrived at their anti-representationalist positions through reacting to "the representationalist problematic," and that process is, in my view, a good thing. Surely Rorty would be willing to admit that, according to his own story, his story applies only to right now, at this peculiar point in history. It is waiting around for refutation by new standards, new arguments, new criteria. According to my story, philosophy could never die, only be transformed, because it is the nature of human beings to devise pleasing stories about the objects of their experience. These stories have changed in gross structure throughout millennia, but they have been and will remain stories until the end of time, or at least until the end of language as we know it.

In *Contingency, Irony, and Solidarity,* Rorty develops a picture of the "ironist," to be distinguished from the classical conception of a "metaphysician" primarily by the size and breadth of the objects he chooses to describe and redescribe. Proust is said to be an ironist, in that he spends his time and energy describing and redescribing very minute aspects of his personal experience, while Nietzsche "still," the suggestion seems to be, harbors metaphysical hankerings. He has not "succeeded," the suggestion seems to be, in freeing himself from the metaphysical desire to say "the last word," to paint "the final picture" of the world. By describing himself as an ironist, Rorty somewhat ironically entrenches himself inextricably with the metaphysically minded theorists, suggesting in some ways that he, too, would like to cast off the yoke of philosophical yearning but that he can't. He seems to view himself as trapped.

I wholeheartedly agree with Rorty about the contingency of language, selfhood, and the communities in which we interact. My peculiar contingent self has properties which make it the case that I would never spend *my* life on an exegesis of Kant's *Critique of Pure Reason,* but I have no problem with anyone who wants to do that. And I disagree with the suggestion that the stance of the ironist is somehow more mature or advanced or in any other way intellectually superior to that of the theorist. This may reveal nothing more than that I happen to enjoy reading the work of theorists such as Rorty more than that of ironists such as Proust. But it seems to me deeper than that. It may be that there is no necessary historical progression from the metaphysician to the supposedly "enlightened" ironist, who has somehow recognized the naïveté of his former ways. Indeed, many thinkers follow precisely the reverse path. They commence from the particular and aspire to the more general and all-encompassing description of the phenomena which they encounter. Because many people lack the motivation or ability to leap out of the frames in which they find themselves, forging such a path has been viewed by those who for whatever reason have done so, as a "progression." But it seems to me that neither one of these routes (directions) is inherently preferable. As characterized by Rorty, the ironist seems to me to have come around full circle back to where he started before having embarked upon his peculiar philosophical journey. "Progress" in the sense of "philosophical development" can only be judged as such relative to the point from which a thinker himself commences.

For the purposes of this epilogue, I have adopted a conversational tone and style along the lines of Rorty's, in order to talk about both of our works as though I were someone who had just happened upon them in a library. And I think that one of the values of edifying philosophy is that it provides infinite possibilities for reflection, even for the author herself, who is sometimes surprised by the new meanings it takes on in readings subsequent to its creation.

Because I do not believe in absolute philosophical "progress," it seems to me just as valuable for a philosopher to "reinvent the wheel" as it was for the very first inventer of the wheel. (I am aware that such a person will be unlikely to make a successful career of professional philosophy.) The intrinsic value of philosophical activity is, I think, exhausted by the value of the process, not the results obtained. Accordingly, it may be that the richest philosophical journey that a person could embark upon would necessitate his taking seriously foundationalism and substantive theories of truth. The fact that some persons, who have been honorifically labeled "revolutionary philosophers," have already walked down that path makes it nonetheless valuable for others to do so as well. Even if some thinkers end up coming full circle, back to the point at which they commenced their journey, this will hardly mean that their time has been wasted.

Historians of philosophy tell stories about stories, and I have just offered a story about my story of philosophy. I would be happy if the reader found something pleasing in my work. But, above all, I hope that my stories, whether you happen to like them or not, will make you think.

Notes

INTRODUCTION

1. My addendum.
2. *Of Mind and Other Matters*, p. 36.
3. *Reconceptions*, p. 51.
4. Kant's notion of a "rational and willing subject" seems to have (inconsistently) involved appeal to the noumena.
5. *Ways of Worldmaking*, p. 6.

CHAPTER ONE
Perspectivism, Interpretation, and "The World"

1. *Jenseits von Gut und Böse*, §16.
2. According to Husserl, our concept of the "otherness" of other persons importantly requires our inability to see all of their aspects (§§49, 50). "Hidden aspects" are a part of our concept of persons. But *that "persons" have hidden aspects* cannot be hidden from those grasping the concept of "person," if perspectivism is true.
3. The scare quotes warn against thinking of "events" absolutistically, as though a single event might have two disparate interpretations. The interpretation itself determines the identity of the event. One is constrained by quasi-absolutistic language and concepts when describing what a perspectivist world would be like. In general, a person is constrained by his own language in describing anything, and his powers of reasoning, in judging anything.
4. I explain below why this is no constraint at all, given the conventional nature of linguistic symbols.
5. The so-called "private language argument" seems to define languages as intersubjective (in the ordinary sense, i.e., between subjects, people, as ordinarily conceived) but assumes a distinction between appearance and reality that is untenable on the perspectivist's view. The "argument" suggests that the "correct" application of the rules governing language requires the veridicality of memory. But the distinction between memory and imagination is socially inculcated, if perspectivism is true. It suffices that an individual conceptualizer believe himself to

be correctly applying a rule in order for him to be doing so in his own private world. In fact, under one interpretation, Wittgenstein's point seems to be the stronger claim that the very application (tout court) of rules requires the possibility of error. As we shall see, individual conceptualizers in worlds suitably relativized are infallible, if perspectivism is true. Does this mean that (under this interpretation of the late Wittgenstein) Wittgenstein was not a perspectivist? Or did he perhaps value human society more than solitude?

6. Cf. *Cartesianische Meditationen*, V.

7. Gilbert Harman discusses conservatism in Chapters Four and Five of *Change in View*. Harman admits that the argument for a conservative policy about belief revision is circular. But circularity is not vicious to coherentists; it appears to be the only alternative to skepticism.

8. Paul Churchland has claimed that the human mind exhibits a sort of plasticity that makes it possible for us radically to refigure our conceptual frameworks. However, his manifesto to the effect that we should refigure our concepts in terms of the constructs of neuroscience is undermined by his claiming (incoherently) both that our current world view is radically false and misguided and that we *should* adopt the framework of neuroscience. Obviously, if it is true that our current world view is false and misguided, then our normative theories, there subsumed, are too.

The blunder is irreparable, since even if we believed that, among our entire sets of theories, only one (viz., the normative theory according to which we should switch our conceptual framework to that of neuroscience) was not false, that very belief would still be undermined by the first claim. Either every newly appended belief, purportedly true, would be undermined similarly, or a substantive set of our original beliefs would be recovered through the process of securing the needed vindication of our normative theory. So the manifesto, assuming its motivating premise, can be no more than an article of faith, à la tertullienne. And without that premise (that our current world view is radically false and misguided), the proposed course of action would be irrational, enjoining us to abandon a more or less correct theory.

9. *Cartesianische Meditationen*, §55.

10. In "The Truth in Relativism," Bernard Williams makes a similar point in his discussion of "real" vs. "notional" conflict. His is the narrower claim that moral judgments cannot be made of those world views that are not real possibilities for us.

11. One might attempt to make the same point in the converse manner, e.g., by observing that 'maison', 'Haus', and 'casa' bear no resemblance to one another. However, the first route is preferable, since it is a philosophically respectable idea that no word translates perfectly into any other language. (Rien ne se traduit.) In other words, one might deny the supposition to the argument, that the meanings of 'maison', 'Haus', and 'casa' are the same.

12. *Essai sur L'origine des Langues.*

13. Ultimately this will depend upon one's view about the necessity of "correct" pronunciation to an utterance's being identified as of the language in question. There seems to be widespread agreement that people with egregious accents are still speaking the language in question, though egregiously. A notable exception might seem to be the French. However, it is unclear whether the French, who often refuse to speak to an egregious speaker of French, do not understand the speaker's utterances or simply refuse to discourse with him.

14. Concerns about the purely conventional or necessarily falsificatory nature of language need not lead one to a reactionary "back to nature" policy. Rien n'entraîne rien. (Ou bien?)

15. In *Change in View*, Gilbert Harman argues that it would be impossible for us to "keep track" of the justifications for our beliefs, so it cannot be the case that we ought to.

16. I should perhaps point out that experts can change their minds and decide that they were formerly wrong. But if perspectivism is true, then "being wrong" must be reinterpreted, since it cannot be in virtue of the way "the world" is.

17. Some indoctrinators probably believe that they are the messiah or a deity. Others are simply engaged in a business for profit.

18. This description is slightly misleading, since if perspectivism is correct, the notions of "responsibility" and "choice" involved are radically attenuated.

19. My own impression is that Sartre was not subtle enough to have been playing a trick on his readers. Then again, maybe the trick was to persuade his readers that he was not subtle.

20. *Reconceptions*, p. 54.

21. Again, scare quotes are meant to alert the reader to the impropriety of considering "the thing" from two perspectives as identical.

22. In *Nietzsche: Life as Literature*, Nehamas' denial (pp. 64–73) that perspectivism implies relativism is equally unilluminating. It is tantamount to a rejection of the obviously false claim that "judgments cannot be made if perspectivism is true."

23. Perhaps they shouldn't be so bothered, given that it serves merely to highlight an ineluctable feature of all normative theory justification, that all moral agents are ultimately constrained by their own intuitions about what constitutes "justification."

24. This label comes from Bernard Williams' discussion: "An Inconsistent Form of Relativism."

25. My own view is that this interpretation of the thesis of so-called "vulgar relativism" is itself vulgar, confusing as it does a statement in the meta-language with a statement in some (arbitrarily selected?) normative theory. In other words, the word 'wrong' used in articulating a meta-thesis could not possibly mean "morally wrong," since meta-theories are entirely devoid of normative content.

26. Truth is relevant to interpretation, whether or not within a specific world it is believed that interpretations can be "true." The statement that an interpretation is correct (valuable, good, etc.) can be rephrased: "It is true that this interpretation is correct (valuable, good, etc.)."

27. In *Pensées*, Pascal, by exhorting those seeking a most radical change in view to engage in certain activities as a means to the acquisition of beliefs, seems to evince skepticism about the degree to which change in belief is directly controllable by volition in the way in which we commonly think that actions are.

CHAPTER TWO
Art, Psychiatry, and Intelligence

1. The reviewer is R. E. Reinert for the *Bulletin of the Menninger Clinic*.

2. The view may be traceable to Mill, whose fervent defense of the value of tolerance (in *On Liberty*) is at least not self-contradictory. The problems with Mill's view are its simplistic conceptions of tolerance and harm.

3. Louis Pasteur discovered the enantiomers of tartaric acid in just this manner.

4. "Epistemology Today," p. 12.

5. The reader will recall that the distinction between conceptualization and interpretation is intersubjectively inculcated. Without communication with others, it, along with the distinction between memories and imaginings, is no longer real to the estranged individual.

CHAPTER THREE
Science and Academic Philosophy

1. "The Will to Believe," in *Essays in Pragmatism*, p. 92.

2. The institution to which I am referring is commonly referred to as "classical music," although it covers many others in addition to the classical period. It is distinguished from popular music in its having a relatively stable core canon, comprising the musical compositions of what are deemed by the experts to be the "great" composers of the past, and in its being performed by professional musicians who have been trained "classically," i.e., in tonal music, usually commencing with J. S. Bach.

3. In "Epistemology Today," Gilbert Harman claims that there are no "perennial" problems of philosophy, and then proceeds to delimit his own philosophical community by asserting that skepticism is no longer "interesting."

4. For example, Alasdair MacIntyre enumerates and discusses some of the major conflicting views of virtue in *After Virtue*.

5. The cardinality of ∞ would be greater than aleph null, if the number of lower-level hypotheses were infinite, since every hypothesis could be combined

with every other hypothesis. But finite people can devise only a finite number of actual hypotheses, so there is no need to review Cantor's diagonal argument here.

6. *Language, Truth, and Logic*, p. 120.

7. Ibid., p. 48.

8. "Five Milestones of Empiricism," in *Theories and Things*, p. 72.

9. One example that comes to mind is David Wong's *Moral Relativity*, which includes a lengthy excursus on theories of reference, the relevance of which to meta-ethical relativism never became clear to me. Another example is at least the beginning of Alasdair MacIntyre's work *After Virtue*, which includes a strongly Kuhnian-flavored diagnosis of the current state of moral philosophy. But, of course, I do see the relevance of Kuhn's model to philosophy.

CHAPTER FOUR
Metaphilosophy

1. David Hume, *An Enquiry Concerning Human Understanding*, §XII.

2. "The New Riddle of Induction," in *Fact, Fiction, and Forecast*.

3. "Realism, Antirealism, and Reasons for Belief," p. 23.

4. Ibid., p. 15.

5. Ibid.

6. "The Inference to the Best Explanation," p. 89.

7. Ibid.

8. *The Scientific Image*, ch. 7.

9. *Laws and Symmetry*, p. 180.

10. Ibid., p. 172.

11. Harman makes a similar point in "Epistemology Today," pp. 11–12.

12. "Realism, Antirealism, and Reasons for Belief," p. 19.

13. *Languages of Art*, p. 90.

CHAPTER FIVE
Skepticism

1. "Is There a Single True Morality?" p. 363.

2. *On the Plurality of Worlds*, p. 135.

3. *Méditations*, 1. Although the *Meditations* were written in Latin, Descartes himself read and approved the 1647 French translation (Luynes et Clerselier), which is the source used by Jean-Marie and Michelle Beyssade.

4. "Von tausend und einem Ziele," *Also Sprach Zarathustra*.

5. As Gilbert Harman maintains in *Change in View*.

Bibliography

Abbot, Edwin. *Flatland.* New York: Dover, 1952.

Aristotle. *Nicomachean Ethics,* trans. Terence Irwin. Indianapolis: Hackett, 1985.

Ayer, A. J. *Language, Truth and Logic.* New York: Dover, 1946.

Carnap, Rudolph. "Empiricism, Semantics and Ontology," in *Meaning and Necessity.* Chicago: Chicago University Press, 1956.

Churchland, Paul. *Matter and Consciousness.* Cambridge, MA: MIT Press, 1988.

———. *Scientific Realism and the Plasticity of Mind.* Cambridge, MA: MIT Press, 1979.

Descartes, René. *Discours de la Méthode.* Paris: J. Vrin, 1976.

———. *Méditations Métaphysiques.* Présentation par Jean-Marie et Michelle Beyssade. Paris: Garnier-Flammarion, 1979.

Dostoevsky, Fyodor. *The Brothers Karamazov,* trans. Constance Garnett. New York: Dell, 1960.

———. *The Idiot,* trans. Constance Garnett. New York: Dell, 1962.

Feyerabend, Paul. *Against Method,* rev. ed. New York: Verso, 1988.

Flaubert, Gustave. *Madame Bovary.* Paris: Garnier-Flammarion, 1966.

Foot, Philippa. "The Problem of Abortion and the Doctrine of Double Effect." In *Virtues and Vices,* 19–32. Berkeley: University of California Press, 1978.

Goodman, Nelson. *Fact, Fiction, and Forecast.* Indianapolis: Bobbs-Merrill, 1965.

———. *Languages of Art.* Indianapolis: Hackett, 1976.

———. *Of Mind and Other Matters.* Cambridge, MA: Harvard University Press, 1984.

———. *Ways of Worldmaking.* Indianapolis: Hackett, 1978.

Goodman, Nelson, and Catherine Elgin. *Reconceptions in Philosophy & Other Arts and Sciences.* Cambridge, MA: Harvard University Press, 1988.

Harman, Gilbert. *Change in View.* Cambridge, MA: MIT Press, 1986.

———. "Epistemology Today." In *Philosophy in Mind: The Place of Philosophy in the Mind,* eds. M. Michael and J. O'Leary-Hawthorne, 203–14. Dordrecht: Kluwer, 1994.

———. "The Inference to the Best Explanation." In *Philosophical Review* 74 (1965): 89–95.

————. "Is There a Single True Morality?" In *Morality, Reason and Truth: New Essays on the Foundations of Ethics,* eds. D. Copp and D. Zimmerman, 27–48, 1984.

————. "Moral Relativism Defended." In *Philosophical Review* 94 (1975): 3–22.

————. "Pragmatism and Reasons for Belief." In *Realism/Antirealism and Epistemology,* ed. Christopher B. Kulp. Totowa, NJ: Rowman & Littlefield, forthcoming.

Hume, David. *An Enquiry Concerning Human Understanding.* LaSalle, IL: Open Court, 1963.

————. *Treatise of Human Nature.* New York: Prometheus Books, 1992.

Husserl, Edmund. *Cartesianische Meditationen,* 1929. In English translation: *Cartesian Meditations,* trans. Dorion Cairns. The Hague: M. Nijhoff, 1960.

James, William. *Essays in Pragmatism.* New York: Hafner, 1948.

Kant, Immanuel. *Critique of Pure Reason,* trans. Norman Kemp Smith. New York: Modern Library, 1958.

Kierkegaard, Soren. *Concluding Unscientific Postscript,* trans. David Swenson. Princeton, NJ: Princeton University Press, 1968.

————. *Either/Or,* trans. Howard and Edna Hong. Princeton, NJ: Princeton University Press, 1987.

————. *Fear and Trembling,* trans. Walter Lowrie. Princeton, NJ: Princeton University Press, 1954.

Krausz & Meiland, eds. *Relativism: Cognitive and Moral.* West Bend, IN: University of Notre Dame Press, 1982.

Kuhn, Thomas. *The Structure of Scientific Revolutions,* 2d ed. Chicago: University of Chicago Press, 1970.

La Rochefoucauld, Francois de. *Réflexions ou Sentences et Maximes Morales.* Paris: Garnier Flammarion, 1988.

Leibniz, Gottfried. *Essais sur Théodicée.* Paris: Garnier-Flammarion, 1969.

Lewis, David. *On the Plurality of Worlds.* New York: Oxford University Press, 1986.

MacIntyre, Alasdair. *After Virtue,* 2d ed. West Bend, IN: University of Notre Dame Press, 1984.

Mill, John Stewart. *On Liberty.* Indianapolis: Hackett, 1978.

Nehamas, Alexander. *Nietzsche: Life as Literature.* Cambridge, MA: Harvard University Press, 1985.

Nietzsche, Friedrich. *Werke,* herausgegeben von Karl Schlechta. Berlin: Ullarwin Materiallen, 1984.

Orwell, George. *Animal Farm.* New York: Harcourt Brace, 1954.

Pascal, Blaise. *Pensées.* Paris: Mercure de France, 1976.

Plato. *Dialogues,* trans. R. E. Allen. New Haven, CT: Yale University Press, 1984.

Popper, Karl. *The Logic of Scientific Discovery.* New York: Basic Books, 1959.

Quine, W. v. O. *From a Logical Point of View*, 2 ed. rev. Cambridge, MA: Harvard University Press, 1961.

———. *Theories and Things*. Cambridge, MA: Harvard University Press, 1981.

———. *The Ways of Paradox and Other Essays*, rev. ed. Cambridge, MA: Harvard University Press, 1976.

Rawls, John. *A Theory of Justice*. Cambridge, MA: Belknap Press, 1971.

Rorty, Richard. *Consequences of Pragmatism*. Minneapolis: University of Minnesota Press, 1982.

———. *Contingency, Irony, and Solidarity*. New York: Cambridge University Press, 1989.

———. *Objectivity, Relativism, and Truth*. New York: Cambridge University Press, 1991.

———. *Philosophy and the Mirror of Nature*. Princeton, NJ: Princeton University Press, 1979.

Rousseau, Jean-Jacques. *Essai sur l'origine des langues*. In English translation: *On the Origin of Language,* trans. John Moran and Alexander Gode. Chicago: University of Chicago Press, 1986.

de Sablé, Madame. *Réflexions*. In La Rochefoucauld.

Sartre, Jean-Paul. *L'Etre et le Néant*. Paris: Gallimard, 1943.

van Fraassen, Bastiaan C. *Laws and Symmetry*. New York: Oxford University Press, 1989.

———. *The Scientific Image*. New York: Oxford University Press, 1980.

Voltaire. *Candide*. Paris: Librairie Larousse, 1970.

Williams, Bernard. "An Inconsistent Form of Relativism." In *Relativism: Cognitive and Moral,* eds. Kraus and Meiland, 171–74, 1982.

———. "The Truth in Relativism." In *Relativism: Cognitive and Moral,* eds. Kraus and Meiland, 175–85, 1982.

Wittgenstein, Ludwig. *Tractatus Logico-Philosophicus*. Frankfurt am Main: Suhrkamp, 1984.

———. *Philosophische Untersuchungen*. Frankfurt am Main: Suhrkamp, 1984.

Wong, David. *Moral Relativity*. Berkeley: University of California Press, 1984.

Index

Cantor, Georg, 198n5
Carnap, Rudolf, 61, 69, 72–80
Churchland, Paul, 196n8
Climacus, Johannes, 24, 142
Coherence, 55, 179
Coherentism, 76, 102–4, 112, 124–25,
129–32
Communities, 23
conceptual, 5
Comprehensibility, 5, 67–68, 116
in academia, 65–66
of art, 65
and levels, 57–58
and normality, 13–14
and public language, 10, 20
of worlds, 28
See also Incomprehensibility
Conceptualization, 2–3, 32, 41, 48,
111
and comprehensibility, 14–16, 20,
116–17
and perspectivism, 5–14
self-, 29–30
Conceptualizers, 8–10, 52, 56, 108,
124–25, 131, 158
Conditionalization, principle of, 99–
101
Conservatism
of belief systems, 25, 102, 142
epistemic, 12–13, 104, 124–25, 127,
129, 131
of institutions, 26
Constructive empiricism, 103–4
Contradiction, 16, 71, 99–100, 104–5,
115, 126, 136–37, 147, 151, 165,
179, 190
Conventions
and deviance, 49, 53–54
and facts, 6–7
and language, 15–16, 107–8, 138,
152, 158, 161
and "the real," 11, 35

Conversion, ix–x, 21–22, 44, 57, 103,
106, 139
to interests, 69
and metaphysicians, 71, 92
in philosophy, 150, 168, 171–72,
177, 180
and science, 62
Correspondence theory of truth, 112
Cordelia, 24, 142
Corngold, Stanley, xi
Creative writing, 38
Critical intelligence, 112
Crittenden, Charles, xi
Cullen, Jane, xi

Death, 111
of metaphilosophy, 168
of philosophy, 77, 110, 124, 128,
129, 168, 190
symbolized, 15
Debriefing, 22, 119, 140
Deception, ix, 21, 24, 47, 139, 141
self-, 27, 30, 103, 106
Deontologists, 58
Derrida, Jacques, 178, 185, 187
DesAutels, Peggy, xi
Descartes, René, 7–8, 71, 77, 104,
124–25, 199n3
Deviance, 11, 37, 53
in academia, 65–66, 77, 135
artistic, 40, 43, 45
and intelligence, 55–57
in society, 134
Dewey, John, 178, 187
Discreteness, 17, 28, 95, 108, 190
Dostoevsky, Fyodor, 68, 181
Duchamp, Marcel, 39, 43–44, 180
Dutch books, 99–100, 104
Dutton, Denis, xi

Eckhardt, Meister, 169
Egoism, 113

Incomprehensibility (*continued*)
  explanation of, 78
  of God, 116–17
  and inappropriateness, 49
  of philosophers, 137, 172
  of psychotics, 51
  See also Comprehensibility
Indoctrination, ix–x, 54, 113, 119–20
  leading to conversion, 21–24, 139,
    169
  in medical school, 133
Indoctrinators, 22–23, 140–41
Induction, 123
  enumerative, 101–2
  new riddle of, 18, 98
  problem of, 97–98
Inductive ascent, 18, 95, 106, 130
Inductive logic, 72
Inference
  ampliative, 99–101
  to the best explanation, 74, 98–99,
    103, 105, 109, 130, 171
Insanity, 35, 39, 43, 46
  and Kuhn, 62
  and metaphysics, 71
  of outsiders, 23, 77, 119, 140
  of philosophers, 155, 165, 169, 172
  of revolutionary work, 85
Institutions, ix, 26, 37, 54, 132, 134,
    163–64
  evolving, 64
  and homogeneity, 65, 67, 82
Intelligence, 55–57, 72, 79, 123, 130,
    134, 146, 151, 153–57, 162–63,
    165, 177–78, 187, 191
  and interests, 157
  and intuitions, 159
  types of, 112
Intentional fallacy, the, 41
Intentionality, 46, 81
Intentions, the artist's, 41, 42
Intuitions, 148, 156, 159

James, William, 61, 185
Jeffrey, Richard, xi
Journals, professional, 83–84, 86, 134

Kant, Immanuel, 2, 78, 178, 193,
  195n4
Kellenberger, James, xi
Kuhn, Thomas, 61–64, 84–89, 145,
  159, 184, 199n9

Lakatos, Imre, 62
Lang, Berel, xi
Language, 114, 163, 179
  and conceptualization, 6–11
  and learning, 17, 152
  and objects, 57, 69, 95, 107–8
  philosophy of, 82, 108, 128, 150,
    182–83
  world-constrained, 43
  written versus spoken, 17
Law
  of the excluded middle, 15, 126,
    128, 178
  of Leibniz, 155–56
  of nature, 103–4
  of noncontradiction, 15, 57, 126,
    128, 148, 178
  of science, 98
Leap of faith, 94–95, 130
Leibniz, Gottfried, 117, 155–56, 169–
  70
Lewis, David, 122–23, 154, 183
Luynes et Clerselier, 199

Machan, Tibor, xi
MacIntyre, Alasdair, 198n4, 199n9
Madness, 51, 53–54, 170. *See also*
  Abnormal; Insanity; Paranoia
Medicine, 133
Meta-
  language, 32, 108–9
  thesis, 32

Professionalization, 83, 194
Professors of philosophy, 65–69, 79,
    82, 114, 132, 135–36, 177, 182,
    188, 191
Projectibility, 98, 106
Protagoras, 58
Proust, Marcel, 192–93
Psychiatrists, as society's experts, 44,
    51, 132
Psychiatry, 52–53, 132–33

Quine, W. v. O., 15, 80–81, 143, 176

Radical doubt, 124–25
Ramsey, Frank, 61
Rationality, 45–46, 54, 94, 102, 104–
    5, 131–32, 143, 165, 179
    and ampliative inference, 99–100
    and fallibility, 58
    and responsibility, 165
    and science, 61, 74
Rawls, John, 86–87
Realism
    metaphysical, 180
    modal, 122
    scientific, 103, 112
Reality, 5, 10, 54, 95–96, 123, 181
    as logical, 15, 57
    as mind-independent, 48
    psychotic break from, 51
Reichenbach, Hans, 61
Reinert, R. E., 198n1
Relativism
    about art, 43
    metaethical, 58, 112, 179–80, 191
    radical, 31–32, 104
    about value, 54
    vulgar, 33
Repleteness, 17–18, 28, 49, 91, 95–96,
    102, 190
Revolutionary work, 85, 184

Revolutions, normal, 145
Rorty, Richard, xi, 175–94
Rousseau, Jean-Jacques, 17–18,
    197nn12–14
Russell, Bertrand, 28, 87
Ryle, Gilbert, 86

Sablé, Madame de, 173
Sartre, Jean-Paul, 30, 180, 197n19
Science, 110, 112
    and Kuhn, 61–64, 145–46
    normal, 84
    and positivism, 72–73, 79
    as religious, 62–63, 80
    and scientists, 46, 59
    skeptical attitudes toward, 103–4
    worlds of, 5
Seduction, ix–x, 44, 119–20, 141
    and Kuhn, 61, 64
    to new interests, 69, 92
    in philosophy, 151, 154, 168, 171–
    72, 177
Self, the
    elusiveness of, 29
    Humean, 30
    as the subject, 20, 109, 111–12, 132,
    146, 153–54, 158, 161, 167, 193
    as text, 31
Self-abnegation, 131
Self-deception, 27, 30, 94, 103, 106,
    122, 132, 137, 182, 184, 190–92
    and Kuhn, 63
Self-defense, 134
Self-destruction, 30, 37, 64, 67, 91,
    94, 111–12, 130
Self-knowledge, 59, 170
Sellars, Wilfrid, 86, 176
Simplicity, 74–75
Skepticism, ix, 97–98, 110, 112
    in academia, 135–36
    and coherentism, 132

Verification criterion, the, 77
Vienna Circle, 78
Voltaire, 169

West Coast semantics, 82–83, 145
Williams, Bernard, 196n10, 197n24

Wishful thinking, 24, 43–44, 62, 73, 95, 106, 109, 122, 130, 138, 141, 171
Wittgenstein, Ludwig, xi, 19, 91, 110, 131, 171, 187–88, 190, 195n5
Wong, David, 199n9